A CONCISE GUIDE TO THE CATHOLIC CHURCH II

A CONCISE GUIDE TO THE CATHOLIC CHURCH II

HISTORY • SAINTS • FEASTS • GLOSSARY

Felician A. Foy, O.F.M.
Rose M. Avato

Our Sunday Visitor Publishing Division
Our Sunday Visitor, Inc.
Huntington, Indiana 46750

Imprimi Potest: Rev. Matthew T. Conlin, O.F.M.
Vicar Provincial
Province of the Most Holy Name

Nihil Obstat:
Rev. Vincent P. Molloy
Censor Librorum

Imprimatur:
✠Frank J. Rodimer, D.D.
Bishop of Paterson
March 4, 1986

The Nihil Obstat and Imprimatur are official declarations that a book or pamphlet is free of doctrinal or moral error. No implication is contained therein that those who have granted the Nihil Obstat and the Imprimatur agree with the contents, opinions, or statements expressed.

International Standard Book Number: 0-87973-585-6
Library of Congress Catalog Card Number: 85-63527

Cover design by James E. McIlrath

PRINTED IN THE UNITED STATES OF AMERICA

ACKNOWLEDGMENTS

Scripture quotations in this work are taken from the *New American Bible*, © 1970 by the Confraternity of Christian Doctrine, Washington, D.C., and are used by permission of said copyright owner. No part of the *New American Bible* may be reproduced in any form without permission in writing from the copyright owner. Quotations from documents of the Second Vatican Council, with permission, are from *The Documents of Vatican II*, ed. W.M. Abbott, S.J. (Herder and Herder, America Press: New York, 1966; copyright 1966 by The America Press; all rights reserved). The authors are grateful to the Rev. John J. Manning, O.F.M., for theological consultation. If any copyrighted materials have been inadvertently used in this book without proper credit being given, please notify Our Sunday Visitor Publishing Division, Our Sunday Visitor, Inc., in writing so that future printings of this work may be corrected accordingly.

CONTENTS

Foreword • viii

Foreword

This book, a companion volume to *A Concise Guide to the Catholic Church*, is a concise guide to the history of the Church.

It contains a century-by-century record of dates, events and popes in the worldwide history of the Church, together with a broad sketch of its history in the United States.

Biographical sketches cover Mary and the saints, persons who exemplified the holiness and mission of the Church through the centuries.

The Church in worship through the centuries is portrayed in its holy days and feasts.

The concluding portion of the book is a selective glossary of terms derived from the history and experience of the Church and its people.

Chapter One

Dates and Events in Church History

Following is a chronological list of significant dates, events and persons, including the popes by centuries, in the history of the Catholic Church.

FIRST CENTURY

c. 33 First Christian Pentecost: descent of the Holy Spirit upon the disciples; preaching of St. Peter in Jerusalem; conversion, baptism and aggregation of some 3,000 persons to the first Christian community. The solemnity of Pentecost is popularly called the birthday of the Church.

St. Stephen, deacon, was stoned to death at Jerusalem; he is venerated as the first Christian martyr.

c. 34 St. Paul, formerly Saul the persecutor of Christians, was converted and baptized. After three years of solitude in the desert, he joined the college of the Apostles; he made three major missionary journeys and became known as the Apostle to the Gentiles; he was imprisoned twice in Rome and was beheaded there between 64 and 67.

39 Cornelius (the Gentile) and his family were baptized by St. Peter; a significant event signaling the mission of the Church to all peoples.

42 Persecution of Christians in Palestine broke out during the reign of Herod Agrippa. St. James the Greater, the first Apostle to die, was beheaded in 44; St. Peter was imprisoned for a short time; many Christians fled to Antioch, marking the beginning of the dispersion of Christians beyond the confines of Palestine. At Antioch, the followers of Christ were called Christians for the first time.

49 Christians at Rome, considered members of a Jewish sect, were adversely affected by a decree of Claudius which forbade Jewish worship there.

51 The Council of Jerusalem, in which all the Apostles participated under the presidency of St. Peter, decreed that circumcision, dietary regulations and various other prescriptions of Mosaic Law were not obligatory for Gentile converts to the Christian community. This crucial decree was issued in opposition to Judaizers who contended that observance of the Mosaic Law in its entirety was necessary for salvation.

64   Persecution broke out at Rome under Nero, the emperor said to have accused Christians of starting a fire which destroyed half of the city.

c. 64 or 67   Martyrdom, by crucifixion, of St. Peter at Rome during the Neronian persecution. He established his see and spent his last years there after preaching in Palestine and several other provinces, establishing a see at Antioch, and presiding at the Council of Jerusalem.

70   Destruction of Jerusalem.

88-97   Pontificate of St. Clement I, third successor of St. Peter as Bishop of Rome, one of the Apostolic Fathers. The *First Epistle of Clement to the Corinthians*, with which he has been identified, was addressed by the Church of Rome to the Church at Corinth, the scene of irregularities and divisions in the Christian community.

95   Persecution under Emperor Domitian, principally at Rome.

c. 100   Death of St. John, Apostle and Evangelist, marking the end of the Age of the Apostles.

By the end of the century, Antioch, Alexandria and Ephesus in the East and Rome in the West were established centers of Christian population and influence.

Popes   St. Peter (d. c. 64 or 67), St. Linus (67-76), St. Anacletus (Cletus) (76-88), St. Clement (88-97).

SECOND CENTURY

c. 107   St. Ignatius of Antioch, the second successor of St. Peter in that see, was martyred at Rome. He was the first writer to use the expression, "Catholic Church."

112   Emperor Trajan, in a rescript in Pliny the Younger, governor of Bithynia, instructed him not to search out Christians but to punish them if they were publicly denounced and refused to do homage to the gods of the Romans. This rescript set a pattern for Roman magistrates in dealing with Christians.

117-38   Persecution under Emperor Hadrian. Many accounts of the sufferings of martyrs (*Acta*) date from this period.

c. 125   Spread of Gnosticism, a combination of elements of Platonic philosophy and Eastern mystery religions. Its adherents claimed that its secret-knowledge principle provided a deeper insight into Christian doctrine than divine revelation and faith. One gnostic thesis denied the divinity of Christ; others denied the reality of his humanity, calling it mere appearance (Docetism, Phantasiasm).

c. 144 Excommunication of Marcion, bishop and heretic, who claimed that there was total opposition and no connection at all between the Old Testament and the New Testament, between the God of the Jews and the God of the Christians; and that the Canon (list of inspired books) of the Bible consisted only of parts of St. Luke's Gospel and ten letters of St. Paul. Marcionism was condemned again by a council at Rome about 260. The heresy was checked at Rome by 200, but persisted for several centuries in the East and had some adherents as late as the Middle Ages.

c. 155 St. Polycarp, bishop of Smyrna and disciple of St. John the Evangelist, was martyred.

c. 156 Beginning of Montanism, a form of religious extremism. Its principal tenets were: the imminent second coming of Christ, denial of the divine nature of the Church and its power to forgive sin, and excessively rigorous morality. The heresy, preached by Montanus of Phrygia and others, was condemned by Pope St. Zephyrinus (199-217).

161-80 Reign of Emperor Marcus Aurelius. His persecution, launched in the wake of natural disasters, was more violent than those of his predecessors.

165 St. Justin, an important early Christian writer called the Apologist, was martyred at Rome.

c. 180 St. Irenaeus, bishop of Lyons, called the Father of Theologians, wrote *Adversus Haereses*, in which he stated that the teaching and tradition of the Roman See is the norm of belief.

196 Easter Controversy, concerning the day of the celebration — a Sunday, according to practice in the West, or the 14th of Nisan no matter what day of the week, according to practice in the East. The controversy was not resolved at this time.

The *Didache*, whose extant form dates from the second century, is an important record of Christian belief, practice and governance in the first century.

Latin was introduced as a language of the liturgy in the West. Other liturgical languages were Aramaic and Greek.

The Catechetical School of Alexandria, founded about the middle of the century, gained increasing influence on doctrinal study and instruction, and interpretation of the Bible.

Popes   St. Evaristus (97-105), St. Alexander I (105-15), St. Sixtus I (115-25), St. Telesphorus (125-36), St. Hyginus (136-40), St. Pius I (140-55), St. Anicetus (155-66), St. Soter (166-75), St. Eleutherius (175-89), St. Victor I (189-99).

THIRD CENTURY

202   Persecution under Emperor Septimius Severus, who wanted to establish a single common religion in the Roman Empire.

206   Tertullian, a convert since 197 and the first great ecclesiastical writer in Latin, joined the heretical Montanists; he died in 230.

215   Death of Clement of Alexandria, a founding father of the School of Alexandria and a teacher of Origen.

217-35   St. Hippolytus, the first antipope; he was reconciled to the Church while in prison during persecution in 235.

232-54   Origen established the School of Caesarea after being deposed in 231 as head of the School of Alexandria; he died in 254. A scholar and voluminous writer, he was one of the pioneers of systematic theology and exerted wide influence for many years.

c. 242   Manichaeism originated in Persia: a combination of errors based on the assumption that two supreme principles (good and evil) are operative in creation and life, and that the supreme objective of human endeavor is liberation from evil (matter). The heresy denied the humanity of Christ, the sacramental system, the authority of the Church (and state), and endorsed a moral code which threatened the fabric of society. In the 12th and 13th centuries it took on the features of Albigensianism and Catharism.

249-51   Persecution under Emperor Decius. Many of those who denied the Faith (*lapsi*, fallen-aways) sought readmission to the Church at the end of persecution in 251. Pope St. Cornelius agreed with St. Cyprian that *lapsi* were to be readmitted to the Church after satisfying the requirements of appropriate penance.

Antipope Novatian, on the other hand, contended that persons who fell away from the Church under persecution and/or those guilty of serious sin after baptism could not be absolved and readmitted to communion with the Church. The heresy was condemned by a Roman synod in 251.

256   Pope St. Stephen I upheld the validity of baptism properly administered by heretics, in the Rebaptism Controversy.

257 Persecution under Emperor Valerian, who attempted to destroy the Church as a social structure.

258 Martyrdom of St. Cyprian, bishop of Carthage.

c. 260 St. Lucian founded the School of Antioch, a center of influence on biblical studies.

Pope St. Dionysius condemned Sabellianism, a form of Modalism (like Monarchianism and Patripassianism). The heresy contended that the Father, Son and Holy Spirit are not distinct divine persons but are only three different modes of being and self-manifestation of the one God.

St. Paul of Thebes became a hermit.

261 Emperor Gallienus issued an edict of toleration which freed Christians from general persecution for a period of about 40 years.

c. 292 Emperor Diocletian divided the Roman Empire into East and West. The division emphasized political, cultural and other differences between the two parts of the Empire, and influenced different developments in the Church in the East and West. The prestige of Rome began to decline.

Popes St. Zephyrinus (199-217), St. Callistus I (217-22), St. Urban I (222-30), St. Pontian (230-35), St. Anterus (235-36), St. Fabian (236-50), St. Cornelius (251-53), St. Lucius I (253-54), St. Stephen I (254-57), St. Sixtus II (257-58), St. Dionysius (259-68), St. Felix I (269-74), St. Eutychian (275-83), St. Caius (283-96).

Antipopes St. Hippolytus (217-35), Novatian (251).

FOURTH CENTURY

303 Persecution broke out under Diocletian; it was particularly violent in 304 but ended in the West in 306.

305 St. Anthony of Heracles established a foundation for hermits near the Red Sea in Egypt.

c. 306 The first local legislation on clerical celibacy was enacted by a council held at Elvira, Spain; bishops, priests, deacons and other ministers were forbidden to have wives.

311 An edict of toleration issued by Galerius, at the urging of Constantine and Licinius, officially ended persecution in the West; some persecution continued in the East.

313 The Edict of Milan, issued by Emperors Constantine and Licinius, recognized Christianity as a lawful religion in the Empire.

314 A council of Arles condemned Donatism, declaring that baptism properly administered by heretics is valid. The

heresy was condemned in view of the principle that sacraments have their efficacy from Christ, not from the spiritual condition of their human ministers.

318 St. Pachomius established the first foundation of the cenobitic (community) life, as compared with the solitary life of hermits in Upper Egypt.

325 Ecumenical Council of Nicaea (I). Its principal action was the condemnation of Arianism, the most devastating of the early heresies, which denied the divinity of Christ. The heresy was authored by Arius of Alexandria, a priest. Arians and several kinds of Semi-Arians propagandized their tenets widely, established their own hierarchies and churches, and raised havoc in the Church for several centuries.

The council contributed to formulation of the Nicene Creed (Creed of Nicaea-Constantinople); fixed the date for the observance of Easter; passed regulations concerning clerical discipline; adopted the civil divisions of the Empire as the model for the jurisdictional organization of the Church.

326 Discovery of the True Cross on which Christ was crucified.

337 Baptism and death of Constantine.

c. 342 Beginning of a 40-year persecution in Persia.

343-44 A council of Sardica reaffirmed doctrine formulated by Nicaea I and also declared that bishops had the right of appeal to the pope as the highest authority in the Church.

361-63 Emperor Julian the Apostate waged an unsuccessful campaign against the Church in an attempt to restore paganism in the Empire.

c. 365 Persecution under Emperor Valens in the East.

c. 376 Beginning of the barbarian invasion in the West.

379 Death of St. Basil, Father of Monasticism in the East. His writings contributed greatly to the development of rules for the life of Religious.

381 Ecumenical Council of Constantinople (I). It condemned various brands of Arianism as well as Macedonianism (which denied the divinity of the Holy Spirit); contributed to formulation of the Nicene Creed; approved a canon acknowledging Constantinople as the second see after Rome in honor and dignity.

382 The Canon of Sacred Scripture (official list of the inspired books of the Bible) was listed in the *Decree of Pope St. Damasus* and published by a regional council of Carthage in 397. The canon was formally defined by the Council of Trent in the 16th century.

382-c. 406 St. Jerome translated the Old and New Testaments into Latin; his work is called the Vulgate Version of the Bible.

396 St. Augustine became bishop of Hippo in North Africa.

Popes St. Marcellinus (296-304), St. Marcellus I (308-09), St. Eusebius (309-10), St. Melchiades (Miltiades) (311-14), St. Sylvester I (314-35), St. Marcus (336), St. Julius I (337-52), Liberius (352-66), St. Damasus I (366-84), St. Siricius (384-99).

Antipopes Felix II (355-65), Ursinus (366-67).

FIFTH CENTURY

410 Visigoths sacked Rome.

411 Donatism was condemned by a council of Carthage (see year 314).

430 Death of St. Augustine, bishop of Hippo for 35 years. He was a strong defender of orthodoxy against Manichaeism, Donatism and Pelagianism. The depth and range of his writings made him a dominant influence in Christian thought for centuries.

431 Ecumenical Council of Ephesus. It condemned Nestorianism, which denied the unity of the divine and human natures in the Person of Christ; defined *Theotokos* (Bearer of God) as the title of Mary, Mother of the Son of God made Man; condemned Pelagianism. The heresy of Pelagianism, proceeding from the assumption that Adam had a natural right to supernatural life, held that man could attain salvation through the efforts of his natural powers and free will; it involved errors concerning the nature of original sin, the meaning of grace and other matters. Related Semi-Pelagianism was condemned by a council of Orange in 529.

432 St. Patrick arrived in Ireland. By the time of his death in 461, most of the country had been converted, monasteries founded and the hierarchy established.

438 The Theodosian Code, a compilation of decrees for the Empire, was issued by Theodosius II; it had great influence on subsequent civil and church law.

449 The Robber Council of Ephesus, which did not have ecclesiastical sanction, declared itself in favor of the opinions of Eutyches, who contended that Christ had only one, the divine, nature (Monophysitism).

451 Ecumenical Council of Chalcedon. Its principal action was the condemnation of Monophysitism (also called Eutychianism), which denied the humanity of Christ by holding that he had only one, the divine, nature.

452   Pope St. Leo the Great persuaded Attila the Hun to spare Rome.

455   Vandals sacked Rome. The decline of imperial Rome dates approximately from this time.

484   Patriarch Acacius of Constantinople was excommunicated for signing the *Henoticon*, a document which capitulated to the Monophysite heresy. The excommunication triggered a schism which lasted for 35 years.

494   Pope St. Gelasius I declared in a letter to Emperor Anastasius that the pope had power and authority over the emperor in spiritual matters.

496   Clovis, king of the Franks, was converted and became the defender of Christianity in the West. The Franks became a Catholic people.

Popes   St. Anastasius I (399-401), St. Innocent I (401-17), St. Zozimus (417-18), St. Boniface I (418-22), St. Celestine I (422-32), St. Sixtus III (432-40), St. Leo I (the Great) (440-61), St. Hilary (461-68), St. Simplicius (468-83), St. Felix III (II) (483-92), St. Gelasius I (492-96), Anastasius II (496-98).

Antipopes   Eulalius (418-19), Lawrence (498).

SIXTH CENTURY

520 on   Irish monasteries flourished as centers for spiritual life, missionary training and scholarly activity.

529   The Second Council of Orange condemned Semi-Pelagianism.

c. 529   St. Benedict founded the Monte Cassino Abbey. Some years before his death in 543 he wrote a monastic rule which exercised tremendous influence on the form and style of religious life. He is called the Father of Monasticism in the West.

533   John II became the first pope to change his name. The practice did not become general until the time of Sergius IV (1009).

533-534   Emperor Justinian promulgated the *Corpus Juris Civilis* for the Roman world. Like the Theodosian Code, it influenced subsequent civil and ecclesiastical law.

c. 545   Death of Dionysius Exiguus, who was the first to date history from the birth of Christ, a practice which resulted in use of the B.C. (Before Christ) and A.D. (Anno Domini; In the Year of the Lord) abbreviations. His calculations were at least four years late.

553 Ecumenical Council of Constantinople (II). It condemned the *Three Chapters*, Nestorian-tainted writings of Theodore of Mopsuestia, Theodoret of Cyrus and Ibas of Edessa.

585 St. Columban founded an influential monastic school at Luxeuil in France.

589 The most important of several councils of Toledo was held. The Visigoths renounced Arianism, and St. Leander began the organization of the Church in Spain.

590-604 Pontificate of Pope St. Gregory I (the Great). He set the form and style of the papacy which prevailed throughout the Middle Ages; exerted great influence on doctrine and liturgy; was strong in support of monastic discipline and clerical celibacy; authored writings on many subjects. Gregorian Chant is named in his honor.

596 Pope St. Gregory I (the Great) sent St. Augustine of Canterbury and 40 monks to do missionary work in England.

597 St. Columba died. He founded an important monastery at Iona, established schools and did notable missionary work in Scotland.

By the end of the century, monasteries of nuns were common; Western monasticism was flourishing; monasticism in the East, under the influence of Monophysitism and other factors, was losing its vigor.

Popes St. Symmachus (498-514), St. Hormisdas (514-23), St. John I, Martyr (523-26), St. Felix IV (III) (526-30), Boniface II (530-32), John II (first pope to change his name, from Mercury) (533-35), St. Agapitus I (535-36), St. Silverius, Martyr (536-37), Vigilius (537-55), Pelagius I (556-61), John III (561-74), Benedict I (575-79), Pelagius II (579-90).

Antipopes Lawrence (501-05, second time), Dioscorus (530).

SEVENTH CENTURY

613 St. Columban established the influential monastery of Bobbio in northern Italy; he died there in 615.

622 The Hegira (flight) of Mohammed from Mecca to Medina signaled the beginning of Islam, which by the end of the century claimed almost all of the southern Mediterranean area.

628 Heraclius, Eastern Roman emperor, recovered the True Cross from the Persians.

649   A Lateran council condemned two erroneous formulas (*Ecthesis* and *Type*) issued by emperors Heraclius and Constans II as means of reconciling Monophysites with the Church.

664   Actions of the Synod of Whitby advanced the adoption of Roman usages in England, especially regarding the date for the observance of Easter.

680-81   Ecumenical Council of Constantinople (III). It condemned Monothelitism, which held that Christ had only one will, the divine; censured Pope Honorius I for a letter to Sergius, bishop of Constantinople, in which he made an ambiguous but not infallible statement about the unity of will and/or operation in Christ.

692   Trullan Synod. Eastern-Church discipline on clerical celibacy was settled, permitting marriage before ordination to the diaconate and continuation in marriage afterwards, but prohibiting marriage following the death of the wife thereafter. Anti-Roman canons contributed to East-West alienation.

During the century, the monastic influence of Ireland and England increased in Western Europe; schools and learning declined; regulations regarding clerical celibacy became more strict in the East.

Popes   St. Gregory I (the Great) (590-604), Sabinian (604-06), Boniface III (607), St. Boniface IV (608-15), St. Deusdedit (Adeodatus) (615-18), Boniface V (619-25), Honorius I (625-38), Severinus (640), John IV (640-42), Theodore I (642-49), St. Martin I, Martyr (649-55; in exile from June, 653), St. Eugene I (654-57; elected during the exile of Martin I, who is believed to have endorsed him as pope), St. Vitalian (657-72), Adeodatus II (672-76), Donus (676-78), St. Agatho (678-81), St. Leo II (682-83), St. Benedict II (684-85), John V (685-86), Conon (686-87), St. Sergius I (687-701).

Antipopes   Theodore and Paschal (with alleged pontificates that ended in 687).

EIGHTH CENTURY

711   Moslems began the conquest of Spain.

726   Emperor Leo III, the Isaurian, launched a campaign against the veneration of sacred images and relics; called Iconoclasm (image-breaking), it caused turmoil in the East until about 843.

731   Pope Gregory III and a synod at Rome condemned

Iconoclasm, with a declaration that the veneration of sacred images was in accord with Catholic tradition.

Venerable Bede issued his *Ecclesiastical History of the English People.*

732 Charles Martel defeated the Moslems at Poitiers, halting their advance in the West.

744 The Monastery of Fulda was established by St. Sturmi, a disciple of St. Boniface; it was influential in the evangelization of Germany.

754 A council of more than 300 Byzantine bishops endorsed Iconoclast errors. This council and its actions were condemned by the Lateran Synod of 769.

Pope Stephen II (III) crowned Pepin ruler of the Franks. Pepin twice invaded Italy, in 754 and 756, to defend the pope against the Lombards. His land grants to the papacy, called the Donation of Pepin, were later extended by Charlemagne (773) and formed part of the States of the Church.

c. 755 St. Boniface (Winfrid) was martyred. He was called the Apostle of Germany for his missionary work and organization of the hierarchy there.

781 Alcuin was chosen by Charlemagne to organize a palace school which became a center of intellectual leadership.

787 Ecumenical Council of Nicaea (II). It condemned Iconoclasm, which held that the use of images was idolatry, and Adoptionism, which claimed that Christ was not the Son of God by nature but only by adoption. This was the last council regarded as ecumenical by Orthodox Churches.

792 A council at Ratisbon condemned Adoptionism.

Popes John VI (701-05), John VII (705-07), Sisinnius (708), Constantine (708-15), St. Gregory II (715-31), St. Gregory III (731-41), St. Zachary (741-52), Stephen II (III) (752-57), St. Paul I (757-67), Stephen III (IV) (768-72), Adrian I (772-95).

Antipopes Constantine (767-69), Philip (768, July 31, retired to a monastery the same day).

NINTH CENTURY

800 Charlemagne was crowned Emperor of the Holy Roman Empire by Pope Leo III on Christmas Day.

Egbert became king of West Saxons; he unified England and strengthened the See of Canterbury.

813 Emperor Leo V, the Armenian, revived Iconoclasm, which persisted until about 843.

814 Charlemagne died.

843 The Treaty of Verdun split the Frankish kingdom among Charlemagne's three grandsons.

844 A Eucharistic controversy involving the writings of St. Paschasius Radbertus, Ratramnus and Rabanus Maurus occasioned the development of terminology regarding the doctrine of the Real Presence.

846 The Moslems invaded Italy and attacked Rome.

847-52 Period of composition of the *False Decretals*, a collection of forged documents attributed to popes from St. Clement (88-97) to Gregory II (715-31). The *Decretals*, which strongly supported the autonomy and rights of bishops, were suspect for a long time before being repudiated entirely about 1628.

848 The Council of Mainz condemned Gottschalk for heretical teaching regarding predestination. He was also condemned by a council of Quierzy in 853.

857 Photius displaced Ignatius as patriarch of Constantinople. This marked the beginning of the Photian Schism, a confused state of East-West relations which has not yet been cleared up by historical research. Photius, a man of exceptional ability, died in 891.

865 St. Ansgar, Apostle of Scandinavia, died.

869 St. Cyril died and his brother, St. Methodius (d. 885), was ordained a bishop. The Apostles of the Slavs devised an alphabet and translated the Gospels and liturgy into the Slavonic language.

869-70 Ecumenical Council of Constantinople (IV). It issued a second condemnation of Iconoclasm, condemned and deposed Photius as patriarch of Constantinople, restored Ignatius to the patriarchate. This was the last ecumenical council held in the East. It was first called ecumenical by canonists toward the end of the 11th century.

871-c. 900 Reign of Alfred the Great, the only English king ever anointed by a pope at Rome.

Popes St. Leo III (795-816), Stephen IV (V) (816-17), St. Paschal I (817-24), Eugene II (824-27), Valentine (827), Gregory IV (827-44), Sergius II (844-47), St. Leo IV (847-55), Benedict III (855-58), St. Nicholas I (the Great) (858-67), Adrian II (867-72), John VIII (872-82), Marinus (882-84), St. Adrian III (884-85), Stephen V (VI) (885-91), Formosus (891-96), Boniface VI (896), Stephen VI (VII) (896-97), Romanus (897), Theodore II (897), John IX (898-900).

Antipopes John (with alleged pontificate that ended in 844), Anastasius (855).

TENTH CENTURY

910   William, duke of Aquitaine, founded the Benedictine Abbey of Cluny, which became a center of monastic and ecclesiastical reform especially in France.

915   Pope John X played a leading role in the expulsion of Saracens from central and southern Italy.

955   St. Olga, of the Russian royal family, was baptized.

962   Otto I, the Great, crowned by Pope John XII, revived Charlemagne's Holy Roman Empire.

966   Mieszko, first of a royal line in Poland, was baptized; he brought Latin Christianity to Poland.

989   Vladimir, ruler of Russia, was baptized. Russia was subsequently Christianized by Greek missionaries.

993   John XV was the first pope to decree the official canonization of a saint (Ulrich) for the universal Church.

997   St. Stephen became ruler of Hungary. He assisted in organizing the hierarchy and establishing Latin Christianity in that country.

999-1003   Pontificate of Sylvester II (Gerbert of Aquitaine), a Benedictine monk and the first French pope.

Popes   Benedict IV (900-03), Leo V (903), Sergius III (904-11), Anastasius III (911-13), Landus (913-14), John X (914-28), Leo VI (928), Stephen VII (VIII) (928-31), John XI (931-35), Leo VII (936-39), Stephen VIII (IX) (939-42), Marinus II (942-46), Agapitus II (946-55), John XII (955-64, year of his death), Leo VIII (963-65; confusion exists regarding the legitimacy of his claim to the pontificate), Benedict V (964-66; confusion exists regarding the legitimacy of his claim to the pontificate), John XIII (965-72), Benedict VI (973-74), Benedict VII (974-83), John XIV (983-84), John XV (985-96), Gregory V (996-99).

Antipopes   Christopher (903-04), Boniface VII (974, 984-85), John XVI (997-98).

ELEVENTH CENTURY

1009   Beginning of lasting East-West schism in the Church, marked by dropping of the name of Pope Sergius IV from the Byzantine diptychs (the listing of persons prayed for during the liturgy). The deletion was made by Patriarch Sergius II of Constantinople.

1012   St. Romuald founded the Camaldolese Hermits.

1025   The Council of Arras, and other councils later, condemned the Cathari (Neo-Manichaeans, Albigenses; see "Heresy").

1027 The Council of Elne proclaimed the Truce of God as a means of stemming violence. The truce involved armistice periods of varying lengths, which were later extended.

1038 St. John Gualbert founded the Vallombrosians.

1043-59 Constantinople patriarchate of Michael Cerularius, the key figure in a controversy concerning the primacy of the papacy. His and the Byzantine synod's refusal to acknowledge this primacy in 1054 widened and hardened the East-West schism in the Church.

1047 Pope Clement II died. He was the only pope ever buried in Germany.

1049-54 Pontificate of St. Leo IX, who inaugurated a movement of papal, diocesan, monastic and clerical reform.

1059 A Lateran council issued new legislation regarding papal elections. Voting power was entrusted to the Roman cardinals.

1066 Death of St. Edward the Confessor, king of England from 1042 and restorer of Westminster Abbey.

Defeat, at Hastings, of Harold by William I, who subsequently exerted strong influence on the lifestyle of the Church in England.

1073-85 Pontificate of St. Gregory VII (Hildebrand). A strong pope, he carried forward programs of clerical and general ecclesiastical reform and struggled against Henry IV and other rulers to end the evils of lay investiture. He introduced the Latin liturgy in Spain and set definite dates for the observance of ember days.

1077 Emperor Henry IV, excommunicated and suspended from the exercise of imperial powers by Gregory VII, sought absolution from the pope at Canossa. Henry later repudiated this action and in 1084 forced Gregory to leave Rome.

1079 The Council of Rome condemned Eucharistic errors (denial of the Real Presence of Christ under the appearances of bread and wine) of Berengarius, who retracted.

1084 St. Bruno founded the Carthusians.

1097-99 The first of several Crusades undertaken between this time and 1265. Recovery of the Holy Places and gaining free access to them for Christians were the original purposes, but these were diverted to less worthy objectives in various ways. Results included: a Latin Kingdom of Jerusalem, 1099-1187; a military and political misadventure in the form of a Latin Empire of Constantinople, 1204-61; acquisition, by treaties, of visiting rights for Christians in the Holy Land. East-West economic and cultural relationships increased during the period. In the religious sphere, actions of the Crusaders had the effect of increasing the alienation of the East from the West.

1098   St. Robert founded the Cistercians.

Popes   Sylvester II (999-1003), John XVII (1003), John XVIII (1004-09), Sergius IV (1009-12), Benedict VIII (1012-24), John XIX (1024-32), Benedict IX (1032-44), Sylvester III (1045, he was an antipope if the forcible removal of Benedict IX was not legitimate), Benedict IX (1045, second time), Gregory VI (1045-46), Clement II (1046-47). (If the resignation of Benedict IX in 1045 and his removal at the December, 1046, synod were not legitimate, Gregory VI and Clement II were antipopes.) Benedict IX (1047-48, third time), Damasus II (1048), St. Leo IX (1049-54), Victor II (1055-57), Stephen IX (X) (1057-58), Nicholas II (1059-61), Alexander II (1061-73), St. Gregory VII (1073-85), Bl. Victor III (1086-87), Bl. Urban II (1088-99).

Antipopes   Gregory (with alleged pontificate that ended in 1012), Benedict X (1058-59), Honorius II (1061-72), Clement III (1080-1100), Theodoric (with alleged pontificate that ended in 1100).

TWELFTH CENTURY

1108   Beginnings of the influential Abbey and School of St. Victor in France.

1115   St. Bernard established the Abbey of Clairvaux and inaugurated the Cistercian Reform.

1118   Christian forces captured Saragossa, Spain; the beginning of the Moslem decline in that country.

1121   St. Norbert established the original monastery of the Praemonstratensians near Laon, France.

1122   The Concordat of Worms (*Pactum Callixtinum*) was formulated and approved by Pope Callistus II and Emperor Henry V to settle controversy concerning the investiture of prelates. The concordat provided that the emperor could invest prelates with symbols of temporal authority but had no right to invest them with spiritual authority, which came from the Church alone, and that the emperor was not to interfere in papal elections. This was the first concordat in history.

1123   The Ecumenical Council of the Lateran (I), the first of its kind in the West. It endorsed provisions of the Concordat of Worms concerning the investiture of prelates and approved reform measures in 25 canons.

1139   Ecumenical Council of the Lateran (II). It adopted measures against a schism organized by antipope Anacletus and approved 30 canons related to discipline and other matters; one of the canons stated that holy orders is an invalidating impediment to marriage.

1140   St. Bernard met Abélard in debate at the Council of Sens. Abélard, whose rationalism in theology was condemned for the first time in 1121, died in 1142 at Cluny.

1148   The Synod of Rheims enacted strict disciplinary decrees for communities of women Religious.

1152   The Synod of Kells reorganized the Church in Ireland.

1160   Gratian, whose *Decretum* became a basic text of canon law, died.
           Peter Lombard, compiler of the *Four Books of Sentences*, a standard theology text for nearly 200 years, died.

1170   St. Thomas Becket, archbishop of Canterbury, who clashed with Henry II over church-state relations, was murdered in his cathedral.

1171   Pope Alexander III reserved the process of canonization of saints to the Holy See.

1179   Ecumenical Council of the Lateran (III). It enacted measures against Waldensianism and Albigensianism (see year 242 regarding Manichaeism), approved reform decrees in 27 canons, provided that popes be elected by a two-thirds vote of the cardinals.

1184   Waldenses and other heretics were excommunicated by Pope Lucius III.

Popes   Paschal II (1099-1118), Gelasius II (1118-19), Callistus II (1119-24), Honorius II (1124-30), Innocent II (1130-43), Celestine II (1143-44), Lucius II (1144-45), Bl. Eugene III (1145-53), Anastasius IV (1153-54), Adrian IV (1154-59), Alexander III (1159-81), Lucius III (1181-85), Urban III (1185-87), Gregory VIII (1187), Clement III (1187-91), Celestine III (1191-98).

Antipopes   Albert (with alleged pontificate that ended in 1102), Sylvester IV (1105-11), Gregory VIII (1118-21), Celestine II (with alleged pontificate that ended in 1124), Anacletus II (1130-38), Victor IV (1138), Victor IV (1159-64; he did not recognize the previous Victor IV), Paschal III (1164-68), Callistus III (1168-78), Innocent III (1179-80).

THIRTEENTH CENTURY

1198-1216   Pontificate of Innocent III, during which the papacy reached its medieval peak of authority, influence and prestige in the Church and in its relations with all civil rulers.

1208 Innocent III called for a crusade, the first in Christendom itself, against the Albigensians, whose beliefs and practices threatened the fabric of society in southern France and northern Italy.

1209 Verbal approval was given by Innocent III to a rule of life for the Order of Friars Minor, started by St. Francis of Assisi.

1212 The Second Order of Franciscans, the Poor Clares, was founded.

1215 Ecumenical Council of the Lateran (IV). It ordered annual reception of the sacraments of penance and the Eucharist; defined and made the first official use of the term transubstantiation to explain the change of bread and wine into the body and blood of Christ; adopted additional measures to counteract teachings and practices of the Albigensians and Cathari; approved 70 canons.

1216 Formal papal approval was given to a rule of life for the Order of Preachers, started by St. Dominic.

The Portiuncula Indulgence was granted by the Holy See at the request of St. Francis of Assisi.

1221 The Third Order of St. Francis for lay persons was founded.

1226 Death of St. Francis of Assisi.

1231 Pope Gregory IX authorized establishment of the Papal Inquisition for dealing with heretics. It was a creature of its time, when crimes against faith and heretical doctrines of extremists like the Cathari and Albigenses threatened the good of the Christian community, the welfare of the state and the very fabric of society. The institution, which was responsible for excesses in punishment, was most active in the second half of the century in southern France, Italy and Germany.

1245 Ecumenical Council of Lyons (I). It confirmed the deposition of Emperor Frederick II and approved 22 canons.

1247 Preliminary approval was given by the Holy See to a Carmelite rule of life.

1270 St. Louis IX, king of France, died.

1274 Ecumenical Council of Lyons (II). It accomplished a temporary reunion of separated Eastern Churches with the Roman Church; issued regulations concerning conclaves for papal elections; approved 31 canons.

Death of St. Thomas Aquinas, Doctor of the Church, of lasting influence.

1280 Pope Nicholas III, who made the *Breviary* the official prayer book for clergy of the Roman Church, died.

1281   The excommunication of Eastern Emperor Michael Palaeologus by Pope Martin IV ruptured the union effected with the Eastern Church in 1274.

Popes   Innocent III (1198-1216), Honorius III (1216-27), Gregory IX (1227-41), Celestine IV (1241), Innocent IV (1243-54), Alexander IV (1254-61), Urban IV 1261-64), Clement IV (1265-68), Bl. Gregory X (1271-76), Bl. Innocent V (1276), Adrian V (1276), John XXI (1276-77), Nicholas III (1277-80), Martin IV (1281-85), Honorius IV (1285-87), Nicholas IV (1288-92), St. Celestine V (1294).

FOURTEENTH CENTURY

1302   Pope Boniface VIII issued the bull *Unam Sanctam*, concerning the unity of the Church and the temporal power of princes, against the background of a struggle with Philip IV of France; it was the most famous medieval document on the subject.

1308-78   For a period of approximately 70 years, seven popes resided at Avignon because of unsettled conditions in Rome and other reasons.

1311-12   Ecumenical Council of Vienne. It suppressed the Knights Templar and enacted a number of reform decrees.

1321   Dante Alighieri died a year after completing the *Divine Comedy.*

1324   Marsilius of Padua completed *Defensor Pacis*, a work condemned by Pope John XXII as heretical because of its denial of papal primacy and the hierarchical structure of the Church, and for other reasons. It was a charter for Conciliarism (an ecumenical council is superior to the pope in authority).

1337-1453   Period of the Hundred Years' War, a dynastic struggle between France and England.

1338   Four years after the death of Pope John XXII, who had opposed Louis IV of Bavaria in a years-long controversy, electoral princes declared at the Diet of Rhense that the emperor did not need papal confirmation of his title and right to rule. Emperor Charles IV later (1356) said the same thing in a *Golden Bull*, eliminating papal rights in the election of emperors.

1347-50   The Black Death swept across Europe, killing perhaps one-fourth to one-third of the total population; an estimated 40 percent of the clergy succumbed.

1374   Petrarch, poet and humanist, died.

1378   Return of the papacy from Avignon to Rome.
Beginning of the Western Schism.

Popes   Boniface VIII (1294-1303), Bl. Benedict XI (1303-04), Clement V (1305-14, first of the seven Avignon popes), John XXII (1316-34), Benedict XII (1334-42), Clement VI (1342-52), Innocent VI (1352-62), Bl. Urban V (1362-70), Gregory XI (1370-78, last of the seven Avignon popes), Urban VI (1378-89).

Antipopes   Nicholas V (1328-30), Clement VII (1378-94 — first of four antipopes of the Western Schism).

FIFTEENTH CENTURY

1409   The Council of Pisa, without canonical authority, tried to end the Western Schism but succeeded only in complicating it by electing a third claimant to the papacy.

1414-18   Ecumenical Council of Constance. It took successful action to end the Western Schism involving rival claimants to the papacy; rejected the teachings of Wycliff; condemned Hus as a heretic. One decree — passed in the earlier stages of the council but later rejected — asserted the superiority of an ecumenical council over the pope (Conciliarism).

1431   St. Joan of Arc was burned at the stake.

1431-49   The Council of Basel, which began with convocation by Pope Martin V in 1431, turned into an anti-papal forum of conciliarists seeking to subject the primacy and authority of the pope to the overriding authority of an assembly of bishops. It was not an ecumenical council.

1438   The Pragmatic Sanction of Bourges was enacted by King Charles VII and the French Parliament to curtail papal authority over the Church in France, in the spirit of Conciliarism. It found expression in Gallicanism and had effects lasting at least until the French Revolution.

1438-45   Ecumenical Council of Florence (also called Basel-Ferrara-Florence).It reaffirmed the primacy of the pope against the claims of conciliarists that an ecumenical council is superior to the pope. It also formulated and approved decrees of union with several separated Eastern Churches — Greek, Armenian, Jacobite — which failed to gain general or lasting acceptance.

1453   The fall of Constantinople to the Turks.

c. 1456   Gutenberg issued the first edition of the Bible printed from movable type, at Mainz, Germany.

1476   Pope Sixtus IV ordered observance of the feast of the Immaculate Conception on Dec. 8 — throughout the Church.

1478 Pope Sixtus IV, at the urging of King Ferdinand of Spain, approved establishment of the Spanish Inquisition for dealing with Jewish and Moorish converts accused of heresy. The institution, which was peculiar to Spain and its colonies in America, acquired jurisdiction over other cases as well and fell into disrepute because of its procedures, cruelty and the manner in which it served the Spanish crown, rather than the accused and the good of the Church. Protests by the Holy See failed to curb excesses of the Inquisition, which lingered in Spanish history until early in the 19th century.

1492 Columbus discovered the Americas.

1493 Pope Alexander VI issued a *Bull of Demarcation* which determined spheres of influence for the Spanish and Portuguese in the Americas.

The Renaissance, a humanistic movement which originated in Italy in the 14th century, spread to France, Germany, the Low Countries and England. A transitional period between the medieval world and the modern secular world, it introduced profound changes which affected literature and the other arts, general culture, politics and religion.

Popes Boniface IX (1389-1404), Innocent VII (1404-06), Gregory XII (1406-15), Martin V (1417-31), Eugene IV (1431-47), Nicholas V (1447-55), Callistus III (1455-58), Pius II (1458-64), Paul II (1464-71), Sixtus IV (1471-84), Innocent VIII (1484-92).

Antipopes Benedict XIII (1394-1423, second antipope of the Western Schism), Alexander V (1409-10), third antipope of the Western Schism), John XXIII (1410-15, last of the four antipopes of the Western Schism), Felix V (1439-49).

SIXTEENTH CENTURY

1512-17 Ecumenical Council of the Lateran (V). It stated the relation and position of the pope with respect to an ecumenical council; acted to counteract the Pragmatic Sanction of Bourges and exaggerated claims of liberty by the Church in France; condemned erroneous teachings concerning the nature of the human soul; stated doctrine concerning indulgences. The council reflected concern for abuses in the Church and the need for reforms but failed to take decisive action in the years immediately preceding the Reformation.

1517   Martin Luther signaled the beginning of the Reformation by posting 95 theses at Wittenberg. Subsequently, he broke completely from doctrinal orthodoxy in discourses and three published works (1519 and 1520); was excommunicated on more than 40 charges of heresy (1521); remained the dominant figure in the Reformation in Germany until his death in 1546.

1519   Zwingli triggered the Reformation in Zurich and became its leading proponent there until his death in combat in 1531.

1524   Luther's encouragement of German princes in putting down the two-year Peasants' Revolt gained political support for his cause.

1528   The Order of Friars Minor Capuchin was approved as an autonomous division of the Franciscan Order; like the Jesuits, the Capuchins became leaders in the Counter-Reformation.

1530   The *Augsburg Confession* of Lutheran faith was issued; it was later supplemented by the *Smalcald Articles* approved in 1537.

1533   King Henry VIII divorced Catherine of Aragon, married Anne Boleyn, was excommunicated. In 1534 he decreed the Act of Supremacy, making the sovereign the head of the Church in England, under which Sts. John Fisher and Thomas More were executed in 1535. Despite his rejection of papal primacy and actions against monastic life in England, he generally maintained doctrinal orthodoxy until his death in 1547.

1536   John Calvin, leader of the Reformation in Switzerland until his death in 1564, issued the first edition of *Institutes of the Christian Religion*, which became the classical text of Reformed (non-Lutheran) theology.

1540   The constitutions of the Society of Jesus (Jesuits), founded by St. Ignatius of Loyola, were approved.

1541   Start of the 11-year career of St. Francis Xavier as a missionary to the East Indies and Japan.

1545-63   Ecumenical Council of Trent. It issued a great number of decrees concerning doctrinal matters opposed by the Reformers, and mobilized the Counter-Reformation. Definitions covered the Canon of the Bible, the rule of faith, the nature of justification, grace, faith, original sin and its effects, the seven sacraments, the sacrificial nature of the Mass, the veneration of saints, use of sacred images, belief in purgatory, the doctrine of indulgences, the jurisdiction of the pope over the whole Church. It initiated many reforms for renewal in the liturgy and general discipline in the Church, the promotion of religious instruction, the education of the clergy through the foundation of seminaries, etc. Trent ranks with Vatican II as the greatest ecumenical council held in the West.

1549   The first *Book of Common Prayer* of the Church of England was issued by Edward VI. Revised editions were published in 1552, 1559, 1662 and later.

1553   Start of the five-year reign of Mary Tudor, who tried to counteract actions of Henry VIII against the Roman Church.

1555   Enactment of the Peace of Augsburg, an arrangement of religious territorialism rather than toleration, which recognized the existence of Catholicism and Lutheranism in the German Empire and provided that citizens should adopt the religion of their respective rulers.

1558   Beginning of the reign of Elizabeth I, during which the Church of England took on its definitive form.

1559   Establishment of the hierarchy of the Church of England, with the consecration of Matthew Parker as archbishop of Canterbury.

1563   The first text of the *39 Articles* of the Church of England was issued. Also enacted were a new Act of Supremacy and Oath of Succession to the English throne.

1570   Elizabeth I was excommunicated. Penal measures against Catholics subsequently became more severe.

1571   Defeat of the Turkish armada at Lepanto staved off the invasion of Eastern Europe.

1577   The *Formula of Concord*, the classical statement of Lutheran faith, was issued; it was, generally, a Lutheran counterpart of the canons of the Council of Trent. In 1580, along with other formulas of doctrine, it was included in the *Book of Concord*.

1582   The Gregorian Calendar, named for Pope Gregory XIII, was put into effect and was eventually adopted in most countries; England delayed adoption until 1752.

Popes   Alexander VI (1492-1503), Pius III (1503), Julius II (1503-13), Leo X (1513-21), Adrian VI (1522-23), Clement VII (1523-34), Paul III (1534-49), Julius III (1550-55), Marcellus II (1555), Paul IV (1555-59), Pius IV (1559-65), St. Pius V (1566-72), Gregory XIII (1572-85), Sixtus V (1585-90), Urban VII (1590), Gregory XIV (1590-91), Innocent IX (1591).

SEVENTEENTH CENTURY

1605 The Gunpowder Plot, an attempt by Catholic fanatics to blow up James I of England and the houses of Parliament, resulted in an anti-Catholic Oath of Allegiance.

1610 Death of Matteo Ricci, outstanding Jesuit missionary to China, pioneer in cultural relations between China and Europe.

Founding of the first community of Visitation Nuns by Sts. Francis de Sales and Jane de Chantal.

1611 Founding of the Oratorians.

1613 Catholics were banned from Scandinavia.

1625 Founding of the Congregation of the Mission (Vincentians) by St. Vincent de Paul. He founded the Sisters of Charity in 1633.

1642 Death of Galileo, scientist who was censured by the Congregation of the Holy Office for supporting the Copernican theory of the sun-centered planetary system.

Founding of the Sulpicians by Jacques Olier.

1643 Start of publication of the Bollandist *Acta Sanctorum*, a critical work on lives of the saints.

1648 Provisions in the Peace of Westphalia, ending the Thirty Years' War, extended terms of the Peace of Augsburg (1555) to Calvinists and gave equality to Catholics and Protestants in the 300 states of the Holy Roman Empire.

1649 Oliver Cromwell invaded Ireland and began a severe persecution of the Church there.

1653 Pope Innocent X condemned five propositions of Jansenism, a complex theory which distorted doctrine concerning the relations between divine grace and human freedom. Jansenism was also a rigoristic movement which seriously disturbed the Church in France, the Low Countries and Italy in this and the 18th century.

1673 The Test Act in England barred from public office Catholics who would not deny the doctrine of transubstantiation and receive communion in the Church of England.

1678 Many English Catholics suffered death as a consequence of the Popish Plot, a false allegation by Titus Oates that Catholics planned to assassinate Charles II, land a French army in the country, burn London and turn over the government to the Jesuits.

1682 The four articles of the *Gallican Declaration*, asserted political and ecclesiastical immunities of France from papal control. The articles, which rejected the primacy of the pope, were condemned in 1690.

1689   The Toleration Act granted a measure of freedom of worship to other English dissenters, but not to Catholics.

Popes   Clement VIII (1592-1605), Leo XI (1605), Paul V (1605-21), Gregory XV (1621-23), Urban VIII (1623-44), Innocent X (1644-55), Alexander VII (1655-67), Clement IX (1667-69), Clement X (1670-76), Bl. Innocent XI (1676-89), Alexander VIII (1689-91), Innocent XII (1691-1700).

EIGHTEENTH CENTURY

1704   Chinese Rites — involving the Christian adaptation of elements of Confucianism, veneration of ancestors and Chinese terminology in religion — were condemned by Pope Clement XI.

1720   The Passionists were founded by St. Paul of the Cross.

1724   Persecution in China.

1732   The Redemptorists were founded by St. Alphonsus Liguori.

1738   Freemasonry was condemned by Clement XII and Catholics were forbidden to join, under penalty of excommunication; the prohibition was repeated by Benedict XIV in 1751 and by later popes. (The penalty of excommunication is no longer in force, but the strict prohibition against membership by Catholics remains.)

1760s   Josephinism, a theory and system of state control of the Church, was initiated in Austria; it remained in force until about 1850.

1764   Febronianism, an unorthodox theory and practice regarding the constitution of the Church and relations between Church and state, was condemned for the first of several times. Proposed by an auxiliary bishop of Trier using the pseudonym Justinus Febronius, it had the effects of minimizing the office of the pope and supporting national churches under state control.

1773   Pope Clement XIV issued a brief of suppression against the Jesuits, following their expulsion from Portugal in 1759, from France in 1764 and from Spain in 1767. Political intrigue and unsubstantiated accusations were principal factors in these developments. The ban, which crippled the society, contained no condemnation of the Jesuit constitutions, particular Jesuits or Jesuit teaching. The society was restored in 1814.

1778   Catholics in England were relieved of some civil disabilities dating back to the time of Henry VIII, by an act which permitted them to acquire, own and inherit property. Additional liberties were restored by the Roman Catholic Relief Act of 1791 and subsequent enactments of Parliament.

1789 Religious freedom in the United States was guaranteed under the First Amendment to the Constitution.

Beginning of the French Revolution which resulted in: the secularization of church property and the Civil Constitution of the Clergy in 1790; the persecution of priests, Religious and lay persons loyal to papal authority; invasion of the Papal States by Napoleon in 1796; renewal of persecution from 1797 to 1799; attempts to dechristianize France and establish a new religion; the occupation of Rome by French troops and the forced removal of Pope Pius VI to France in 1798.

This century is called the age of Enlightenment or Reason because of the predominating rational and scientific approach of its leading philosophers, scientists and writers with respect to religion, ethics and natural law. This approach downgraded the fact and significance of revealed religion. Also characteristic of the Enlightenment were subjectivism, secularism and optimism regarding human perfectibility.

Popes Clement XI (1700-21), Innocent XIII (1721-24), Benedict XIII (1724-30), Clement XII (1730-40), Benedict XIV (1740-58), Clement XIII (1758-69), Clement XIV (1769-74), Pius VI (1775-99).

NINETEENTH CENTURY

1809 Pope Pius VII was made a captive by Napoleon and deported to France where he remained in exile until 1814. During this time he refused to cooperate with Napoleon who sought to bring the Church in France under his own control.

The turbulence in church-state relations in France at the beginning of the century recurred in connection with the Bourbon Restoration, the July Revolution, the second and third Republics, the Second Empire and the Dreyfus case.

1814 The Society of Jesus, suppressed since 1773, was restored.

1817 Reestablishment of the Congregation for the Propagation of the Faith (Propaganda) by Pius VII was an important factor in increasing missionary activity during the century.

1820 Years-long persecution, during which thousands died for the faith, ended in China. Thereafter, communication with the West remained cut off until about 1834. Vigorous missionary work got under way in 1842.

1822 The Pontifical Society for the Propagation of the Faith, inaugurated in France by Pauline Jaricot for the support of missionary activity, was established.

1829 The Catholic Emancipation Act relieved Catholics in England and Ireland of most of the civil disabilities to which they had been subject from the time of Henry VIII.

1832 Pope Gregory XVI, in the encyclical *Mirari Vos*, condemned Indifferentism, one of the many ideologies at odds with Christian doctrine which were proposed during the century.

1833 Start of the Oxford Movement which affected the Church of England and resulted in some notable conversions, including that of John Henry Newman in 1845, to the Catholic Church.

Frederic Ozanam founded the Society of St. Vincent de Paul in France. The society, whose objective was works of charity, became worldwide.

1848 The *Communist Manifesto* was issued.

1850 The hierarchy was reestablished in England and Nicholas Wiseman made the first archbishop of Westminster. He was succeeded in 1865 by Henry Manning, an Oxford convert and proponent of the rights of labor.

1853 The Catholic hierarchy was reestablished in Holland.

1854 Pope Pius IX proclaimed the dogma of the Immaculate Conception in the bull *Ineffabilis Deus.*

1858 The Blessed Virgin Mary appeared to St. Bernadette at Lourdes, France.

1864 Pius IX issued the encyclical *Quanta Cura* and the *Syllabus of Errors* in condemnation of some 80 propositions derived from the scientific mentality and rationalism of the century. The subjects in question had deep ramifications in many areas of thought and human endeavor; in religion, they explicitly and/or implicitly rejected divine revelation and the supernatural order.

1867 The first volume of *Das Kapital* was published. Together with the Communist First International, formed in the same year, it had great influence on the subsequent development of Communism and socialism.

1869 The Anglican Church was disestablished in Ireland.

1869-70 Ecumenical Council of the Vatican (I). It defined papal primacy and infallibility in a dogmatic constitution on the Church; covered natural religion, revelation, faith, and the relations between faith and reason in a dogmatic constitution on the Catholic faith.

1870-71 Victor Emmanuel II of Sardinia, crowned king of Italy after defeating Austrian and papal forces, marched into Rome in 1870 and expropriated the Papal States after a plebiscite in which Catholics, at the order of Pius IX, did not vote. In 1871, Pius IX refused to accept a Law of Guarantees. Confiscation of church property and hindrance of ecclesiastical administration by the regime followed.

1871 The German Empire, a confederation of 26 states, was formed. Government policy launched a Kulturkampf whose May Laws of 1873 were designed to annul papal jurisdiction in Prussia and other states and to place the Church under imperial control. Resistance to the enactments, and the persecution they legalized, forced the government to modify its anti-Church policy by 1887.

1878 Beginning of the pontificate of Leo XIII. His encyclical *Rerum Novarum* greatly influenced the course of Christian social thought and the labor movement. His other accomplishments included promotion of a revival of Scholastic philosophy and the impetus he gave to scriptural studies.

1881 The first International Eucharistic Congress was held in Lille, France.

Alexander II of Russia died. His policies of Russification — as well as those of his two predecessors and a successor during the century — caused great suffering to Catholics, Jews and Protestants in Poland, Lithuania, the Ukraine and Bessarabia.

1882 Charles Darwin died. His theory of evolution by natural selection, one of several scientific highlights of the century, had extensive repercussions in the faith-and-science controversy.

1889 The Catholic University of America was founded in Washington, D.C.

1893 The U.S. Apostolic Delegation was set up in Washington, D.C.

Popes Pius VII (1800-23), Leo XII (1823-29), Pius VIII (1829-30), Gregory XVI (1831-46), Pius IX (1846-78), Leo XIII (1878-1903).

TWENTIETH CENTURY

1901 Restrictive measures in France forced the Jesuits, Benedictines, Carmelites and other religious orders to leave the country. Subsequently, 14,000 schools were suppressed; religious orders and congregations were expelled; the concordat was renounced in 1905; church property was confiscated in 1906. For some years the Holy See, refusing to comply with government demands for the control of bishops' appointments, left some ecclesiastical offices vacant.

1903   End of the pontificate of Leo XIII. (See Twentieth Century Popes.)

1903-14   Pontificate of St. Pius X. He stimulated frequent reception of the Eucharist, ordered establishment of the Confraternity of Christian Doctrine in parishes throughout the world, condemned Modernism. (See Twentieth Century Popes.)

1908   The United States and England, long under the jurisdiction of the Congregation for the Propagation of the Faith as mission territories, were removed from its control and placed under the common law of the Church.

1910   Laws of separation were enacted in Portugal, marking a point of departure in church-state relations.

1911   The Catholic Foreign Mission Society of America — Maryknoll, the first U.S.-founded society of its type — was established.

1914-18   World War I.

1914-22   Pontificate of Benedict XV. Much of his pontificate was devoted to seeking ways and means of minimizing the havoc of World War I. (See Twentieth Century Popes.)

1917   The Blessed Virgin Mary appeared to three children at Fatima, Portugal.

A new constitution, embodying repressive laws against the Church, was enacted in Mexico. Its implementation resulted in persecution in the 1920s and 1930s.

Bolsheviks seized power in Russia and set up a communist dictatorship. The event marked the establishment of Communism in Russian and world affairs. One of its immediate, and lasting, results was persecution of the Church, Jews and other segments of the population.

1918   The Code of Canon Law, in preparation for more than 10 years, went into effect in the Western Church.

1919   Benedict XV stimulated missionary work through the decree *Maximum Illud*, in which he urged the recruiting and training of native clergy in places where the Church was not firmly established.

1920-22   Ireland was partitioned by two enactments of the British government which (1) made the six counties of Northern Ireland part of the United Kingdom in 1920 and (2) gave dominion status to the Irish Free State in 1922. The Irish Free State became an independent republic in 1949.

1922-39 Pontificate of Pius XI. He settled the Roman Question, resisted efforts by Mussolini to dominate the Church and Catholic Action, issued key encyclical letters on Christian marriage, social justice and Communism. (See Twentieth Century Popes.)

1926 The Catholic Relief Act repealed virtually all legal disabilities of Catholics in England.

1931 Leftists proclaimed Spain a republic and proceeded to disestablish the Church, confiscate church property, deny salaries to the clergy, expel the Jesuits and ban teaching of the Catholic faith. These actions were preludes to the civil war of 1936-39.

1933 Emergence of Adolf Hitler to power in Germany. By 1935 two of his aims were clear, the elimination of Jews and control of a single national church. Six million Jews were killed in the Holocaust of persecution. The Church was subject to repression, which Pius XI protested futilely in the encyclical letter *Mit Brennender Sorge* in 1937.

1936-39 Civil war in Spain between leftist Loyalist and rightist Franco forces. Priests, Religious and lay persons fell victims of persecution by Loyalists.

1939-45 World War II.

1939-58 Pontificate of Pius XII. He condemned Communism, proclaimed the dogma of the Assumption of Mary in 1950, in various documents and other enactments provided ideological background for many of the accomplishments of the Second Vatican Council. (See Twentieth Century Popes.)

1940 Start of a decade of communist conquest in more than 13 countries, resulting in conditions of persecution for a minimum of 60 million Catholics, as well as members of other faiths.

Persecution diminished in Mexico through nonenforcement of anti-religious laws still on record.

1957 The communist regime of China established the Patriotic Association of Chinese Catholics in opposition to the Church in union with the pope.

1958-63 Pontificate of John XXIII. His principal accomplishment was the convocation of the Second Vatican Council, the twenty-first ecumenical council in the history of the Church. (See Twentieth Century Popes.)

1962-65 Ecumenical Council of the Vatican (II). It formulated and promulgated 16 documents — two dogmatic and two pastoral constitutions, nine decrees and three declarations — reflecting pastoral orientation toward renewal and reform in the Church, and making explicit dimensions of doctrine

and Christian life requiring emphasis for the full development of the Church and the better accomplishment of its
mission in the contemporary world.

1963-78   Pontificate of Paul VI. His main purpose and effort was to
give direction and provide guidance for the authentic
trends of church renewal set in motion by the Second Vatican Council. (See Twentieth Century Popes.)

1978   The thirty-four-day pontificate of John Paul I. (See Twentieth Century Popes.)

Start of the pontificate of John Paul II. (See Twentieth
Century Popes.)

1983   The revised Code of Canon Law, embodying reforms enact-
ed by the Second Vatican Council, went into effect in the
Church of Roman Rite. (Revision of the Canon Law of
Eastern Churches was still in process.)

1985   Formal ratification of a Vatican-Italy concordat replacing
the Lateran Treaty of 1929.

Popes   St. Pius X (1903-14), Benedict XV (1914-22), Pius XI
(1922-39), Pius XII (1939-58), John XXIII (1958-63), Paul VI
(1963-78), John Paul I (1978), John Paul II (1978 —).

Chapter Two

Twentieth Century Popes

LEO XIII

Leo XIII (Gioacchino Vincenzo Pecci) was born May 2, 1810, in Carpineto, Italy. Although all but three years of his life and pontificate were of the 19th century, his influence extended well into the 20th century. He was educated at the Jesuit college in Viterbo, the Roman College, the Academy of Noble Ecclesiastics, and the University of the Sapienza. He was ordained to the priesthood in 1837.

He served as an apostolic delegate to two States of the Church, Benevento from 1838 to 1841 and Perugia in 1841 and 1842. Ordained titular archbishop of Damietta, he was papal nuncio to Belgium from January, 1843, until May, 1846; in the post, he had controversial relations with the government over education issues and acquired his first significant experience of industrialized society.

He was archbishop of Perugia from 1846 to 1878. He became a cardinal in 1853 and chamberlain of the Roman Curia in 1877. He was elected to the papacy Feb. 20, 1878. He died July 20, 1903.

Canonizations: He canonized 18 saints and beatified a group of English martyrs.

Church Administration: He established 300 new dioceses and vicariates; restored the hierarchy in Scotland; set up an English, as contrasted with the Portuguese, hierarchy in India; approved the action of the Congregation for the Propagation of the Faith in reorganizing missions in China.

Encyclicals: He issued 86 encyclicals, on subjects ranging from devotional to social. In the former category were *Annum Sacrum*, on the Sacred Heart, in 1899, and 11 letters on Mary and the Rosary.

Interfaith Relations: He was unsuccessful in unity overtures made to Orthodox and Slavic Churches. He declared Anglican orders invalid in the apostolic bull *Apostolicae Curae* Sept. 13, 1896.

International Relations: Leo was frustrated in seeking solutions to the Roman Question arising from the seizure of church lands by the Kingdom of Italy in 1870. He also faced anticlerical situations in Belgium and France and in the Kulturkampf policies of Bismarck in Germany.

Social Questions: Much of Leo's influence stemmed from social doctrine stated in numerous encyclicals, concerning liberalism, liberty, the divine origin of authority; socialism, in *Quod Apostolici Muneris*, 1878; the Christian concept of the family, in *Arcanum*, 1880; socialism and economic liberalism, relations between capital and labor, in *Rerum Novarum*, 1891. Two of his social encyclicals were against the African slave trade.

Studies: In the encyclical *Aeterni Patris* of Aug. 4, 1879, he ordered a renewal of philosophical and theological studies in seminaries along scholastic, and especially Thomistic, lines, to counteract influential trends of liberalism and Modernism. He issued guidelines for biblical exegesis in *Providentissimus Deus* Nov. 18, 1893, and established the Pontifical Biblical Commission in 1902.

In other actions affecting scholarship and study, he opened the Vatican Archives to scholars in 1883 and established the Vatican Observatory.

United States: He authorized establishment of the Apostolic Delegation in Washington, D.C., on Jan. 24, 1893. He refused to issue a condemnation of the Knights of Labor. With a document entitled *Testem Benevolentiae*, he eased resolution of questions concerning what was called an American heresy in 1899.

ST. PIUS X

St. Pius X (Giuseppe Melchiorre Sarto) was born June 2, 1835 in Riese, Italy. Educated at the college of Castelfranco and the seminary at Padua, he was ordained to the priesthood Sept. 18, 1858. He served as a curate in Trombolo for nine years before beginning an eight-year pastorate at Salzano. He was chancellor of the Treviso Diocese from November, 1875, and bishop of Mantua from 1884 until 1893. He was cardinal-patriarch of Venice from that year until his election to the papacy by the conclave held from July 31 to Aug. 4, 1903. He died Aug. 20, 1914. He was beatified in 1951 and canonized May 29, 1954; his feast is observed Aug. 21.

Aims: Pius' principal objectives as pope were "to restore all things in Christ, in order that Christ may be all and in all," and "to teach (and defend) Christian truth and law."

Canonizations, Encyclicals: He canonized four saints and issued 16 encyclicals. One of the encyclicals was issued in commemoration of the 50th anniversary of the proclamation of the dogma of the Immaculate Conception of Mary.

Catechetics: He introduced a whole new era of religious instruction and formation with the encyclical *Acerbo Nimis* of Apr. 15, 1905, in which he called for vigor in establishing and conducting parochial programs of the Confraternity of Christian Doctrine.

Catholic Action: He outlined the role of official Catholic Action in two encyclicals in 1905 and 1906. Favoring organized action by Catholics themselves, he had serious reservations about interconfessional collaboration.

He stoutly maintained claims to papal rights in the anticlerical climate of Italy. He authorized bishops to relax prohibitions against participation by Catholics in some Italian elections.

Church Administration: With the motu proprio *Arduum Sane* of Mar. 19, 1904, he inaugurated the work which resulted in the Code of Canon Law published in 1917 and placed in effect the following year. He reorganized and strengthened the Roman Curia with the apostolic constitution *Sapienti Consilio* of June 29, 1908. While promoting the expansion of missionary work, he removed from the jurisdiction of the Congregation for the Propagation of the Faith the Church in the United States, Canada, Newfoundland, England, Ireland, Holland and Luxembourg.

International Relations: He ended traditional prerogatives of Catholic governments with respect to papal elections, in 1904. He opposed anti-Church and anticlerical actions in several countries: Bolivia in 1905, because of anti-religious legislation; France in 1906, for its 1901 action in annulling its concordat with the Holy See, and for the 1905 Law of Separation by which it decreed separation of church and state, ordered the confiscation of church property, and blocked religious education and the activities of religious orders; Portugal in 1911, for the separation of church and state, and repressive measures which resulted in persecution later.

In 1912 he called on the bishops of Brazil to work for the improvement of conditions among Indians.

Liturgy: "The Pope of the Eucharist," he strongly recommended the frequent reception of Holy Communion in a decree dated Dec. 20, 1905; in another decree, *Quam Singulari,* of Aug. 8, 1910, he called for the early reception of the sacrament by children. He initiated measures for liturgical reform with new norms for sacred music and the start of work on revision of the *Breviary* for recitation of the Divine Office (Liturgy of the Hours).

Modernism: Pius was a vigorous opponent of "the synthesis of all heresies," which threatened the integrity of doctrine through its influence in philosophy, theology and biblical exegesis. In opposition, he condemned 65 of its propositions as erroneous in the decree *Lamentabili* July 3, 1907; issued the encyclical *Pascendi* in the same vein Sept. 8, 1907; backed both of these with censures, and published the Oath against Modernism in September, 1910, to be taken by all the clergy. Ecclesiastical studies suffered to some extent from these actions, necessary as they were at the time.

Pius followed the lead of Leo XIII in promoting the study of scholastic philosophy. He established the Pontifical Biblical Institute May 7, 1909.

BENEDICT XV

Benedict XV (Giacomo della Chiesa) was born Nov. 21, 1854, in Pegli, Italy. He was educated at the Royal University of Genoa and Gregorian University in Rome. He was ordained to the priesthood Dec. 21, 1878.

He served in the papal diplomatic corps from 1882 to 1907: as secretary to the nuncio to Spain from 1882 to 1887, as secretary to the papal secretary of state from 1887, and as undersecretary from 1901.

He was ordained archbishop of Bologna Dec. 22, 1907, and spent four years completing a pastoral visitation there. He was made a cardinal just three months before being elected to the papacy Sept. 3, 1914. He died Jan. 22, 1922.

Two key efforts of his pontificate were for peace and the relief of human suffering caused by World War I.

Canonizations: Benedict canonized three saints; one of them was Joan of Arc.

Canon Law: He published the Code of Canon Law, developed by the commission set up by St. Pius X, June 28, 1917; it went into effect the following year.

Curia: He made great changes in the personnel of the Curia. He established the Congregation for the Oriental Churches May 1, 1917, and founded the Pontifical Oriental Institute in Rome later in the year.

Encyclicals: He issued 12 encyclicals. Peace was the theme of three of them. In another, published two years after the cessation of hostilities, he wrote about child victims of the war. He followed the lead of Leo XIII in *Spiritus Paraclitus,* Sept. 15, 1920, on biblical studies.

International Relations: He was largely frustrated on the international level because of the events and attitudes of the World War I period. The number of diplomats accredited to the Vatican nearly doubled, from 14 to 26, between the time of his accession to the papacy and his death.

Peace Efforts: Benedict's stance on World War I was one of absolute impartiality but not of uninterested neutrality. Because he would not take sides, he was suspected by both sides, and the seven-point peace plan he offered to all belligerents Aug. 1, 1917, was turned down. The points of the plan were: recognition of the moral force of right; disarmament; acceptance of arbitration in cases of dispute; guarantee of freedom of the seas; renunciation of war indemnities; evacuation and restoration of occupied territories; examination of territorial claims in dispute.

Relief Efforts: Benedict assumed personal charge of Vatican relief efforts during the war. He set up an international missing persons bureau for contacts between prisoners and their families, but was forced to close it because of the suspicion of warring nations that it was a front for espionage operations. He persuaded the Swiss government to admit into the country military victims of tuberculosis.

Roman Question: Benedict arranged a meeting of Benito Mussolini and the papal secretary of state, which marked the first step toward settlement of the question in 1929.

PIUS XI

Pius XI (Ambrogio Damiano Achille Ratti) was born May 31, 1857, in Desio, Italy. Educated at seminaries in Seviso and Milan, and at the Lombard College, Gregorian University and Academy of St. Thomas in Rome, he was ordained to the priesthood Dec. 20, 1879.

He taught at the major seminary of Milan from 1882 to 1888. Appointed to the staff of the Ambrosian Library in 1888, he remained there until 1911, acquiring a reputation for publishing works on paleography and serving as director from 1907 to 1911. He then moved to the Vatican Library, of which he was prefect from 1914 to 1918. In 1919, he was named apostolic visitor to Poland in April, nuncio in June, and was made titular archbishop of Lepanto Oct. 28. He was made archbishop of Milan and cardinal June 13, 1921, before being elected to the papacy Feb. 6, 1922. He died Feb. 10, 1939.

Aim: The objective of his pontificate, as stated in the encyclical *Ubi Arcano,* Dec. 23, 1922, was to establish the reign and peace of Christ in society.

Canonizations: He canonized 34 saints, including the Jesuit Martyrs of North America, and conferred the title of Doctor of the Church on Sts. Peter Canisius, John of the Cross, Robert Bellarmine and Albert the Great.

Eastern Churches: He called for better understanding of the Eastern Churches in the encyclical *Rerum Orientalium* of Sept. 8, 1928, and developed facilities for the training of Eastern-Rite priests. He inaugurated steps for the codification of Eastern church law in 1929. In 1935 he made Syrian Patriarch Tappouni a cardinal.

Encyclicals: His first encyclical, *Ubi Arcano,* in addition to stating the aims of his pontificate, blueprinted Catholic Action and called for its development throughout the Church. In *Quas Primas,* Dec. 11, 1925, he established the feast of Christ the King for universal observance. Subjects of some of his other encyclicals were: Christian education, in *Rappresentanti in Terra,* Dec. 31, 1929; Christian marriage, in *Casti Connubii,* Dec. 31, 1930; social conditions and pressure for social change in line with the teaching in *Rerum Novarum,* in *Quadragesimo Anno,* May 15, 1931; atheistic Communism, in *Divini Redemptoris,* Mar. 19, 1937; the priesthood, in *Ad Catholici Sacerdotii,* Dec. 20, 1935.

Missions: Following the lead of Benedict XV, Pius called for the training of native clergy in the pattern of their own respective cultures, and promoted missionary developments in various ways. He ordained six native bishops for China in 1926, one for Japan in 1927, and others for regions of Asia, China and India in 1933. He placed 40 mission dioceses under native bishops, saw the number of native priests increase from about 2,600 to more than 7,000 and the number of Catholics in missionary areas more than double from nine million. In the apostolic constitution *Deus Scientiarum Dominus* of May 24, 1931, he ordered the introduction of missiology into theology courses.

Interfaith Relations: Pius was negative to the ecumenical movement among Protestants but approved the Malines Conversations, 1921 to 1926, between Anglicans and Catholics.

International Relations: Relations with the Mussolini government deteriorated from 1931 on, as indicated in the encyclical *Non Abbiamo Bisogno*, when the regime took steps to curb liberties and activities of the Church; they turned critical in 1938 with the emergence of racist policies. Relations deteriorated also with Germany from 1933 on, resulting finally in condemnation of the Nazis in the encyclical *Mit Brennender Sorge*, Mar. 14, 1937.

Pius sparked a revival of the Church in France by encouraging Catholics to work within the democratic framework of the Republic rather than foment trouble over restoration of a monarchy. He was powerless to influence developments related to the civil war which erupted in Spain in July, 1936, sporadic persecution and repression by the Calles regime in Mexico, and systematic persecution of the Church in the Soviet Union.

Roman Question: Pius negotiated for two and one-half years with the Italian government to settle the Roman Question by means of the Lateran Agreement of 1929. The agreement provided independent status for the State of Vatican City; made Catholicism the official religion of Italy, with pastoral and educational freedom and state recognition of Catholic marriages, religious orders and societies; and provided a financial payment to the Vatican for expropriation of the former States of the Church. (The Lateran Agreement was superseded by a concordat formally approved in 1985.)

PIUS XII

Pius XII (Eugenio Maria Giovanni Pacelli) was born Mar. 2, 1876, in Rome. Educated at the Gregorian University and the Lateran University, in Rome, he was ordained to the priesthood Apr. 2, 1899.

He entered the Vatican diplomatic service in 1901, worked on the codification of canon law, and was appointed secretary of the Congregation for Ecclesiastical Affairs in 1914. Three years later he was ordained titular archbishop of Sardis and made apostolic nuncio to Bavaria. He was nuncio to Germany from 1920 to 1929, when he was made a cardinal, and took office as papal secretary of state in the following year. His diplomatic negotiations resulted in concordats between the Vatican and Bavaria (1924), Prussia (1929), Baden (1932), Austria and the German Republic (1933). He took part in negotiations which led to settlement of the Roman Question in 1929.

He was elected to the papacy Mar. 2, 1939. He died Oct. 9, 1958, at Castel Gandolfo after the 12th longest pontificate in history.

Canonizations: He canonized 34 saints, including Mother Frances X. Cabrini, the first U.S. citizen-saint.

Cardinals: He raised 56 prelates to the rank of cardinal in two consistories held in 1946 and 1953. There were 57 cardinals at the time of his death.

Church Organization and Missions: He increased the number of dioceses from 1,696 to 2,048. He established native hierarchies in China (1946), Burma (1955) and parts of Africa, and extended the native structure of the Church in India. He ordained the first black bishop for Africa.

Communism: In addition to opposing and condemning Communism on numerous occasions, he decreed in 1949 the penalty of excommunication for all Catholics holding formal and willing allegiance to the Communist Party and its policies. During his reign the Church was persecuted in some 15 countries which fell under communist domination.

Doctrine and Liturgy: He proclaimed the dogma of the Assumption of the Blessed Virgin Mary Nov. 1, 1950, in the apostolic constitution *Munificentissimus Deus*.

In various encyclicals and other enactments, he provided background for the *aggiornamento* introduced by his successor, John XXIII: by his formulations of doctrine and practice regarding the Mystical Body of Christ, the liturgy, sacred music and biblical studies; by the revision of the Rites of Holy Week; by initiation of the work which led to the calendar-missal-breviary reform ordered into effect Jan. 1, 1961; by the first of several modifications of the Eucharistic fast; by extending the time of Mass to the evening. He instituted the feasts of Mary, Queen, and of St. Joseph the Worker, and clarified teaching concerning devotion to the Sacred Heart.

Encyclicals: His 41 encyclicals and nearly 1,000 public addresses made Pius one of the greatest teaching popes. His concern in all his communications was to deal with specific points at issue and/or to bring Christian principles to bear on contemporary world problems.

Peace Efforts: Before the start of World War II, he tried unsuccessfully to get the contending nations — Germany and Poland, France and Italy — to settle their differences peaceably. During the war, he offered his services to mediate the widened conflict, spoke out against the horrors of war and the suffering it caused, mobilized relief work for its victims, proposed a five-point program for peace in Christmas messages from 1939 to 1942, and secured a generally open status for the City of Rome. After the war, he endorsed the principles and intent of the United Nations and continued efforts for peace.

United States: Pius appointed more than 200 of the 265 American bishops resident in the U.S. and abroad in 1958, erected 27 dioceses in this country, and raised seven dioceses to archiepiscopal rank.

JOHN XXIII

John XXIII (Angelo Roncalli) was born Nov. 25, 1881, at Sotte il Monte, Italy. He was educated at the seminary of the Bergamo Diocese and the Pontifical Seminary in Rome, where he was ordained to the priesthood Aug. 10, 1904.

He spent the first nine or 10 years of his priesthood as secretary to the bishop of Bergamo and as an instructor in the seminary there. He served as a medic and chaplain in the Italian army during World War I. Afterwards, he resumed duties in his own diocese until he was called to Rome in 1921 for work with the Society for the Propagation of the Faith.

He began diplomatic service in 1925 as titular archbishop of Areopolis and apostolic visitor to Bulgaria. A succession of offices followed: apostolic delegate to Bulgaria (1931-35); titular archbishop of Mesembria, apostolic delegate to Turkey and Greece, administrator of the Latin vicariate apostolic of Istanbul (1935-44); apostolic nuncio to France (1944-53). On these missions he was engaged in delicate negotiations involving Roman, Eastern-Rite and Orthodox relations; the needs of people suffering from the consequences of World War II; and unsettling suspicions arising from wartime conditions.

He was made a cardinal Jan. 12, 1953, and three days later was appointed patriarch of Venice, the position he held until his election to the papacy Oct. 28, 1958. He died of stomach cancer June 3, 1963.

John was a strong and vigorous pope whose influence far outmeasured both his age and the shortness of his time in the papacy.

Second Vatican Council: John announced Jan. 25, 1959, his intention of convoking the 21st ecumenical council in history to renew life in the Church, to reform its structures and institutions, and to explore ways and means of promoting unity among Christians; he presided at the opening session in 1962. Through the council, which completed its work two and one-half years after his death, he ushered in a new era in the history of the Church.

Canon Law: He established a commission Mar. 28, 1963, for revision of the Code of Canon Law. The revised code was promulgated in 1983.

Canonizations: He canonized 10 saints and beatified Mother Elizabeth Ann Seton, the first native of the U.S. ever so honored. He named St. Lawrence of Brindisi a Doctor of the Church.

Cardinals: He created 52 cardinals in five consistories, raising membership of the College of Cardinals above the traditional number of 70; at one time in 1962, the membership was 87. He made the College more international in representation than it had ever been, appointing the first cardinals from the Philippines, Japan and Africa. He ordered episcopal ordination for all cardinals. He relieved the suburban bishops of Rome of ordinary jurisdiction over their dioceses so they might devote all their time to business of the Roman Curia.

Eastern Rites: He made all Eastern-Rite patriarchs members of the Congregation for the Oriental Churches.

Ecumenism: He assigned to the Second Vatican Council the task of finding ways and means of promoting unity among Christians. He established the Vatican Secretariat for Promoting Christian Unity June 5, 1960. He showed his desire for more cordial relations with the Orthodox by sending personal representatives to visit Patriarch Athenagoras I June 27, 1961. He approved a mission of five delegates to the General Assembly of the World Council of Churches which met in New Delhi, India, in November, 1961. He removed a number of pejorative references to Jews in the Roman-Rite liturgy for Good Friday.

Encyclicals: Of the eight encyclicals he issued, the two outstanding ones were *Mater et Magistra* ("Christianity and Social Progress"), in which he recapitulated, updated and extended the social doctrine stated earlier by Leo XIII and Pius XI; and *Pacem in Terris* ("Peace on Earth"), the first encyclical ever addressed to all men of good will as well as to Catholics, on the natural-law principles of peace.

Liturgy: In forwarding liturgical reforms already begun by Pius XII, he ordered a calendar-missal-breviary reform into effect Jan. 1, 1961. He authorized the use of vernacular languages in the administration of the sacraments and approved giving Holy Communion to the sick in afternoon hours. He selected the liturgy as the first topic of major discussion by the Second Vatican Council.

Missions: He issued an encyclical on the missionary activity of the Church; established native hierarchies in Indonesia, Vietnam and Korea; and called on North American superiors of religious institutes to have one-tenth of their members assigned to work in Latin America by 1971.

Peace: John spoke and used his moral influence for peace in 1961 when tension developed over Berlin, in 1962 during the Algerian revolt from France, and later the same year in the Cuban missile crisis. His efforts were singled out for honor by the Balzan Peace Foundation. In 1963, he was posthumously awarded the U.S. Presidential Medal of Freedom.

PAUL VI

Paul VI (Giovanni Battista Montini) was born Sept. 26, 1897, at Concesio in northern Italy. Educated at Brescia, he was ordained to the priesthood May 29, 1920. He pursued additional studies at the Pontifical Academy for Noble Ecclesiastics and the Pontifical Gregorian University. In 1924 he began 30 years of service in the Secretariat of State. As undersecretary from 1937 until 1954, he was closely associated with Pius XII and was heavily engaged in organizing informational and relief services during and after World War II.

He was ordained archbishop of Milan Dec. 12, 1954, and was inducted into the College of Cardinals Dec. 15, 1958. He was elected to the papacy June 21, 1963, two days after the conclave began. He died of a heart attack Aug. 6, 1978.

Second Vatican Council: He reconvened the Second Vatican Council after the death of John XXIII, presided over its second, third and fourth sessions, formally promulgated the 16 documents it produced, and devoted the whole of his pontificate to the task of putting them into effect throughout the Church. The main thrust of his pontificate — in a milieu of cultural and other changes in the Church and the world — was toward institutionalization and control of the authentic trends articulated and set in motion by the council.

Canonizations: He canonized 84 saints. They included groups of 22 Ugandan martyrs and 40 martyrs of England and Wales, as well as two Americans — Elizabeth Ann Bayley Seton and John Nepomucene Neumann.

Cardinals: He created 144 cardinals and gave the College a more international complexion than it ever had before. He limited participation in papal elections to 120 cardinals under the age of 80.

Collegiality: He established the Synod of Bishops in 1965 and called it into session five times. He stimulated the formation and operation of regional conferences of bishops, and of consultative bodies on other levels.

Creed and Holy Year: On June 30, 1968, he issued a Creed of the People of God in conjunction with the celebration of a Year of Faith. He proclaimed and led the observance of a Holy Year from Christmas Eve of 1974 to Christmas Eve of 1975.

Diplomacy: He met with many world leaders, including Soviet President Nikolai Podgorny in 1967, Marshal Tito of Yugoslavia in 1971 and President Nicolae Ceausescu of Romania in 1973. He worked constantly to reduce tension between the Church and the intransigent regimes of Eastern European countries by means of a detente type of policy called Ostpolitik. He agreed to significant revisions of the Vatican's concordat with Spain and initiated efforts to revise the concordat with Italy. More than 40 countries established diplomatic relations with the Vatican during his pontificate.

Encyclicals: He issued seven encyclicals, three of which are the best known. In *Populorum Progressio* ("Development of Peoples") he appealed to wealthy countries to take "concrete action" to promote human development and to remedy imbalances between richer and poorer nations; this encyclical, coupled with other documents and related actions, launched the Church into a new depth of involvement as a public advocate for human rights and for humanizing social, political and economic policies. In *Sacerdotalis Caelibatus* ("Priestly Celibacy") he reaffirmed the strict observance of priestly celibacy throughout the Western Church. In *Humanae Vitae* ("Of Human Life") he condemned abortion, sterilization and artificial birth control, in line with traditional teaching and in "defense of life, the gift of God, the glory of the family, the strength of the people."

Interfaith Relations: He initiated formal consultation and informal dialogue on international and national levels between Catholics and non-Catholics — Orthodox, Anglicans, Protestants, Jews, Moslems, Buddhists, Hindus, and unbelievers. He and Greek Orthodox Patriarch Athenagoras I of Constantinople nullified in 1965 the mutual excommunications imposed by their respective churches in 1054.

Liturgy: He carried out the most extensive liturgical reform in history, involving a new Order of the Mass effective in 1969, a revised church calendar in 1970, revisions and translations into vernacular languages of all sacramental rites and other liturgical texts.

Ministries: He authorized the restoration of the permanent diaconate in the Roman Rite and the establishment of new ministries of lay persons.

Peace: In 1968, he instituted the annual observance of a World Day of Peace on New Year's Day as a means of addressing a message of peace to all the world's political leaders and the peoples of all nations. The most dramatic of his many appeals for peace and efforts to ease international tensions was his plea for "No more war!" before the United Nations Oct. 4, 1965.

Pilgrimages: A "Pilgrim Pope," he made pastoral visits to the Holy Land and India in 1964, the United Nations and New York City in 1965, Portugal and Turkey in 1967, Colombia in 1968, Switzerland and Uganda in 1969, and Asia, Pacific islands and Australia in 1970. While in Manila in 1970, he was stabbed by a Bolivian artist who made an attempt on his life.

Roman Curia: He reorganized the central administrative organs of the Church in line with provisions of the apostolic constitution *Regimini Ecclesiae Universae,* streamlining procedures for more effective service and giving the agencies a more international perspective by drawing officials and consultors from all over the world. He also instituted a number of new commissions and other bodies. Coupled with curial reorganization was a simplification of papal ceremonies.

JOHN PAUL I

John Paul I (Albino Luciani) was born Oct. 17, 1912, in Forno di Canale (now Canale d'Agordo) in northern Italy. Educated at the minor seminary in Feltre and the major seminary of the Diocese of Belluno, he was ordained to the priesthood July 7, 1935. He pursued further studies at the

Pontifical Gregorian University in Rome and was awarded a doctorate in theology. From 1937 to 1947 he was vice rector of the Belluno seminary, where he taught dogmatic and moral theology, canon law and sacred art. He was appointed vicar general of his diocese in 1947 and served as director of catechetics.

Ordained bishop of Vittorio Veneto Dec. 27, 1958, he attended all sessions of the Second Vatican Council, participated in three assemblies of the Synod of Bishops (1971, 1974 and 1977), and was vice president of the Italian Bishops' Conference from 1972 to 1975.

He was appointed archbishop and patriarch of Venice Dec. 15, 1969, and was inducted into the College of Cardinals Mar. 5, 1973.

He was elected to the papacy Aug. 26, 1978, on the fourth ballot cast by the 111 cardinals participating in the largest and one of the shortest conclaves in history. The quickness of his election was matched by the brevity of his pontificate of 33 days, during which he delivered 19 addresses. He died of a heart attack Sept. 28, 1978.

JOHN PAUL II

John Paul II (Karol Wojtyla) was born May 18, 1920, in Wadowice, Poland. He began studies for the priesthood in 1942 in the underground seminary of Cracow and was ordained Nov. 1, 1946. He pursued higher studies at the University of Lublin where he also began teaching in 1953. He wrote more than 100 articles and several books on ethics and other themes; phenomenology was one of his fields of expertise.

He was ordained auxiliary bishop of Kracow Sept. 28, 1958, became vicar capitular in 1962 and archbishop Jan. 13, 1964. He attended all sessions of the Second Vatican Council, was one of the writers of the *Pastoral Constitution on the Church in the Modern World* and contributed to the *Declaration on Religious Freedom* and the *Decree on the Instruments of Social Communication*. He also attended assemblies of the Synod of Bishops. He was inducted into the College of Cardinals June 26, 1967, and subsequently served in the Congregations for the Sacraments and Divine Worship, for the Clergy, and for Catholic Education. He was a theological consultant to Pope Paul VI.

In his own diocese and native Poland, he was a strong defender of human and religious rights, the rights of workers and rights to religious freedom and education. In company with fellow bishops, he negotiated the tightrope of Catholic survival in a nation under communist control. With them, and as their spokesman at times, he was stalwart in resisting efforts of the regime to impose atheism, materialism and secularism on the people and culture of Poland.

He was elected Bishop of Rome Oct. 16, 1978, on the seventh or eighth ballot cast on the second day of voting at a conclave of 111 cardinals. He chose the name John Paul II and was invested with the pallium, the symbol of his papal office, Oct. 22 in ceremonies witnessed by more than 250,000 persons in St. Peter's Square.

The 263rd successor of St. Peter as Bishop of Rome and Supreme Pastor of the Universal Church, he is the first non-Italian pope since Adrian VI (1522-23), the first Polish pope in the history of the Church, and the youngest at the time of his election since Pius IX (1846-78).

The aim of John Paul's pontificate is the same as that of Paul VI: to institutionalize and guide, within the limits of sound doctrine and discipline, the authentic trends of renewal and reform set in motion by the Second Vatican Council.

Canon Law: He ordered into effect, as of Nov. 27, 1983, the revised Code of Canon Law, calling it the final act of the Second Vatican Council.

Cardinals: He inducted three groups of cardinals into the Sacred College: 14 in 1979, 18 in 1983 and 28 in May, 1985, when membership totaled a record high of 152.

Causes of Saints: By the end of 1985, he had canonized 110 saints (including 103 martyrs of Korea) and beatified more than 140 candidates for sainthood.

Diocesan Ministry: Since the beginning of his pontificate, John Paul has been active as Bishop of Rome, with frequent visits to parishes and institutions of the diocese for the celebration of Mass and participation in other events. During these visits, as well as others to places of pilgrimage and historic significance in Italy, he has had more personal contact with the faithful than any other pope. The number of attendants at weekly general audiences at the Vatican and Castel Gandolfo has been unprecedented.

Ecumenism: From the beginning of his pontificate, the Pope has established and maintained direct, as well as indirect, contact with leaders and representatives of separated Eastern Churches, the Anglican Communion and other Christian churches. He has encouraged interfaith relations at all levels.

While visiting at the headquarters of the World Council of Churches in June, 1984, in Geneva, he said the Church's engagement in the quest for Christian unity is irreversible. At the same time, he mentioned two points of extreme significance in Catholic doctrine and practice. The Church is convinced "that in the ministry of the bishop of Rome it has preserved the visible pole and guarantee of unity in full fidelity to the apostolic tradition and to the faith of the Fathers." He also reiterated doctrinal opposition to sharing the Eucharist until full unity is achieved: "It is not yet possible for us to celebrate the Eucharist together and communicate at the same table."

Nevertheless, he placed emphasis on things Christians have in common, among them: baptism, reverence for Scripture, prayer, a rediscovery of the "whole role of the Holy Spirit," and cooperation in work for social justice and human rights.

The Pope has sought deepening relations with Jews and Moslems in particular, and also with other non-Christian peoples.

Encyclical Letters, Other Writings, Addresses: The key document on the Pope's doctrinal and pastoral concern is his first encyclical letter, *Redemptor Hominis*, a treatise on Christian anthropology dealing with the divine and human aspects of redemption and the mission of the Church to carry on a dialogue of salvation with all peoples. Three other encyclicals have the titles *Dives in Misericordia*, on divine mercy (1980); *Laborem Exercens*, on work as a way of holiness (1981); and *Slavorum Apostoli*, honoring Sts. Cyril and Methodius on the 1100th anniversary of the death of St. Methodius (1985).

He also wrote three apostolic exhortations — on the family (1981), Religious (1984), penance and reconciliation (1984) — and two apostolic letters — on suffering and on Jerusalem — in 1984.

Writings such as these, in conjunction with hundreds of addresses and homilies delivered by the Pontiff on various occasions, especially during pastoral trips abroad and at general audiences, form a compendium of dogmatic, moral, pastoral and social teaching rooted in tradition and expressive of the spirit and letter of the Second Vatican Council.

Holy Year: He proclaimed and led in observance of a Jubilee celebration of the 1950th anniversary of the Redemption from the solemnity of the Annunciation of the Lord, Mar. 25, 1983, to Easter Sunday, Apr. 22, 1984.

International Affairs: On the international level, the Pope has had unique status as a moral spokesman and advocate of: human dignity and rights, life, peace, nuclear and conventional disarmament, reconciliation among nations and peoples, aid and relief for distressed peoples and nations. Time and time again, on world travels and at the Vatican, he has called for and supported the priority of people over things.

In the first seven years of his pontificate, new concordats were negotiated with Spain, Peru and Italy; Great Britain and the United States became two of the 113 nations with diplomatic representation to the Vatican; papal-sponsored negotiations were instrumental in resolving the years-long Beagle Channel dispute between Argentina and Chile.

Synods: He convoked a particular synod of the bishops of Holland in 1980 to deal with serious problems of the Church in that country.

He also convoked three assemblies of the Synod of Bishops: in 1980, on the Christian family; in 1983, on penance and reconciliation; in 1985, an extraordinary assembly, to assess the effects of the Second Vatican Council.

Pastoral Trips: With 28 trips abroad between 1979 and 1985, John Paul, the most widely traveled Pope in history, added to the universal pastoral ministry of the pope a new dimension of personal presence in countries throughout the world.

There were four trips in 1979, to: the Dominican Republic and Mexico, Jan. 5 to Feb. 1; Poland, June 2 to 10; Ireland and the United States, Sept. 29 to Oct. 7; Turkey, Nov. 28 to 30.

There were four trips in 1980, to: Zaire, Congo Republic, Kenya, Ghana, Burkina Fasso (Upper Volta), Ivory Coast, May 2 to 12; France, May 30 to June 2; Brazil, June 30 to July 12; West Germany, Nov. 15 to 19.

There was only one trip in 1981, to the Philippines, Guam and Japan, with stopovers in Pakistan and Alaska, Feb. 16 to 27.

There were seven trips in 1982, to: Nigeria, Benin, Gabon, Equatorial Guinea, Feb. 12 to 19; Portugal, May 12 to 15; Great Britain, May 28 to June 2; Argentina, June 11 and 12; Switzerland, June 15; San Marino, Aug. 29; Spain, Oct. 31 to Nov. 9.

There were four trips in 1983, to: Costa Rica, Nicaragua, Panama, El Salvador, Guatemala, Belize, Honduras, Haiti, Mar. 2 to 10; Poland, June 16 to 23; France (Lourdes), Aug. 14 and 15; Austria, Sept. 10 to 13.

There were four trips in 1984, to: South Korea, Papua New Guinea, Solomon Islands, Thailand, May 2 to 12; Switzerland, June 12 to 17; Canada, Sept. 9 to 20; Spain, Dominican Republic, Puerto Rico, Oct. 10 to 12.

There were four trips in 1985, to: Venezuela, Ecuador, Peru, Trinidad and Tobago, Jan. 26 to Feb. 6; Belgium, The Netherlands, Luxembourg, May 11 to 21; Togo, Ivory Coast, Cameroon, Central African Republic, Zaire, Kenya, Morocco, Aug. 8 to 19; Liechtenstein, Sept. 8.

Near Tragedy: The Pope narrowly escaped death May 13, 1981, when he was fired upon at close range by Mehmet Ali Agca as he entered St. Peter's Square to address a general audience. Wounded more seriously than realized at first, he underwent emergency surgery and remained in Gemelli Polyclinic Hospital until June 3. On release, he stayed at the Vatican until June 20, when he was hospitalized a second time until Aug. 14.

Agca told reporters July 8, 1983, that the Bulgarian secret service and the KGB were involved in his attempt on the life of the Pope, but hard and convincing evidence appeared to be missing, despite exhaustive investigation by Italian authorities who assumed jurisdiction in the case. Results of the conspiracy trial under way in 1985 were inconclusive.

Chapter Three

History of the Catholic Church in the United States

The starting point of the mainstream of Catholic history in the United States was Baltimore at the end of the Revolutionary War. Long before that, however, Catholic explorers had traversed much of the country and missionaries had done considerable work among Indians in the Southeast, Northeast and Southwest, leaving cultural and spiritual legacies that became a permanent part of the heritage — especially Catholic — of the country.

Spanish and French Missions

Missionaries from Spain evangelized Indians in Florida (which included a large area of the Southeast), New Mexico, Texas and California. Franciscan Juan de Padilla, killed in 1542 in what is now central Kansas, was the first of numerous martyrs among the early missionaries. The city of St. Augustine, settled by the Spanish in 1565, was the first permanent settlement in the United States and also the site of the first parish, established the same year with secular Father Martin Francisco Lopez de Mendoza Grajales as pastor. Italian Jesuit Eusebio Kino (1645-1711) established Spanish missions in lower California and southern Arizona, where he founded San Xavier del Bac mission in 1700. Junípero Serra (1713-84), who established nine of the famous chain of 21 Franciscan missions in California, was perhaps the most noted of the Spanish missionaries.

French missionary efforts originated in Canada and extended to parts of Maine, New York and areas around the Great Lakes and along the Mississippi River as far south as Louisiana. Sts. Isaac Jogues, René Goupil and John de Brébeuf, three of eight Jesuit missionaries of New France martyred between 1642 and 1649 (canonized in 1930), met their deaths near Auriesville, New York. Jesuit explorer-missioner Jacques Marquette (1637-75), who founded St. Ignace Mission at the Straits of Mackinac in 1671, left maps and a diary of his exploratory trip down the Mississippi River with Louis Joliet in 1673. Claude Allouez (1622-89), another French Jesuit, worked for 32 years among Indians in the Midwest, baptizing an estimated 10,000. French Catholics founded the colony of Louisiana in 1699. In 1727, Ursuline nuns from France founded a convent in New Orleans, the oldest in the United States.

English Settlements

Catholics were excluded by penal law from English settlements along the Atlantic coast.

The only colony established under Catholic leadership was Maryland, granted to George Calvert (Lord Baltimore) as a proprietary colony in 1632; its first settlement at St. Mary's City was established in 1634 by a contingent of Catholic and Protestant colonists who had arrived from England on the *Ark* and the *Dove*. Jesuits Andrew White and John Altham, who later evangelized Indians of the area, accompanied the settlers. The principle of religious freedom on which the colony was founded was enacted into law in 1649 as the Act of Toleration. It was the first such measure passed in the colonies and, except for a four-year period of Puritan control, remained in effect until 1688, when Maryland became a royal colony, and the Anglican Church was made the official religion in 1692. Catholics were disenfranchised and persecuted until 1776.

The only other colony where Catholics were assured some degree of freedom was Pennsylvania, founded by the Quaker William Penn in 1681.

One of the earliest permanent Catholic establishments in the English colonies was St. Francis Xavier Mission, Old Bohemia, in northern Maryland, founded by the Jesuits in 1704 to serve Catholics of Delaware, Maryland and southeastern Pennsylvania. Its Bohemia Academy, established in the 1740s, was attended by sons of prominent Catholic families in the area.

Catholics and the Revolution

Despite their small number, which accounted for about one percent of the population, Catholics made significant contributions to the cause for independence from England.

Father John Carroll (1735-1815) and his cousin, Charles Carroll (1737-1832), a signer of the Declaration of Independence, were chosen by the Continental Congress to accompany Benjamin Franklin and Samuel Chase to Canada to try to secure that country's neutrality. Father Pierre Gibault (1737-1804) gave important aid in preserving the Northwest Territory for the revolutionaries. Thomas FitzSimons (1741-1811) of Philadelphia gave financial support to the Continental Army, served in a number of campaigns and later, with Daniel Carroll of Maryland, became one of the two Catholic signers of the Constitution. John Barry (1745-1803), commander of the *Lexington*, the first ship commissioned by Congress, served valiantly and is considered a founder of the U.S. Navy. There is no record of the number of Catholics who served in Washington's armies, although 38 to 50 percent had Irish surnames.

Casimir Pulaski (1748-79) and Thaddeus Kosciusko (1746-1817) of Poland served the cause of the Revolution. Assisting also were the Catholic nations of France, with a military and naval force, and Spain, with money and the neutrality of its colonies.

Acknowledgment of Catholic aid in the war and the founding of the Republic was made by General Washington in his reply to a letter from prominent Catholics seeking justice and equal rights: "I presume your fellow citizens of all denominations will not forget the patriotic part which you took in the accomplishment of our Revolution and the establishment of our government, or the important assistance which they received from a nation [France] in which the Roman Catholic faith is professed."

In 1789, religious freedom was guaranteed under the First Amendment to the Constitution. Discriminatory laws against Catholics remained in force in many of the states, however, until well into the 19th century.

Beginning of Organization

Father John Carroll's appointment as superior of the American mission on June 9, 1784, was the first step toward organization of the Church in this country. According to a report he submitted to Rome the following year, there were 24 priests and approximately 25,000 Catholics, mostly in Maryland and Pennsylvania, in a general population of four million. For the most part they were a virtually unknown minority laboring under legal and social handicaps.

Establishment of the Hierarchy

Father Carroll was named the first American bishop in 1789 and placed in charge of the Diocese of Baltimore, whose boundaries were coextensive with those of the United States. Ordained in England Aug. 15, 1790, he was installed in his see the following Dec. 12.

Ten years later, Father Leonard Neale became his coadjutor and the first bishop ordained in the United States. Bishop Carroll became an archbishop in 1808, when Baltimore was designated a metropolitan see and the new dioceses of Boston, New York, Philadelphia and Bardstown (now Louisville) were established. These jurisdictions were later subdivided and by 1840 there were, in addition to Baltimore, 15 dioceses, 500 priests and 663,000 Catholics in the total population of 17 million.

Priests and First Seminaries

The original number of the 24 priests noted in Bishop Carroll's 1785 report was gradually augmented with the arrival of others from France and other countries. Among arrivals from France, after the Civil Constitution of the Clergy went into effect in 1790, were Jean Louis Lefebvre de Cheverus and Sulpicians Ambrose Maréchal, Benedict Flaget, and William Dubourg, who later became bishops.

The first seminary in the country was St. Mary's, established in 1791 in Baltimore and placed under the direction of the Sulpicians. French seminarian Stephen T. Badin (1768-1853), who fled to the U.S. in 1792 and became a pioneer missionary in Kentucky, Ohio and Michigan, was the first priest ordained (1793) in this country. Demetrius Gallitzin (1770-1840), a Russian prince and convert to Catholicism who did pioneer missionary work in western Pennsylvania, was ordained to the priesthood in 1795; he was the first to receive all his orders in the U.S. St. Mary's Seminary had 30 ordained alumni by 1815.

Two additional seminaries — Mt. St. Mary's at Emmitsburg, Md., and St. Thomas at Bardstown, Ky. — were established in 1809 and 1811, respectively. These and similar institutions founded later played key roles in the development and growth of the American clergy.

Early Schools

Early educational enterprises included the establishment in 1791 of a school at Georgetown which later became the first Catholic university in the U.S.; the opening of a secondary school for girls, conducted by Visitation nuns, in 1792 at Georgetown; and the start of a similar school in the first decade of the 19th century at Emmitsburg, Md., by St. Elizabeth Ann Seton.

By the 1840s, which saw the beginnings of the present public school system, more than 200 Catholic elementary schools, half of them west of the Alleghenies, were in operation. From this start, the Church subsequently built the greatest private system of education in the world.

Sisterhoods

Institutes of women Religious were largely responsible for the development of educational and charitable institutions. Among them were Ursuline Nuns in Louisiana from 1727 and Visitation Nuns at Georgetown in the 1790s.

The first contemplative foundation in the country was established in 1790 at Port Tobacco, Md., by three American-born Carmelites trained at an English convent in Belgium.

The first community of American origin was that of the Sisters of Charity of St. Joseph, founded in 1808 at Emmitsburg, Md., by Mother Elizabeth Ann Bayley Seton (canonized in 1975). Other early American communities were the Sisters of Loretto and the Sisters of Charity of Nazareth, both founded in 1812 in Kentucky, and the Oblate Sisters of Providence, a black community founded in 1829 in Baltimore.

Among pioneer U.S. foundresses of European communities were

Mother Rose Philippine Duchesne (beatified in 1940), who established the Religious of the Sacred Heart in Missouri in 1818, and Mother Théodore Guérin, who founded the Sisters of Providence of St.-Mary-of-the-Woods in Indiana in 1840.

The number of sisters' communities, most of them branches of European institutes, increased apace with needs for their missions in education, charitable service and spiritual life.

Trusteeism

The initial lack of organization in ecclesiastical affairs, nationalistic feeling among Catholics and the independent action of some priests were factors involved in several early crises.

In Philadelphia, some German Catholics, with the reluctant consent of Bishop Carroll, founded Holy Trinity in 1788, the first national parish in the U.S. They refused to accept the pastor appointed by the bishop and elected their own. This and other abuses led to formal schism in 1796, a condition which existed until 1802 when they returned to canonical jurisdiction. Philadephia was also the scene of the Hogan Schism, which developed in the 1820s when Father William Hogan, with the aid of lay trustees, seized control of St. Mary's Cathedral. His movement, for churches and parishes controlled by other than canonical procedures and run in extralegal ways, was nullified by a decision of the Pennsylvania Supreme Court in 1822.

Similar troubles seriously disturbed the peace of the Church in other places, principally New York, Baltimore, Buffalo, Charleston and New Orleans.

Dangers arising from the exploitation of lay control were gradually diminished with the extension and enforcement of canonical procedures and with changes in civil law in the middle of the 19th century.

Bigotry

Bigotry against Catholics waxed and waned during the 19th century and into the 20th. The first major campaign of this kind, which developed in the wake of the Panic of 1819 and lasted for about 25 years, was mounted in 1830 when the number of Catholic immigrants began to increase to a noticeable degree. Nativist anti-Catholicism generated a great deal of violence, represented by climaxes in loss of life and property in Charlestown, Mass., in 1834, and in Philadelphia 10 years later. Later bigotry was fomented by the Know-Nothings, in the 1850s; the Ku Klux Klan, from 1866; the American Protective Association, from 1887, and the Guardians of Liberty. Perhaps the last major eruption of virulently overt anti-Catholicism occurred during the campaign of Alfred E. Smith for the presidency in 1928. Observers feel the issue was muted to a considerable extent in the political area with the election of John F. Kennedy to the presidency in 1960.

The Catholic periodical press had its beginnings in response to the attacks of bigots. The *U.S. Catholic Miscellany* (1822-61), the first Catholic newspaper in the U.S., was founded by Bishop John England of Charleston to answer critics of the Church. This remained the character of most of the periodicals of the 19th and into the 20th century.

Growth and Immigration

Between 1830 and 1900, the combined factors of natural increase, immigration and conversion raised the Catholic population to 12 million. A large percentage of the growth figure represented immigrants: some 2.7 million, largely from Ireland, Germany and France, between 1830 and 1880; and another 1.25 million during the 1880s when Eastern and Southern Europeans came in increasing numbers. By the 1860s the Catholic Church, with most of its members concentrated in urban areas, was one of the largest religious bodies in the country.

The efforts of progressive bishops to hasten the acculturation of Catholic immigrants occasioned a number of controversies, which generally centered around questions concerning national or foreign-language parishes. One of them, called Cahenslyism, arose from complaints that German Catholic immigrants were not being given adequate pastoral care.

Immigration continued after the turn of the century, but its impact was more easily cushioned through the application of lessons learned earlier in dealing with problems of nationality and language.

Eastern-Rite Catholics

The immigration of the 1890s included large numbers of Eastern-Rite Catholics with their own liturgies and tradition of a married clergy, but without their own bishops. The treatment of their clergy and people by some of the U.S. (Latin-Rite) hierarchy and the prejudices they encountered resulted in the defection of thousands from the Catholic Church.

In 1907, Basilian monk Stephen Ortynsky was ordained the first bishop of Byzantine-Rite Catholics in the U.S. Eventually, jurisdictions were established for most Byzantine- and other Eastern-Rite Catholics in the country.

Councils of Baltimore

Actions taken by the bishops at seven provincial councils between 1829 and 1849, and three plenary councils of Baltimore, had great influence on the growth and development of the Church.

In 1846, they proclaimed the Blessed Virgin Mary patroness of the United States under the title of the Immaculate Conception, eight years before the dogma was proclaimed.

After the establishment of the Archdiocese of Oregon City in 1846 and the elevation to metropolitan status of St. Louis, New Orleans, Cincinnati and New York, the first of the three plenary councils of Baltimore was held.

The first plenary assembly was convoked on May 9, 1852, with Archbishop Francis P. Kenrick of Baltimore as papal legate. The bishops drew up regulations concerning parochial life, matters of church ritual and ceremonies, the administration of church funds and the teaching of Christian doctrine.

The second plenary council, meeting from Oct. 7 to 21, 1866, under the presidency of Archbishop Martin J. Spalding, formulated a condemnation of several current doctrinal errors and established norms affecting the organization of dioceses, the education and conduct of the clergy, the management of ecclesiastical property, parochial duties and general education.

Archbishop (later Cardinal) James Gibbons called into session the third plenary council, which lasted from Nov. 9 to Dec. 7, 1884. Among highly significant results of actions taken by this assembly were the preparation of the line of Baltimore catechisms which became a basic means of religious instruction in this country; legislation which fixed the pattern of Catholic education by requiring the building of elementary schools in all parishes; the establishment of the Catholic University of America in Washington, D.C., in 1889; and the determination of six holy days of obligation for observance in this country.

The enactments of the three plenary councils have had the force of particular law for the Church in the United States.

The Holy See established the Apostolic Delegation in Washington, D.C., on Jan. 24, 1893.

Slavery

In the Civil War period, as before, Catholics reflected attitudes of the general population with respect to the issue of slavery. Some supported it, some opposed it, but not one was prominent in the Abolition Movement. Gregory XVI had condemned the slave trade in 1839, but no contemporary pope or American bishop published an official document on slavery itself. The issue did not split Catholics in schism as it did Baptists, Methodists and Presbyterians.

Catholics fought on both sides in the Civil War. Five hundred members of 20 or more sisterhoods served the wounded of both sides.

One hundred thousand of the four million slaves emancipated in 1863 were Catholics; the highest concentrations were in Louisiana (about

60,000) and Maryland (16,000). Three years later, their pastoral care was one of the subjects covered in nine decrees issued by the Second Plenary Council of Baltimore. The measures had little practical effect with respect to integration of the total Catholic community, predicated as they were on the proposition that individual bishops should handle questions regarding segregation in churches and related matters as best they could in the pattern of local customs.

Long-entrenched segregation practices continued in force through the rest of the 19th century and well into the 20th. The first effective efforts to alter them were initiated by Cardinal Joseph Ritter of St. Louis in 1947, Cardinal (then Archbishop) Patrick O'Boyle of Washington in 1948, and Bishop Vincent Waters of Raleigh in 1953.

Friend of Labor

The Church became known during the 19th century as a friend and ally of labor in seeking justice for the working man. Cardinal Gibbons journeyed to Rome in 1887, for example, to defend and prevent a condemnation of the Knights of Labor by Pope Leo XIII. The encyclical *Rerum Novarum* (1891) was hailed by many American bishops as a confirmation, if not vindication, of their own theories. Catholics have always formed a large percentage of union membership, and some have served unions in positions of leadership.

The American Heresy

Near the end of the century some controversy developed over what was characterized as Americanism, or the Phantom Heresy. It was alleged that Americans were discounting the importance of contemplative virtues, exalting the practical virtues and watering down the purity of Catholic doctrine for the sake of facilitating convert work.

The French translation of Father Walter Elliott's *Life of Isaac Hecker*, which fired the controversy, was one of many factors that led to the issuance of Leo XIII's *Testem Benevolentiae* in January, 1899, in an attempt to end the matter. It was the first time the orthodoxy of the Church in the U.S. was called into question.

Schism

In the 1890s, serious friction developed between Poles and Irish in Scranton, Buffalo and Chicago, resulting in schism and the establishment of the Polish National Church. A central figure in the affair was Father Francis Hodur, who was excommunicated by Bishop William O'Hara of Scranton in 1898. Nine years later, his ordination by an Old Catholic Archbishop of Utrecht gave the new church its first bishop.

Coming of Age

In 1900, there were 12 million Catholics in the total U.S. population of 76 million, 82 dioceses in 14 provinces, and 12,000 priests and members of about 40 communities of men Religious. Many sisterhoods, most of them of European origin and some of American foundation, were engaged in Catholic educational and hospital work, two of their traditional apostolates.

The Church in the United States was removed from mission status with promulgation of the apostolic constitution *Sapienti Consilio* by Pope St. Pius X on June 29, 1908.

Long a recipient of financial assistance from mission-aid societies in France, Bavaria and Austria, the Church in the United States began making contributions of its own, gradually becoming one of the major national contributors to the worldwide Society for the Propagation of the Faith.

An awareness of personnel needs of foreign mission areas also took hold. The first missionary seminary in the U.S. was in operation at Techny, Ill., in 1909 under the auspices of the Society of the Divine Word. Maryknoll, the first American foreign mission society, was established in 1911 and sent its first priests to China in 1918. American foreign missionary personnel increased from 14 or less in 1906 to an all-time high in 1968 of 9,655 priests, brothers, sisters, seminarians and lay persons; they represented more than 250 mission-sending groups and 81 dioceses.

In the home mission field, the Catholic Church Extension Society, founded in 1905 to meet the needs of the Church in isolated and unevangelized areas of the country, generated enthusiasm for missionary endeavors through sponsorship of missionary congresses and material-support activities.

National Catholic Welfare Conference

A highly important apparatus for mobilizing the Church's resources was established in 1917 under the title of the National Catholic War Council. Its success led to the formation of the National Catholic Welfare Conference (NCWC) in 1919 to serve as an advisory and coordinating agency of the American bishops for advancing works of the Church in fields of social significance and impact — education, communications, immigration, social action, legislation, youth and lay organizations.

The forward thrust of the bishops' social thinking was evidenced in a program of social reconstruction they recommended in 1919. By 1945, all but one of their 12 points had been enacted into legislation.

The NCWC was renamed the United States Catholic Conference (USCC) in November, 1966, when the hierarchy also organized itself as a territorial conference with pastoral-juridical authority under the title

National Conference of Catholic Bishops. The USCC is carrying on the functions of the former NCWC.

Catholic Press

The establishment of the National Catholic News Service (NC) in 1920 was an important event in the development of the Catholic press, which had its beginnings about a hundred years earlier. Early in the 20th century, there were 63 weekly newspapers. Fifteen years before the end of the century, there were 179 newspapers with a combined weekly circulation in excess of five million, and 340 magazines with a circulation of about 21 million.

Lay Organizations

A burst of lay organizational growth occurred from the 1930s onwards with the appearance of Catholic Action types of movements and other groups and associations devoted to special causes, social service and assistance for the poor and needy. Several special apostolates were developed under the aegis of the National Catholic Welfare Conference; the outstanding one was the Confraternity of Christian Doctrine.

Nineteenth century organizations of great influence included: the St. Vincent de Paul Society, whose first U.S. office was set up in 1845 in St. Louis; the Catholic Central Union (Verein), dating from 1855; the Knights of Columbus, founded in 1882; the Holy Name Society, organized in the U.S. in 1870; the Rosary Society (1891) and scores of chapters of the Sodality of the Blessed Virgin Mary.

Pastoral Concerns

The potential for growth of the Church in this country by immigration was sharply reduced but not entirely curtailed after 1921 with the passage of restrictive federal legislation. As a result, the Catholic population became more stabilized and, to a certain extent and for many reasons, began to acquire an identity of its own.

Some increase from outside has taken place in the past 50 years, however; from Canada, from Central and Eastern European countries, and from Puerto Rico and Latin American countries since World War II. This influx, while not as great as that of the 19th century and early 20th, has enriched the Church here with a sizable body of Eastern-Rite Catholics for whom eight ecclesiastical jurisdictions were established between 1924 and 1969. It has also created a challenge for pastoral care of millions of Hispanics in urban centers and in agricultural areas where migrant workers are employed.

The Church continues to grapple with serious pastoral problems in rural areas, where about 600 counties are no-priest land. The National Catholic Rural Life Conference was established in 1922 in an attempt to make the Catholic presence felt on the land, and the Glenmary Society since its foundation in 1939 has devoted itself to this single apostolate. Religious communities and diocesan priests are similarly engaged.

Other challenges lie in the cities and suburbs, where 75 percent of the Catholic population live. Conditions peculiar to each segment of the metropolitan area have developed in recent years as the flight to the suburbs has not only altered some traditional aspects of parish life but has also, in combination with many other factors, left behind a complex of special problems in inner-city areas.

Twenty years after the end of Vatican II, the statistics of the Church in the United States were impressive. There were 52,286,000 Catholics in the total population of 237,233,000, 180 archdioceses and dioceses and 445 members of the hierarchy, including 10 cardinals. Priests numbered 57,317; permanent deacons, 7,204; brothers, 7,544; sisters, 115,386; seminarians, 11,000. The educational system included 242 colleges with 550,000 students; 1,425 high schools with 794,000 students; 7,957 elementary schools with 2,163,000 students. Another 4,052,000 public high and elementary school students were in religious instruction programs. The Church's charitable network included 731 hospitals, 607 homes for the aged, 170 orphanages, numerous facilities for handicapped children and adults, and other specialized social services.

Contemporary Factors

The Church in the U.S. is in a stage of transition from a relatively stable and long established order of life and action to a new order of things. Some of the phenomena of this period are:

• differences in trends and emphasis in theology, and in interpretation and implementation of directives of the Second Vatican Council, resulting in situations of conflict;

• the changing spiritual formation, professional education, style of life and ministry of priests and Religious (men and women), which are altering influential patterns of pastoral and specialized service;

• vocations to the priesthood and Religious life, which are generally in decline;

• departures from the priesthood and Religious life which, while small percentagewise, are numerous enough to be a matter of serious concern;

• decline of traditional devotional practices, along with the emergence of new ones;

• exercise of authority along the lines of collegiality and subsidiarity;

• structure and administration, marked by a trend toward greater participation in the life and work of the Church by its members on all levels, from the parish on up;

• alienation from the Church, leading some persons into the catacombs of an underground church, "anonymous Christianity" and religious indifferentism;

• education, undergoing crisis and change in Catholic schools and seeking new ways of reaching out to the young not in Catholic schools and to adults;

• social witness in ministry to the world, which is being shaped by the form of contemporary needs — e.g., race relations, poverty, the peace movement, the Third World;

• ecumenism, involving the Church in interfaith relations on a wider scale than before.

Chapter Four

Mary

Mary has a special place in Catholic doctrine and devotion because of her unique role as the Mother of Jesus and His closest human cooperator in the work of redemption. She was conceived without original sin (her Immaculate Conception) through the application to her of the merits of her Son before His redemptive death and resurrection. She was full of grace and sinless throughout her life. She was a virgin before, in and after the birth of Jesus. She cared for Him in infancy, childhood and adolescence. She witnessed the preaching and work of His ministry. At His crucifixion, Jesus bequeathed her to all peoples as their spiritual mother. She was with the Apostles in prayer as they awaited the coming of the Holy Spirit at Pentecost and the beginning of their mission to preach and to baptize. Pope Pius XII, in proclaiming the dogma of the Assumption, declared: "The Immaculate Mother of God, the ever Virgin Mary, having completed the course of her earthly life, was assumed body and soul into heavenly glory." There, according to the Second Vatican Council's *Dogmatic Constitution on the Church*, her maternity in the order of grace "will last without interruption until the eternal fulfillment of all the elect. For, taken up to heaven, she did not lay aside this saving role, but by her manifold acts of intercession continues to win for us gifts of eternal salvation."

The conciliar document also said: "As it has always existed in the Church, this cult [of Mary] is altogether special. Still, it differs essentially from the cult of adoration which is offered to the Incarnate Word, as well as to the Father and the Holy Spirit. Yet devotion to Mary is most favorable to this supreme cult. The Church has endorsed many forms of piety toward the Mother of God, provided that they were within the limits of sound and orthodox doctrine. . . . While honoring Christ's Mother, these devotions cause her Son to be rightly known, loved and glorified, and all His commands observed."

Feasts

The cult of Mary finds expression in a number of celebrations in the liturgy of the Roman Church, including the following observances.

Annunciation of the Lord: See Holy Days and Feast Days.

Assumption, Aug. 15, a solemnity and holy day of obligation, commemorating the taking into heaven of Mary, soul and body, at the end of her life on earth, a truth of faith that was proclaimed a dogma by Pius XII on Nov. 1, 1950. One of the oldest and most solemn feasts of Mary, it has a history dating back to at least the seventh century when its celebration was already established at Jerusalem and Rome.

Birth of Mary, Sept. 8, a very old feast which originated in the East and found place in the Roman liturgy in the seventh century.

Dedication of St. Mary Major, Aug. 5, an optional memorial commemorating the rebuilding and dedication by Pope Sixtus III (432-40) of a church in honor of Blessed Mary the Virgin. This is the Basilica of St. Mary Major on the Esquiline Hill in Rome. An earlier building was erected during the pontificate of Liberius (352-66); according to legend, it was located on a site covered by a miraculous fall of snow seen by a nobleman favored with a vision of Mary.

Immaculate Conception, Dec. 8, a solemnity and a holy day of obligation, commemorating the fact that Mary, in view of her calling to be the Mother of Christ and in virtue of His merits, was preserved from original sin from the first moment of her conception and was filled with grace from the very beginning of her life. She is the only person so preserved from original sin. The present form of the feast dates from Dec. 8, 1854, when Pius IX defined the dogma of the Immaculate Conception. An earlier feast of the Conception, which testified to long-existing belief in this truth, was observed in the East by the eighth century, in Ireland in the ninth, and subsequently in European countries. In 1846, Mary was proclaimed Patroness of the U.S. under this title.

Immaculate Heart of Mary, Saturday following the second Sunday after Pentecost, an optional memorial. On May 4, 1944, Pius XII ordered this observance throughout the Church in order to obtain Mary's intercession for "peace among nations, freedom for the Church, the conversion of sinners, the love of purity and the practice of virtue." Two years earlier, he consecrated the entire human race to Mary under this title. Devotion to Mary under the title of her Most Pure Heart originated during the Middle Ages. It was given great impetus in the 17th century by the preaching of St. John Eudes, who was the first to celebrate a Mass and Divine Office of Mary under this title. A feast, celebrated in various places and on different dates, was authorized in 1799.

Mary, Mother of God, Jan. 1, a solemnity and holy day of obligation. The calendar in effect since 1970, in accord with Eastern tradition, reinstated the Marian character of this commemoration on the octave day of Christmas. The former feast of the Circumcision, dating at least from the first half of the sixth century, marked the initiation of Jesus (Lk. 2:21) into Judaism, and by analogy focused attention on the initiation of persons in the Christian religion and their incorporation in Christ through baptism. The solemnity supplants the former feast of the Maternity of Mary observed on Oct. 11.

Our Lady of Mt. Carmel, July 16, an optional memorial which originated with the Carmelites in the 14th century and was extended throughout the Roman Rite in 1726. The observance is related to the Scapular Devotion.

Our Lady of the Rosary, Oct. 7, a memorial commemorating the Virgin Mary through recall of the mysteries of the Rosary which recapitulate events in her life and the life of Christ. The feast was instituted to commemorate a Christian victory over invading Mohammedan forces at Lepanto on Oct. 7, 1571, and was extended throughout the Church by Clement XI in 1716.

Our Lady of Sorrows, Sept. 15, a memorial recalling the sorrows experienced by Mary in her association with Christ: the prophecy of Simeon (Lk. 2:34-35), the flight into Egypt (Mt. 2:13-21), the three-day separation from Jesus (Lk. 2:41-50), and four incidents connected with the Passion: her meeting with Christ on the way to Calvary, the crucifixion, the removal of Christ's body from the cross, and His burial (Mt. 27:31-61; Mk. 15:20-47; Lk. 23:26-56; Jn. 19:17-42). A Mass and Divine Office of the feast were celebrated by the Servites, especially, in the 17th century, and in 1817 Pius VII extended the observance to the whole Church.

Presentation of Mary, Nov. 21, a memorial commemorating the dedication in 543 of the Basilica of St. Mary near the site of the Temple of Jerusalem; connected with the commemoration is the legendary presentation of Mary to the service of the Lord at an early age.

Presentation of the Lord: See Holy Days and Feast Days.

Queenship of Mary, Aug. 22, a memorial commemorating the high dignity of Mary as Queen of heaven, angels and men. Universal observance of the memorial was ordered by Pius XII in the encyclical *Ad Caeli Reginam*, Oct. 11, 1954, near the close of a Marian Year observed in connection with the centenary of the proclamation of the dogma of the Immaculate Conception and four years after the proclamation of the dogma of the Assumption. The original date of the memorial was May 31.

Visitation, May 31, a feast commemorating Mary's visit to her cousin Elizabeth after the Annunciation and before the birth of John the Baptist, the precursor of Christ (Lk. 1:39-56). The feast had a medieval origin and was observed in the Franciscan Order before being extended throughout the Church by Urban VI in 1389. It is one of the feasts of the incarnation and is notable for its recall of the *Magnificat*, one of the few New Testament canticles, which acknowledges the unique gifts of God to Mary because of her role in the redemptive work of Christ. The canticle is recited at Evening Prayer in the Liturgy of the Hours.

Mary is also the subject of liturgical veneration in votive commemorations at Mass and in the Liturgy of the Hours on many Saturdays throughout the year.

The Rosary

The most popular private veneration of Mary, and the one with the longest history, is the Rosary, a form of mental and vocal prayer centered on mysteries, or events, in the lives of Jesus and Mary. Its essential elements are meditation on the mysteries and the recitation of a number of decades of Hail Marys, each beginning with the Lord's Prayer. Each decade is customarily concluded with a Glory be to the Father; at the end, it is customary to say the Hail, Holy Queen and a prayer from the liturgy for the feast of the Blessed Virgin Mary of the Rosary. Introductory prayers may include the Apostles' Creed, an initial Our Father, three Hail Marys and a Glory be to the Father.

The Mysteries of the Rosary, which are the subjects of meditation, are: (1) Joyful — the annunciation to Mary that she was to be the Mother of Christ, her visit to Elizabeth, the birth of Jesus, the presentation of Jesus in the Temple, the finding of Jesus in the Temple. (2) Sorrowful — Christ's agony in the Garden of Gethsemani, scourging at the pillar, crowning with thorns, carrying of the Cross to Calvary, and crucifixion. (3) Glorious — the resurrection and ascension of Christ, the descent of the Holy Spirit upon the Apostles, Mary's assumption into heaven and her crowning as Queen of angels and men.

The complete Rosary, called the Dominican Rosary, consists of 15 decades. In customary practice, only five decades are usually said at one time. Rosary beads are used to aid in counting the prayers without distraction.

The Rosary originated through the coalescence of popular devotions to Jesus and Mary from the 12th century onward. Its present form dates from about the 15th century. Carthusians contributed greatly toward its development; Dominicans have been its greatest promoters.

Apparitions, Shrines

Hundreds of shrines and sanctuaries throughout the world bear testimony to private veneration of Mary. Among such places are some which have been the sites of Marian apparitions duly investigated by Church authorities and declared credible (although acceptance of them is not required as a matter of faith or Church teaching).

The sites of the following apparitions have become shrines and centers of pilgrimage. Miracles of the moral and physical orders have been reported as occurring at these places and/or in connection with related practices of prayer and penance.

Banneux, near Liège, Belgium: Mary appeared eight times between Jan. 15 and Mar. 2, 1933, to an 11-year-old peasant girl, Mariette Beco, in a garden before the family cottage in Banneux. She called herself the Virgin of the Poor, and has since been venerated as Our Lady of the Poor, the Sick, and the Indifferent. A small chapel was built by a spring near the site of the apparitions and was blessed Aug. 15, 1933. Approval of devotion to Our Lady of Banneux was given in 1949 by Bishop Louis J. Kerkhofs of Liège, and a statue of that title was solemnly crowned in 1956.

Beauraing, Belgium: Mary appeared 33 times between Nov. 29, 1932, and Jan. 3, 1933, to five children in the garden of a convent school in Beauraing. A chapel, which became a pilgrimage center, was erected on the spot. Reserved approval of devotion to Our Lady of Beauraing was given Feb. 2, 1943, and final approbation July 2, 1949, by Bishop Charue of Namur.

Fatima, Portugal: Mary appeared six times between May 13 and Oct. 13, 1917, to three children in a field called the Cova da Iria near Fatima, north of Lisbon. She recommended frequent recitation of the Rosary; urged works of mortification for the conversion of sinners; called for devotion to herself under the title of her Immaculate Heart; asked that the people of Russia be consecrated to her under this title, and that the faithful make a Communion of reparation on the first Saturday of each month. The apparitions were declared worthy of belief in October, 1930, after a seven-year canonical investigation, and devotion to Our Lady of Fatima was authorized under the title of Our Lady of the Rosary. In October, 1942, Pius XII consecrated the world to Mary under the title of her Immaculate Heart. Ten years later, in the first apostolic letter addressed directly to the peoples of Russia, he consecrated them in a special manner to Mary.

Guadalupe, Mexico: Mary appeared four times in 1531 to an Indian, Juan Diego, on Tepeyac hill outside of Mexico City, and instructed him to tell Bishop Zumarraga of her wish that a church be built there. The bishop complied with the request about two years later after being convinced of the genuineness of the apparition by the evidence of a miraculously painted life-size figure of the Virgin on the mantle of the Indian. The mantle bearing the picture has been preserved and is enshrined in the Basilica of Our Lady of Guadalupe, which has a long history as a center of devotion and pilgrimage in Mexico. The shrine church, originally dedicated in 1709 and subsequently enlarged, has the title of basilica. Benedict XIV, in a decree issued in 1754, authorized a Mass and Office under the title of Our Lady of Guadalupe for celebration on Dec. 12, and named Mary the Patroness of New Spain. Our Lady of Guadalupe was designated Patroness of Latin America by St. Pius X in 1910 and Patroness of the Americas by Pius XII in 1945.

La Salette, France: Mary appeared as a sorrowful and weeping figure Sept. 19, 1846, to two peasant children, Melanie Matthieu, 15, and Maximin Giraud, 11, at La Salette in southern France. The message she confided to them, regarding the necessity of penance, was communicated to Pius IX in 1851 and has since been known at the "Secret" of La Salette. Bishop de Bruillard of Grenoble declared in 1851 that the apparition was credible, and devotion to Mary under the title of Our Lady of La Salette was authorized. The devotion has been confirmed by popes since the time of Pius IX, and a Mass and Office with this title were authorized in 1942. The shrine church was given the title of minor basilica in 1879.

Lourdes, France: Mary, identifying herself as the Immaculate Conception, appeared 18 times between Feb. 11 and July 16, 1858, to 14-year-old Bernadette Soubirous at the grotto of Massabielle near Lourdes in southern France. Her message concerned the necessity of prayer and penance for the conversion of peoples. Mary's request that a chapel be built at the grotto and spring was fulfilled in 1862 after four years of rigid examination established the credibility of the apparitions. Devotion under the title of Our Lady of Lourdes was authorized later, and a Feb. 11 feast commemorating the apparitions was instituted by Leo XIII. St. Pius X extended this feast throughout the Church in 1907. The Church of Notre Dame was made a basilica in 1870, and the Church of the Rosary was built later. The underground Church of St. Pius X, consecrated Mar. 25, 1958, is the second largest church in the world, with a capacity of 20,000 persons.

Our Lady of the Miraculous Medal, France: Mary appeared three times in 1830 to Catherine Labouré in the chapel of the motherhouse of the Daughters of Charity of St. Vincent de Paul, Rue de Bac, Paris. She commissioned Catherine to have made the medal of the Immaculate Conception, now known as the Miraculous Medal, and to spread devotion to her under this title. In 1832, the medal was struck according to the model revealed to Catherine.

Chapter Five

Saints

Saints are holy persons who have died and are in glory with God in heaven. From the early years of the Church they have been honored and held up as models of Christian living: Apostles, martyrs, the Blessed Virgin Mary, persons who practiced Christian virtue to a heroic degree.

Veneration in the liturgy is given only to saints who have been canonized, actually or in an equivalent manner; private veneration may be given to anyone thought to be in heaven. The veneration of saints is essentially different from the adoration given to God alone; by its very nature, however, it terminates in the worship of God.

According to the Second Vatican Council's *Dogmatic Constitution on the Church* (No. 50): "It is supremely fitting . . . that we love those friends and fellow heirs of Jesus Christ, who are also our brothers and extraordinary benefactors, that we render due thanks to God for them and 'suppliantly invoke them and have recourse to their prayers, their power and help in obtaining benefits from God through His Son, Jesus Christ, our Lord, who is our sole Redeemer and Savior.' For by its very nature every genuine testimony of love which we show to those in heaven tends toward and terminates in Christ, who is the 'crown of all saints.' Through Him it tends toward and terminates in God, who is wonderful in His saints and is magnified in them."

The saints and blessed (candidates for sainthood) whose biographical sketches are given in this chapter form only a small number of those who have been canonized or whose cult has been approved. The official listing of saints and blessed for the Roman Church has been contained in the *Roman Martyrology* and related decrees. Butler's unofficial *Lives of the Saints* (1956) contains 2,565 entries.

Selections for this listing are of saints included in the universal calendar of the Roman Church (indicated by an asterisk), well-known saints who are honored in the calendars of particular churches or are the objects of long-standing devotion, many who have been canonized in the 20th century, and saints and blessed of special interest in North and South America. The feast day of a saint, as a general rule, is observed on the day of death (*dies natalis*, day of birth to glory).

Agatha, dates unknown. Sicilian virgin; martyred at Catania during the reign of Decius (249-51); her feast was introduced in Rome in the sixth century; invoked in Sicily as protectress against eruptions of Mt. Etna. Feb. 5*.

Agnes, d. c. 304. Roman virgin; martyred at the age of 10 or 12; patron of young girls. Jan. 21*.

Albert the Great (Albertus Magnus), c. 1200-80. Doctor of the Church. German Dominican; bishop, philosopher, scientist, writer; teacher of St. Thomas Aquinas; declared a saint (equivalent canonization) and doctor, 1931; proclaimed patron of natural scientists, 1948. Nov. 15*.

Alonso Rodriguez, Blessed, 1598-1628. Spanish Jesuit; missionary in Paraguay, where he was martyred; beatified, 1934. Nov. 17.

Aloysius Gonzaga, 1568-91. Italian Jesuit who died while nursing the plague-stricken; canonized, 1726; patron of youth. June 21*.

Alphonsus Liguori, 1696-1787. Doctor of the Church. Born near Naples, Italy; bishop of St. Agatha of the Goths, 1762-75; founder of the Redemptorists, 1732; spiritual and doctrinal writer; canonized, 1839; proclaimed doctor, 1871; named patron of confessors and moralists, 1950. Aug. 1*.

Alphonsus Rodriguez, 1533-1617. Spanish merchant who became a Jesuit lay brother after the death of his wife; spent most of his religious life as a doorkeeper; canonized, 1888. Oct. 30.

Ambrose, c. 340-97. Father and Doctor of the Church. Born in Trier, Germany, where his father was praetorian prefect; was a provincial governor residing in Milan and still a catechumen when he was acclaimed bishop of Milan by the populace in 374; following his baptism and ordination, he was consecrated and installed as bishop Dec. 7, 374; one of the strongest opponents of Arianism in the West; his writings include homilies and doctrinal works. Dec. 7*.

André Bessette, Blessed (Bro. André), 1845-1937. Canadian Holy Cross brother; doorkeeper of the congregation's College of Notre Dame, Montreal, for 40 years; was the prime mover in the building of St. Joseph's Oratory, Montreal; beatified, 1982. Jan. 6* (U.S.).

Andrew, d. c. 70. Apostle, the first to be called. Brother of Peter and disciple of St. John the Baptist; according to legend, he preached the Gospel in northern Greece, Epirus and Scythia, and was martyred at Patras; is honored as the patron of Russia and Scotland; his emblem is an X-shaped cross. Nov. 30*.

Andrew Bobola, 1592-1657. Polish Jesuit; joined the Jesuits at Vilna; worked for return of the Orthodox to union with Rome; martyred; canonized, 1938. May 16.

Andrew Fournet, 1752-1834. French priest; founder, with St. Jeanne Elizabeth Bichier des Anges, of the Daughters of the Holy Cross of St. Andrew in 1804; canonized, 1933. May 13.

Andrew Kim, Paul Chong and Companions, d. between 1839-67. Korean martyrs (103) killed in persecutions of 1839, 1846, 1866 and 1867; outstanding were Andrew Kim, the first Korean priest, and Paul Chong, lay apostle; canonized May 6, 1984, during Pope John Paul II's visit to Korea. Sept. 20*.

Angela Merici, 1474-1540. Italian Franciscan tertiary; founded the

Company of St. Ursula in 1535, the first teaching order of women Religious in the Church; canonized, 1807. Jan. 27*.

Angelico, Blessed (Fra Angelico; John of Faesulis), 1378-1455. Dominican; Florentine painter of early Renaissance; proclaimed blessed by Pope John Paul II in 1983; patron of artists. Feb. 18.

Ann (Anne), first century B.C. Traditional name given to the mother of Mary; there is no mention of her in Scripture; a church at Constantinople was dedicated to her as early as the sixth century; in the West, devotion became widespread in the 12th century; her feast was placed in the universal calendar in 1584; patron of married women and childless couples. July 26* (with Joachim).

Anne Mary Javouhey, Blessed, 1779-1851. French foundress of the Institute of St. Joseph of Cluny, 1812; beatified, 1950. July 15.

Anselm, 1033-1109. Doctor of the Church. Born in Aosta, Piedmont, Italy; entered the Benedictine monastery at Bec in Normandy; elected archbishop of Canterbury, England, 1093; was twice exiled because of his opposition to lay investiture; theological works include *Cur Deus Homo* on the Atonement and a defense of the *Filioque*; proclaimed doctor, 1720; called Father of Scholasticism. Apr. 21*.

Ansgar, 801-65. Benedictine monk; born near Amiens; archbishop of Hamburg; missionary in Denmark, Sweden, Norway and northern Germany; apostle of Scandinavia. Feb. 3*.

Anthony, c. 251-356. Egyptian hermit, abbot; patriarch of all monks; established communities for hermits which became models for monastic life, especially in the East; friend and supporter of St. Athanasius in the latter's struggle with the Arians. Jan. 17*.

Anthony Claret, 1807-70. Spanish bishop; founder of the Missionary Sons of the Immaculate Heart of Mary (Claretians), 1849, in Spain; archbishop of Santiago, Cuba, 1851-57; canonized, 1950. Oct. 24*.

Anthony Daniel, 1601-48. French Jesuit; missionary among Huron Indians in Canada; martyred by Iroquois, July 4, 1648; one of the Jesuit North American Martyrs. Oct. 19* (U.S.).

Anthony Gianelli, 1789-1846. Italian bishop; bishop of Bobbio, 1838; as parish priest, founded the Daughters of Our Lady of the Garden, 1829; canonized, 1951. June 7.

Anthony Zaccaria, 1502-39. Italian priest; founder of the Barnabites (Clerks Regular of St. Paul), 1530; canonized, 1897. July 5*.

Anthony of Padua, 1195-1231. Doctor of the Church. Born in Lisbon, Portugal; was an Augustinian monk at Coimbra when in 1220, attracted by missionary work in Moslem Africa and possible martyrdom, he joined the Franciscans; circumstances led him instead to Italy; he became the first theologian of the Franciscan Order, a celebrated preacher and wonder worker; he remains one of the most popular saints of the Church; canonized, 1232; declared doctor, 1946; called Evangelical Doctor. June 13*.

Apollonia, d. 249. Deaconess of Alexandria; martyred during the persecution of Decius; her patronage of dentists probably rests on tradition that her teeth were broken with pincers by her persecutors.

Athanasius, c. 297-373. Father and Doctor of the Church. Born in Alexandria, Egypt; bishop of Alexandria, 328-73; exiled from his see five times because of his vigorous opposition to Arianism; called the Father of Orthodoxy. May 2*.

Augustine of Canterbury, d. 604 or 605. Italian monk sent by Pope St. Gregory the Great with 40 companions to evangelize England; arrived in Kent, 597; his mission had a successful beginning with the conversion of King Ethelbert and many of his subjects; first archbishop of Canterbury; Apostle of the English. May 27*.

Augustine of Hippo, 354-430. Father and Doctor of the Church. Born in Tagaste, North Africa, of a pagan father and Christian mother (St. Monica); turned to Manichaeism during his student days at Carthage; converted to Christianity and was baptized at Easter, 387, at Milan where he had gone to teach and had come under the influence of St. Ambrose; from that time on, his life was spent in defense of the Christian faith; he returned to Africa, was ordained a priest and in 395 was named bishop of Hippo; he had a strong and lasting influence on Christian theology and philosophy; his writings include the autobiographical *Confessions* and *City of God*; called Doctor of Grace. Aug. 28*.

Barnabas, first century. Ranked among the Apostles because of his collaboration with Paul. Originally called Joseph, but renamed Barnabas by the Apostles (Acts 4:36); a Jew of the Diaspora and a cousin of Mark; member of the Christian community at Jerusalem; influenced the Apostles to accept Paul, with whom he became a pioneer missionary; according to legend he was martyred in Cyprus during the persecution of Nero. June 11*.

Bartolomea Capitanio, 1807-33. Italian foundress with Vincenza Gerosa of the Sisters of Charity of Lovere; canonized, 1950. July 26.

Bartholomew, first century. Apostle. A friend of Philip; identified with Nathanael (Jn. 1:45-50); nothing for certain is known about him; according to various traditions, he preached the Gospel in Ethiopia, India, Persia and Armenia, where he was martyred by being flayed and beheaded. Aug. 24*.

Basil the Great, c. 329-79. Father and Doctor of the Church. Born in Caesarea, Cappadocia, Asia Minor; bishop of Caesarea, 370-79; writings include works refuting Arian errors, homilies, letters and principles of monastic life which earned him the title Father of Eastern Monasticism. Jan. 2*.

Beatrice da Silva Meneses, 1424-90. Daughter of a Portuguese count; raised in the household of Princess Isabella of Portugal, whom she accompanied to Spain; left court life and became a Cistercian for a time; founded the Congregation of the Immaculate Conception of the Blessed Virgin Mary, 1484; canonized, 1976. Sept. 1.

Bede the Venerable, c. 673-735. Doctor of the Church. Born in Northumberland, England; Benedictine; regarded as probably the most learned man of his time in Western Europe; *Ecclesiastical History of* *the English Nation* is his principal work; proclaimed doctor, 1899. May 25*.

Benedict, c. 480-547. Abbot; founder of monasticism in Western Europe; born at Norcia (Nursia), Italy; lived as a solitary, then founded 12 communities of monks near Subiaco, Italy; established the monastery at Monte Cassino about 529; proclaimed patron of Europe by Pope Paul VI in 1964. July 11*.

Benedict Joseph Labre, 1748-83. French layman; pilgrim-beggar who walked from shrine to shrine throughout Europe for some years before going to Rome; noted for his piety and love of prayer before the Blessed Sacrament; canonized, 1883. Apr. 16.

Benedict the Black (il Moro), 1529-89. Sicilian Franciscan; born a slave, he was freed by his master and became a Franciscan lay brother; appointed guardian and novice master of the convent at Palermo; noted for his sanctity; canonized, 1807. Apr. 4.

Benilde (Peter) Romançon, 1805-62. French Christian Brother; educator; founded a school at Saugues in 1841; canonized, 1967. Aug. 13.

Bernadette of Lourdes (Marie Bernard Soubirous), 1844-79. French peasant girl favored with series of visions of the Blessed Virgin Mary at Lourdes in 1858; joined the Sisters of Notre Dame at Nevers in 1866; canonized, 1933. Apr. 16.

Bernard of Clairvaux, c. 1090-1153. Doctor of the Church. Born near Dijon, France; abbot, monastic reformer; called the second founder of the Cistercian Order; mystical theologian with great influence on devotional life; canonized, 1174; declared doctor, 1830; described as Mellifluous Doctor because of his eloquence. Aug. 20*.

Bernard of Montjoux or Menthon, d. 1081. Italian priest; founded hospices near the two Alpine passes named for him (Great and Little St. Bernard); patron of mountaineers, 1923. May 28.

Bernardine of Feltre, Blessed, 1434-94. Italian Franciscan; popular preacher against evils of gambling, usury and licentiousness; helped found the *monti di pieta* (lending institutions); beatified, 1728. Sept. 28.

Bernardine of Siena, 1380-1444. Italian Franciscan; noted preacher and missioner; spread of devotion to the Holy Name of Jesus is attributed to him; represented in art holding to his breast the monogram IHS; canonized, 1450; patron of advertisers, communications and public relations personnel. May 20*.

Bernardino Realino, 1530-1616. Italian Jesuit; was a lawyer before becoming a Jesuit in Naples at the age of 34; canonized, 1947. July 2.

Bertilla Boscardin, 1888-1922. Italian Religious; joined the Sisters of St. Dorothy at the age of 16 and devoted her life to care of the sick; died of cancer; canonized, 1961. Oct. 20.

Blase, d.c. 316. Bishop, born in Armenia; martyr; the blessing of throats on his feast day probably derives from a legend that he miraculously saved the life of a boy who had half-swallowed a fish-bone. Feb. 3*.

Bonaventure, c. 1217-74. Doctor of the Church. Italian Franciscan, bishop of Albano, 1273-74; cardinal; writings include treatises, scriptural commentaries, mystical works on devotional life and a life of St.

Francis of Assisi; canonized, 1482; proclaimed doctor, 1588; called Seraphic Doctor. July 15*.

Boniface (Winfrid), d. 754. English Benedictine; bishop; martyr; established monastery at Fulda which became the center of missionary work in Germany; archbishop of Mainz; martyred near Dukkum in Holland; Apostle of Germany. June 5*.

Brendan, c. 489-583. Irish abbot; founded monasteries; his patronage of sailors probably rests on a legend that he made a seven-year voyage in search of a fabled paradise; called Brendan the Navigator. May 16.

Bridget (Brigid), c. 450-525. Irish nun; established a religious community at Kildare, the first in Ireland; patron, with Sts. Patrick and Columba, of Ireland. Feb. 1.

Bridget (Birgitta), c. 1303-73. Swedish mystic; widow; foundress of the Order of Our Savior (Brigittines); wrote *Revelationes*, accounts of her visions; canonized, 1391; patroness of Sweden. July 23*.

Bruno, 1030-1101. German monk; chancellor of Rheims; withdrew to the Grand Chartreuse, near Grenoble, France, where in 1084 he founded the Carthusians; called to Rome as a papal counselor by Pope Urban II in 1090; established several Carthusian foundations in Calabria. Oct. 6*.

Cajetan (Gaetano), 1480-1547. Italian lawyer; ordained a priest, 1516; religious reformer; a founder with Bishop Peter Caraffa (later Pope Paul IV) and two other priests, of the Theatines (Congregation of Clerks Regular), 1524; canonized, 1671. Aug. 7*.

Callistus I, d. 222. Pope, 217-22; martyr; condemned Sabellianism and other heresies; advocated a policy of mercy toward repentant sinners; venerated as a martyr from the fourth century. Oct. 14*.

Camillus de Lellis, 1550-1614. Italian priest; addicted to gambling in his youth; reformed in 1575 and joined the Franciscans, but had to leave because of a diseased leg; ordained a priest in 1584 on the advice of St. Philip Neri; founded the Ministers of the Sick (Camillians); canonized, 1746; patron of the sick and of nurses. July 14*.

Casimir, 1458-84. Polish prince, son of King Casimir IV; drawn to life of holiness and retirement from his youth; died while on a visit to Lithuania; his burial place at Vilna has been the site of many miracles; canonized, 1521; patron of Poland and Lithuania. Mar. 4*.

Cassian of Tangier, d. 298. An official court stenographer at the trial of St. Marcellus the Centurion who, according to legend, was converted and suffered martyrdom; patron of stenographers. Dec. 3.

Catherine Labouré, 1806-76. French Religious; favored with a series of visions of the Blessed Virgin soon after she joined the Sisters of Charity of St. Vincent de Paul in Paris in 1830; the first Miraculous Medal was struck in 1832 in accord with one of the visions; canonized, 1947. Nov. 28.

Catherine of Bologna, 1413-63. Italian Poor Clare; mystic, writer, artist; canonized, 1712; patron of artists. May 9.

Catherine of Siena, c. 1347-80. Doctor of the Church. Italian Dominican tertiary; mystic; had great influence in persuading Pope Gregory XI to return the papacy and curia to Rome in 1376, to end the Avignon period of the papacy; authored a long series of letters, mainly concerning spiritual instruction, and *Dialogue*, a spiritual testament; canonized, 1461; the second woman proclaimed doctor, Oct. 4, 1970. Apr. 29*.

Cecilia, date unknown. Roman virgin-martyr; nothing is known for certain about her life; a church was dedicated in her honor as early as 313; traditional patroness of musicians. Nov. 22*.

Charles Borromeo, 1538-84. Italian cardinal, bishop of Milan; influential figure in Church reform in Italy; promoted education of the clergy; established schools for the religious education of children; canonized, 1610. Nov. 4*.

Charles Garnier, c. 1606-49. French Jesuit; missionary among the Hurons in Canada; martyred by Iroquois, Dec. 7, 1649; canonized, 1930; one of the Jesuit North American Martyrs. Oct. 19* (U.S.).

Charles Lwanga and Companions (Martyrs of Uganda), d. between 1885 and 1887. Group of 22 Christians, many of them pages in the court of King Mwanga, who were put to death because they denounced his corrupt lifestyle; Charles Lwanga was master of the pages; they were the first martyrs of black Africa; canonized, 1964. June 3*.

Charles of Sezze, 1616-70. Italian Franciscan lay brother who served in humble capacities as cook, porter or gardener in different monasteries near Rome; noted for sanctity; canonized, 1959. Jan. 6.

Christopher, third century. Early Christian martyr inscribed in the Roman calendar about 1550; his feast was relegated to particular calendars because of the legendary nature of accounts of his life; traditional patron of travelers. July 25.

Clare of Assisi, 1194-1253. Foundress of the Poor Clares; born at Assisi; was joined in religious life by her sisters, Agnes and Beatrice, and eventually her widowed mother; canonized, 1255; patroness of television. Aug. 11*.

Clement I, first century. Pope, 88-97; third successor of St. Peter in the papacy; wrote an important letter to the Church in Corinth, settling disputes there; venerated as a martyr. Nov. 23*.

Clement Hofbauer, 1751-1820. Redemptorist priest, missionary; born in Moravia; was a baker by trade in Vienna; joined the Redemptorists and was ordained in Rome in 1785; missionary in Poland; from 1808 worked in Italian section of Vienna; helped spread Redemptorists north of the Alps; canonized, 1909. Mar. 15.

Columba, 521-97. Irish monk; founded monasteries in Ireland; missionary in Scotland; established monastery at Iona, off the coast of Scotland, which became the center for conversion of Picts, Scots and Northern English; patron of Scotland. June 9.

Columban, 545-615. Irish monk, scholar; founded monasteries in England and Brittany (the famous abbey of Luxeuil); forced into exile because of his criticism of the Frankish court; spent last years in northern Italy, where he founded the abbey at Bobbio. Nov. 23*.

Conrad of Parzham, 1818-94. Bavarian Capuchin lay brother; served as porter at the Marian shrine of Altotting in Upper Bavaria for 40 years; canonized, 1934. Apr. 21.

Contardo Ferrini, Blessed, 1859-1902. Italian layman, secular Franciscan; model of a Catholic professor; recognized as an authority on Roman law; beatified, 1947; patron of universities. Oct. 20.

Cornelius, d. 253. Pope, 251-53; promoted a policy of mercy with respect to the readmission of repentant Christians who had fallen away during the persecution of Decius *(lapsi)*; banished from Rome during the persecution of Gallus; regarded as a martyr. Sept. 16* (with Cyprian).

Cosmas and Damian, d. c. 303. Arabian twin brothers, physicians who gave their services free of charge; martyred during the Diocletian persecution; patrons of physicians. Sept. 26*.

Crispin and Crispinian, third century. Early Christian martyrs said to have met their deaths in Gaul; patrons of shoemakers, a trade they pursued according to legend. Oct. 25.

Crispin of Viterbo, 1668-1750. Italian Capuchin; renowned during his life for miracles and the gift of prophecy; beatified, 1806; canonized, 1982. May 21.

Cyprian, d. 258. Early ecclesiastical writer; born in Africa; bishop of Carthage, 249-58; supported Pope St. Cornelius concerning readmission of repentant Christians who had apostasized in time of persecution. Sept. 16* (with Cornelius).

Cyril and Methodius, ninth century. Greek missionaries; brothers venerated as apostles of the Slavs; Cyril (Constantine), monk, d. 869, and Methodius, bishop, d. 885, began their missionary work in Moravia in 863; developed a Slavonic alphabet and used the vernacular in the liturgy, a practice that was eventually approved; declared patrons of Europe with St. Benedict, Dec. 31, 1980. Feb. 14*.

Cyril of Alexandria, c. 376-444. Doctor of the Church. Born in Egypt; bishop of Alexandria, 412-44; wrote treatises on the Trinity, the Incarnation and other subjects, mostly in refutation of Nestorian errors; made key contributions to the development of Christology; preached at the Council of Ephesus, 431; proclaimed doctor, 1882. June 27*.

Cyril of Jerusalem, c. 315-86. Doctor of the Church. Bishop of Jerusalem, 350-87; vigorous opponent of Arianism; his principal work was *Catecheses*, a pre-baptismal explanation of the creed of Jerusalem; proclaimed doctor, 1882. Mar. 18*.

Damasus I, d. 384. Pope, 366-84; opposed Arians and Apollinarians; published a canon of Sacred Scripture; commissioned St. Jerome to translate the Bible into Latin; developed the Roman liturgy. Dec. 11*.

Damian. See Cosmas and Damian.

David, fifth or sixth century. Name of the patron saint of Wales; nothing for certain is known of his life; said to have founded a monastery at Menevia. Mar. 1.

Denis and Companions, d. third century. Denis, bishop of Paris, and two companions identified by early writers as Rusticus, a priest, and Eleutherius, a deacon; martyred near Paris; Denis is popularly regarded as the apostle and a patron saint of France. Oct. 9*.

Dismas, first century. Name given to the repentant thief (Good Thief) to whom Jesus promised salvation (Lk. 23:40-43); regarded as the patron of prisoners. Mar. 25.

Dominic (Dominic de Guzman), 1170-1221; Spanish priest; founded the Order of Preachers (Dominicans), 1215, in France; preached against the Albigensian heresy; a contemporary of St. Francis of Assisi; canonized, 1234. Aug. 8*.

Dominic Savio, 1842-57. Italian youth, pupil of St. John Bosco; died before his 15th birthday; canonized, 1954; patron of choirboys. May 6.

Dunstan, c. 910-88. English monk; archbishop of Canterbury; initiated reforms of religious life; counselor to several kings; considered one of the greatest Anglo-Saxon saints; patron of armorers, goldsmiths, locksmiths, jewelers (trades in which he is said to have excelled). May 19.

Dymphna, dates unknown. Nothing certain is known of her life; according to legend she was an Irish maiden murdered by her heathen father at Gheel, near Antwerp, Belgium, where she had fled to escape his advances; her relics were discovered there in the 13th century; since that time cures of mental illness and epilepsy have been attributed to her intercession; patron of those suffering from mental illness. May 15.

Edmund Campion, 1540-81. English Jesuit; convert, 1573; martyred at Tyburn; canonized, 1970; one of the Forty English and Welsh Martyrs. Dec. 1.

Edward the Confessor, d.1066. King of England, 1042-66; canonized, 1161. Oct. 13.

Eligius, c. 590-660. Bishop, born in Gaul; famous worker in gold and silver; founded monasteries and convents; was generous to the poor; bishop of Noyon and Tournai; patron of metalworkers. Dec. 1.

Elizabeth Ann Seton, 1774-1821. American foundress; convert, 1805, two years after the death of her husband; founded the Sisters of Charity in the U.S.; beatified, 1963; canonized, Sept. 14, 1975; the first American-born saint. Jan. 4* (U.S.).

Elizabeth of Hungary, 1207-31. Daughter of King Andrew II of Hungary; married the Landgrave of Thuringia at the age of 14 and was widowed six years later; always generous to the poor, she devoted her life completely to the needy and destitute as a Franciscan tertiary; canonized, 1235; a patron of the Secular Franciscan Order. Nov. 17*.

Elizabeth of Portugal, 1271-1336. Queen of Portugal; born in Spain; married to King Denis of Portugal; known for her charity and piety; became a Franciscan tertiary after her husband's death in 1325; canonized, 1626, July 4*.

Emily de Rodat, 1787-1852. French foundress of the Congregation of the Holy Family of Villefranche; canonized, 1950. Sept. 19.

Emily de Vialar, 1797-1856. French foundress of the Sisters of St. Joseph of the Apparition; canonized, 1951. June 17.

Ephraem (Ephraim, Ephrem), c. 306-73. Doctor of the Church. Born in Nisibis, Mesopotamia; deacon; counteracted the spread of Gnostic and Arian errors with didactic poems and hymns of his own composition; wrote also on the Eucharist and Mary; proclaimed doctor, 1920; called the Harp of the Holy Spirit. June 9 *.

Erasmus (Elmo), d. 303. Accounts of his life are legendary; martyred during the Diocletian persecution; patron of sailors. June 2.

Ethelbert, d. 616. King of Kent, England; baptized by St. Augustine of Canterbury, 597; issued a legal code; furthered the spread of Christianity. Feb. 26.

Euphrasia Pelletier, 1796-1868. French Religious; founded the Sisters of the Good Shepherd at Angers, 1829; canonized, 1940. Apr. 24.

Eusebius of Vercelli, 283-370. Italian bishop; exiled from his see (Vercelli) for a time because of his opposition to Arianism. Aug. 2*.

Fabian, d. 250. Pope, 236-50; martyred during the Decian persecution. Jan. 20*.

Felicity. See Perpetua and Felicity.

Ferdinand III, 1198-1252. King of Castile and León; waged a successful crusade against Mohammedans in Spain; canonized, 1671. May 30.

Fiacre (Fiachra), d. c. 670. Irish hermit who settled in France; patron of gardeners and Paris cabdrivers. Aug. 30.

Fidelis of Sigmaringen (Mark Rey), 1577-1622. German Capuchin; a lawyer before he joined the Franciscans in 1612; missionary to Swiss Protestants; stabbed to death by peasants who were told he was an agent of the Austrian emperor. Apr. 24*.

Forty Martyrs of England and Wales, d. between 1535 and 1679. Martyrs included 32 priests (Religious and secular), one Jesuit lay brother, four laymen and three laywomen who were executed as traitors for refusal to comply with penal laws enacted by Henry VIII and Elizabeth I in England; canonized, 1970.

Alban Roe, Benedictine (Jan. 21, 1642); Alexander Briant, Jesuit

(Dec. 1, 1581); Ambrose Barlow, Benedictine (Sept. 10, 1641); Ann Line, laywoman (Feb. 27, 1600); Augustine Webster, Carthusian (May 4, 1535); Cuthbert Mayne, diocesan priest (Nov. 30, 1577); David Lewis, Jesuit (Aug. 27, 1679); Edmund Arrowsmith, Jesuit (Aug. 28, 1610); Edmund Campion, Jesuit (Dec. 1, 1581); Edmund Gennings, diocesan priest (Dec. 10, 1591); Eustace White, diocesan priest (Dec. 10, 1591); John Plessington, diocesan priest (July 19, 1679); Henry Morse, Jesuit (Feb. 1, 1645); Henry Walpole, Jesuit (Apr. 7, 1595); John Almond, diocesan priest (Dec. 5, 1610); John Boste, diocesan priest (July 24, 1594); John Houghton, Carthusian (May 4, 1535); John Jones, Franciscan (July 12, 1598); John Kemble, diocesan priest (Aug. 22, 1679); John Lloyd, diocesan priest (July 22, 1679); John Paine, diocesan priest (Apr. 2, 1582); John Rigby, layman (June 21, 1600); John Roberts, Benedictine (Dec. 10, 1610); John Southworth, diocesan priest (June 28, 1654); John Stone, Augustinian (Dec. 27, 1539); John Wall, Franciscan (Aug. 22, 1679); Luke Kirby, diocesan priest (May 30, 1582); Margaret Clitherow, laywoman (Mar. 25, 1586); Margaret Ward, laywoman (Aug. 30, 1588); Nicholas Owen, Jesuit lay brother (Mar. 22, 1606); Philip Evans, Jesuit (July 22, 1679); Philip Howard, layman (Oct. 19, 1595); Polydore Plasden, diocesan priest (Dec. 10, 1591); Ralph Sherwin, diocesan priest (Dec. 1, 1581); Richard Gwyn, layman (Oct. 17, 1584); Richard Reynolds, Brigittine (May 4, 1535); Robert Lawrence, Carthusian (May 4, 1535); Robert Southwell, Jesuit (Feb. 21, 1595); Swithun Wells, layman (Dec. 10, 1591); Thomas Garnet, Jesuit (June 23, 1608).

Frances of Rome, 1384-1440. Italian wife and mother who was happily married for 40 years; after the death of her husband in 1436, she joined a community of Benedictine Oblates she had founded; a model for housewives and widows; canonized, 1608; patron of motorists. Mar. 9*.

Frances Xavier Cabrini (Mother Cabrini), 1850-1917. Foundress; born in Italy; founded Missionary Sisters of the Sacred Heart, 1877; settled in the U.S., 1889; became an American citizen, 1909; worked among Italian immigrants; established schools, hospitals and other institutions; canonized, 1946, the first American citizen so honored. Nov. 13* (U.S.).

Francis Borgia, 1510-72. Spanish Jesuit; upon the death of his wife in 1546 he joined the Jesuits, after providing for his eight children; as superior general of the Order, 1565, was responsible for its revitalization. Oct. 10.

Francis Caracciolo, 1563-1608. Italian priest; founder with Father Augustine Adorno of the Clerks Regular Minor (Adorno Fathers); canonized, 1807. June 4.

Francis de Sales, 1567-1622. Doctor of the Church. Born in Savoy; bishop of Geneva, 1602-22; spiritual writer with strong influence on devotional life through treatises such as *Introduction to a Devout Life* and *The Love of God*; co-founder with St. Jane Frances de Chantal of the

Order of the Visitation; canonized, 1665; proclaimed doctor, 1877; patron of journalists and the Catholic press. Jan. 24*.

Francis of Assisi (Giovanni di Bernardone), 1181/82-1226). Founder of the Franciscans, 1209; received the stigmata, 1224; canonized, 1228; one of the best-known and best-loved saints; patron of Italy, Catholic Action and ecologists. Oct. 4*.

Francis of Paola, 1416-1507. Italian hermit; founder of the Minim Friars; canonized, 1512. Apr. 2*.

Francis Solanus, 1549-1610. Spanish Franciscan; missionary in Paraguay, Argentina and Peru; called the Wonder Worker of the New World; canonized, 1726. July 14.

Francis Xavier, 1506-52. Spanish Jesuit; a student at the University of Paris when he met Ignatius of Loyola; among the original group of Jesuits who professed their first vows at Montmartre in 1534; ordained to the priesthood three years later in Venice; sent as a missionary to the Far East in 1540, he landed at Goa and visited India, Ceylon, Malaya and Japan; died at Sancian when about to enter China, and was buried at Goa; considered one of the greatest Christian missionaries; canonized, 1602; named patron of foreign missions, 1904. Dec. 3*.

Francis Xavier Bianchi, 1743-1815. Italian Barnabite; acclaimed apostle of Naples because of his work there among the poor and abandoned; canonized, 1951. Jan. 31.

François de Montmorency Laval, Blessed, 1623-1708. French-born missionary bishop in Canada; vicar apostolic of Canada, 1658; first bishop of Quebec, 1674-88; his jurisdiction extended over all French-claimed territory in the New World; beatified, 1980. May 6.

Gabriel, Archangel. The messenger of God sent to Daniel (8:16; 9:21-27) to explain the meaning of the prophet's visions, to Zechariah (although his name is not given) to announce the birth of John the Baptist (Lk. 1:11-18) and to Mary to announce the incarnation (Lk. 1:26-38); named patron of telecommunications personnel, Jan. 12, 1951. Sept. 29* (with Michael and Raphael).

Gabriel Lalemant, 1610-49. French Jesuit; missionary among the Hurons in Canada; martyred by the Iroquois, Mar. 17, 1649; canonized, 1930; one of the Jesuit North American Martyrs. Oct. 19* (U.S.).

Gabriel of the Sorrowful Mother (Francis Possenti), 1838-62. Italian Passionist; lived a devoted, ordinary life; canonized, 1920. Feb. 27.

Gaspar (Caspar) del Bufalo, 1786-1836. Italian priest; exiled to Corsica for a time because of his refusal to swear allegiance to Napoleon; founded the Missionaries of the Precious Blood, 1815, for home mission work; canonized, 1954. Jan. 2.

Gemma Galgani, 1878-1903. Italian laywoman prevented by physical infirmities from becoming a Passionist nun; visionary; subject of extraordinary religious experiences; canonized, 1940. Apr. 11.

Genesius, d.c. 300. Roman actor; according to legend, was converted while performing a burlesque of Christian baptism and was subsequently martyred; patron of actors. Aug. 25.

Geneviève, 422-500. French nun; dedicated her life to God at the age of seven, and at 15 received the veil from the bishop of Paris; venerated in Paris as a protectress and patron. Jan. 3.

George, d. c. 300. Martyr, probably in Palestine during the Diocletian persecution; one of the most famous of the early martyrs; incidents of his life, including the story of the dragon, are legendary; patron of England, soldiers and Boy Scouts. Apr. 23*.

Gerard Majella, 1725-55. Italian Redemptorist lay brother; noted for supernatural occurrences in his life, including bilocation and reading of consciences; canonized, 1904; patron of mothers and expectant mothers. Oct. 16.

Gertrude, 1256-1302. German mystic; writer; promoted devotion to the Sacred Heart. Nov. 16*.

Gregory I, the Great, c. 540-604. Pope, Father and Doctor of the Church. Born in Rome; pope, 590-604; enforced papal supremacy and established the position of the pope in relation to the emperor; worked for clerical and monastic reform and the observance of clerical celibacy; sent missionaries under Augustine of Canterbury to evangelize England; writings include scriptural commentaries, a compendium of theology and 14 books of letters. Sept. 3*.

Gregory VII (Hildebrand), 1020?-1085. Pope, 1075-85; Benedictine monk; adviser to several popes; during his papacy he strengthened the interior life of the Church and fought against lay investiture; was driven from Rome by King Henry IV; died in exile; canonized, 1584. May 25*.

Gregory Barbarigo, 1626-97. Italian bishop and cardinal; noted for his works of charity and efforts to bring about the reunion of separated Christians; canonized, 1960. June 18.

Gregory Nazianzen, c. 330-90. Father and Doctor of the Church. Born in Arianzus, Cappadocia, Asia Minor; theologian; bishop of Constantinople, 381-90; vigorous opponent of Arianism; in addition to five theological discourses on the Nicene Creed and the Trinity for which he is best known, wrote letters and poetry. Jan. 2*.

Gregory of Nyssa, c. 335-95. Bishop, theologian; wrote many theological treatises; younger brother of St. Basil the Great. Mar. 9.

Gregory Thaumaturgus, c. 213-68. Bishop of Neocaesarea; missionary, famed as a wonder worker. Nov. 17.

Gregory the Illuminator, 257-332. Bishop; called the apostle of Armenia. Sept. 30.

Hedwig, 1174-1243. Moravian noblewoman; aunt of St. Elizabeth of Hungary; married Henry I, duke of Silesia and head of the Polish royal family; mother of six children; fostered religious life in the country; established the first Cistercian convent in Silesia; died at Trebnitz, Poland; canonized, 1267; patron of Silesia. Oct.16*.

Helena, 250-330. Empress; mother of Constantine the Great; associated with discovery of the True Cross. Aug. 18.

Henry, 972-1024. Bavarian emperor; cooperated with Benedictine abbeys in the restoration of ecclesiastical and social discipline; canonized, 1146. July 13*.

Herman Joseph, 1150-1241. German Premonstratensian; his visions were the subjects of artists; writer; cult approved, 1958. Apr. 7.

Hilary of Poitiers, c. 315-67. Doctor of the Church. Born in Poitiers, France, of pagan parents; became a Christian and shortly afterward was elected bishop of Poitiers; introduced Eastern theology to the West; contributed to the development of hymnology; proclaimed doctor, 1851; called the Athanasius of the West because of his vigorous defense of the divinity of Christ against Arian errors. Jan. 13*.

Hippolytus, d. c. 236. Roman priest; opposed Pope St. Callistus I in his teaching about the readmission to the Church of repentant Christians who had apostasized during persecution; antipope; exiled to Sardinia; was reconciled to the Church before his martyrdom; important ecclesiastical writer. Aug. 13*.

Hubert, d. 727. Bishop of Liège; not much is known of his life; according to legend he was converted to a better life while hunting; patron of hunters. Nov. 3.

Hugh of Cluny (the Great), 1024-1109. Abbot of the Benedictine foundation at Cluny; supported popes in efforts to reform ecclesiastical abuses; canonized, 1120. Apr. 29.

Ignatius of Antioch, d. c. 107. Early ecclesiastical writer whose letters are important sources of information on Christian belief and practice in the early years of the Church; bishop of Antioch in Syria for 40 years; martyred at Rome. Oct. 17*.

Ignatius of Laconi, 1701-81. Italian Capuchin lay brother whose 60 years of religious life were spent in Franciscan simplicity; canonized, 1951. May 11.

Ignatius of Loyola, 1491-1556. Spanish-born founder of the Society of Jesus (Jesuits); was a soldier recovering from wounds received at the siege of Pampeluna (Pamplona) in 1521 when he decided to dedicate his life to God; founded the Jesuits in Paris in 1534; ordained to the priesthood, 1537, in Venice; directed the Order from Rome the rest of his life; wrote *The Book of Spiritual Exercises*; canonized, 1622. July 31*.

Irenaeus of Lyons, 130-202. Early ecclesiastical writer; opposed Gnosticism; bishop of Lyons; traditionally regarded as a martyr. June 28*.

Isaac Jogues, 1607-46. French Jesuit; ordained to the priesthood in

France in 1636; sent to Canada as a missionary to the Hurons; captured by Iroquois in 1642, held for a year and tortured; with the aid of Dutch, escaped to France; returned to Canada in 1644 to resume missionary work; was martyred by a Mohawk war party near the present site of Auriesville, New York; one of the Jesuit North American Martyrs, canonized, 1930. Oct. 19* (U.S.).

Isidore, d. 1170. Spanish layman; worked as a farmer for the same employer all his life; canonized, 1622; patron of farmers. May 15* (U.S.).

Isidore of Seville, c. 560-636. Doctor of the Church. Born in Cartagena, Spain; bishop of Seville, c. 600-36; wrote on theological and historical subjects; his principal work was *Etymologiae*, an encyclopedia of the knowledge of his day; proclaimed doctor, 1722. Apr. 4*.

James the Greater, first century. Apostle. A Galilean, son of Zebedee, brother of John (with whom he was called a "Son of Thunder"), a fisherman; with Peter and John, witnessed the raising of Jairus' daughter to life, the Transfiguration, the agony of Jesus in the Garden of Gethsemani; he was the first of the Apostles to be martyred, by the sword in 44, during the rule of Herod Agrippa; there is doubt about a journey legend says he made to Spain and also about the authenticity of relics said to be his at Santiago de Compostela. July 25*.

James the Less, first century. Apostle. Son of Alphaeus, called "Less" because he was younger in age or shorter in stature than James the Greater; one of the Catholic Letters bears his name; one account of his martyrdom states that he was stoned to death in 62; another, that he was thrown from the top of the temple in Jerusalem and clubbed to death at a later date. May 3* (with St. Philip).

Jane Frances de Chantal, 1572-1641. French widow; foundress, under guidance of St. Francis de Sales, of the Order of the Visitation; canonized, 1767. Dec. 12*.

Januarius (Gennaro), d. 304. Bishop of Benevento; martyred during the Diocletian persecution; his fame rests on liquefaction of some of his blood preserved in a phial at Naples, an unexplained phenomenon which has occurred regularly several times each year for over 400 years; declared patron of the Campania region around Naples, 1980. Sept. 19*.

Jeanne (Joan) de Lestonnac, 1556-1640. French foundress; widowed in 1597, she founded the Religious of Notre Dame in 1607 for the education of girls; canonized, 1949. Feb. 2.

Jeanne Delanoue, 1666-1736. French foundress; preoccupied with management of the family business until 1698, when she had a change of heart and she began to help the poor; founded the Sisters of St. Anne of Providence, 1704; canonized, 1982. Aug. 16.

Jeanne de Valois or **Jeanne of France**, 1464-1505. French foundress; deformed daughter of King Louis XI; was married in 1476 to Duke Louis of Orleans, who had the marriage annulled when he ascended the throne as Louis XII; Jeanne offered no objection to the annulment; she retired to live a secluded life of prayer and founded the Annonciades of Bourges, a contemplative community, in 1504; canonized, 1950. Feb. 4.

Jeanne Elizabeth Bichier des Anges, 1773-1838. French Religious; co-founder with St. Andrew Fournet of the Daughters of the Cross of St. Andrew, 1807; canonized, 1947. Aug. 26.

Jeanne Jugan, Blessed, 1792-1879. French foundress; worked as a domestic and in hospital work; at the age of 50, founded the Little Sisters of the Poor, a congregation devoted to care of the aged poor; beatified, Oct. 5, 1982. Aug. 30.

Jerome, c. 343-420. Father and Doctor of the Church. Born in Stridon, Dalmatia; translated the Old Testament into Latin from the Hebrew and revised the existing Latin translation of the New Testament to produce the Vulgate edition of the Bible; wrote scriptural comment-aries and treatises on matters of controversy; called the Father of Bibli-cal Science. Sept. 30*.

Jerome Emiliani, 1481-1537. Italian priest; founded the Clerks Regu-lar of Somasca (Somascans) in 1534 for the care of orphans; canonized, 1767; named patron of orphans and abandoned children, 1928. Feb. 8*.

Joachim, first century. Name given by tradition to the father of Mary; there is no mention of him in the Gospel. July 16* (with Ann).

Joan Antida Thouret, 1765-1826. French Religious; joined the Sisters of Charity of St. Vincent de Paul in Paris in 1787; forced to return to her home near Besançon during the French Revolution; founded, 1799, the religious congregation now known as the Sisters of Charity of St. Joan Antida; canonized, 1934. Aug. 24.

Joan of Arc, 1412-31. French heroine, the Maid of Orleans, La Pucelle; peasant girl who, in obedience to inner promptings, successful-ly led the French army in 1429 against English invaders besieging Or-leans; captured by Burgundians in another engagement the following year, was sold to the English, turned over to an ecclesiastical court, tried on charges of heresy and witchcraft, found guilty and burned at the stake; a commission appointed by Pope Callistus III in 1456 declared her innocence; canonized, 1920; patroness of France. May 30.

Joaquina de Vedruna de Mas, 1783-1854. Spanish foundress; widowed in 1816; in 1826, after providing for her children, she founded the Car-melite Sisters of Charity; canonized, 1959. Aug. 28.

John, first century. Apostle and Evangelist. A Galilean, son of Zebedee, brother of James the Greater (with whom he was called a "Son of Thunder"), a fisherman, probably a disciple of John the Baptist, called the Beloved Disciple; with Peter and his brother James, wit-nessed the raising of Jairus' daughter to life, the Transfiguration, the agony of Jesus in the Garden of Gethsemani; Mary was commended to his special care by Christ; the fourth Gospel, three Catholic Letters and

Revelation bear his name; according to various accounts, lived at Ephesus in Asia Minor for some time and died a natural death about 100. Dec. 27*.

John I, d. 526. Pope, 523-26; martyr; died in prison at Ravenna. May 18*.

John the Baptist, d. c. 29. Prophet; precursor of Jesus; son of Zechariah and Elizabeth, a kinswoman of Mary; the miraculous circumstances surrounding his birth, his mission as precursor of Christ, his imprisonment and his martyrdom under Herod Antipas during the first year of Christ's public ministry are fully recorded in the Gospels. June 24*, his nativity, a solemnity (the only saint other than the Blessed Virgin Mary whose birthday is liturgically observed). His martyrdom by beheading is observed as a memorial on Aug. 29*.

John Baptist de la Salle, 1651-1719. French priest; founder of the Brothers of the Christian Schools (Christian Brothers), 1680; canonized, 1900; patron of teachers. Apr. 7*.

John Baptist of the Conception, 1561-1613. Spanish Trinitarian reformer; writer; canonized, 1975. Feb. 14.

John Berchmans, 1599-1621. Belgian Jesuit scholastic; canonized, 1888; patron of Mass servers. Nov. 26.

John (Don) Bosco, 1815-88. Italian priest; founder of the Salesians (Society of St. Francis de Sales) in Turin, 1859, for the education of boys; co-founder of the Daughters of Mary Help of Christians for girls; canonized, 1934; Jan. 31*.

John Capistran, 1386-1456. Italian Franciscan; preacher, papal diplomat; canonized, 1690; declared patron of military chaplains, Feb. 10, 1984. Oct. 23*.

John Chrysostom, c. 347-407. Doctor of the Church. Born in Antioch, Asia Minor; archbishop of Constantinople, 398-407; wrote homilies, scriptural commentaries and letters of wide influence in addition to a classical treatise on the priesthood; proclaimed doctor by the Council of Chalcedon, 451; named patron of preachers, 1909; called Golden-Mouthed because of his eloquence. Sept. 13*.

John Damascene, c. 675-749. Doctor of the Church. Born in Damascus, Syria; monk; wrote *Fountain of Wisdom*, a three-part work including a history of heresies and an exposition of the Christian faith, homilies on Mary, biblical commentaries and treatises on moral subjects; proclaimed doctor, 1890; called Golden Speaker because of his eloquence. Dec. 4*.

John de Brébeuf, 1593-1649. French Jesuit; missionary among Huron Indians in Canada; martyred by Iroquois, Mar. 16, 1649; canonized, 1930; one of the Jesuit North American Martyrs. Oct. 19* (U.S.).

John de Castillo, Blessed, 1596-1628. Spanish Jesuit; worked in Indian mission settlements (Reductions) in Paraguay; martyred; beatified, 1934. Nov. 17.

John de Massias (Macias), 1585-1645. Dominican brother, a native of

Spain; entered the Dominican Order in 1622 in Lima, Peru; served as doorkeeper until his death; canonized, 1975. Sept. 16.

John de Ribera, 1532-1611. Spanish bishop and statesman; archbishop of Valencia, 1568-1611, and viceroy of that province; canonized, 1960. Jan. 6.

John Eudes, 1601-80. French priest; founder of the Sisters of Our Lady of Charity of Refuge, 1641, and the men's Congregation of Jesus-Mary (Eudists), 1643; introduced devotion to the Sacred Heart in the liturgy; canonized, 1925. Aug. 19*.

John Fisher, 1469-1535. English prelate, theologian; martyr; bishop of Rochester, 1504; cardinal, 1534; refused to recognize the validity of Henry VIII's marriage to Anne Boleyn; upheld supremacy of the pope; beheaded for refusing to acknowledge Henry as head of the Church in England; canonized, 1935; June 22* (with St. Thomas More).

John Gualbert, d. 1073. Italian priest; founder of the Benedictine Congregation of Vallombrosians, 1039; canonized, 1193. July 12.

John Kanty (Cantius), 1395-1473. Polish priest; scripture scholar and professor at the University of Cracow; canonized, 1767. Dec. 23*.

John Lalande, d. 1646. French lay missionary, companion of St. Isaac Jogues; martyred by Mohawks at Auriesville, New York, Oct. 19, 1646; canonized, 1930; one of the Jesuit North American Martyrs. Oct. 19* (U.S.).

John Leonardi, 1550-1609. Italian priest; worked among prisoners and the sick; founded the Clerks Regular of the Mother of God; canonized, 1938. Oct. 9*.

John Nepomucene, 1345-93. Bohemian priest; martyr; court chaplain, who, by order of King Wenceslaus IV, was thrown into a river and drowned because, according to tradition, he refused to reveal to the king what the queen had told him in sacramental confession; canonized, 1729; patron of Czechoslovakia. May 16.

John Nepomucene Neumann, 1811-60. American prelate; born in Bohemia; ordained to the priesthood in New York, 1836; missionary among Germans near Niagara Falls before joining Redemptorists in 1840; bishop of Philadelphia, 1852; first bishop in the United States to prescribe the Forty Hours devotion in his diocese; beatified, 1963; canonized, June 19, 1977. Jan. 5* (U.S.).

John of Avila, 1499-1569. Spanish priest; preacher; ascetical writer; spiritual adviser of St. Teresa of Jesus (Avila); canonized, 1970. May 10.

John of Britto, 1647-93. Portuguese Jesuit; missionary in India where he was martyred; canonized, 1947. Feb. 4.

John of God, 1495-1550. Portuguese Religious; his work among the sick led to the foundation of the Brothers Hospitallers of St. John of God, 1540, in Spain; canonized, 1690; patron of the sick, nurses, hospitals. Mar. 8*.

John of Matha, 1160-1213. French priest; founder of the Order of the

Most Holy Trinity, whose original purpose was the ransom of prisoners from the Moslems. Feb. 8.

John of the Cross, 1542-91. Doctor of the Church. Born in Old Castile, Spain; Carmelite, co-founder of the reform Order of Discalced Carmelites; mystical theologian; wrote *The Ascent of Mount Carmel, The Dark Night of the Soul, The Spiritual Canticle, The Living Flame of Love*; canonized, 1726; proclaimed doctor, 1926; called Doctor of Mystical Theology. Dec. 14*.

John Ogilvie, 1579-1615. Scottish Jesuit; converted from Calvinism, 1596, while studying at Louvain; joined the Jesuits and was ordained to the priesthood in Paris, 1610; returned to Scotland to minister to persecuted Catholics there; was betrayed and hanged; canonized, 1976, the first canonized Scottish saint since 1250 (St. Margaret of Scotland). Mar. 10.

John Vianney (Curé of Ars), 1786-1859. French parish priest; noted confessor, spent 15 to 18 hours a day in the confessional; canonized, 1925; patron of parish priests. Aug. 4*.

Josaphat Kuncevyc, 1584-1623. Basilian monk, born in Poland; archbishop of Polotsk, Lithuania; worked for the reunion of separated Eastern Christians with Rome; martyred by a mob of schismatics; canonized, 1867. Nov. 12*.

José de Anchieta, Blessed, 1534-97. Portuguese Jesuit, born in the Canary Islands; missionary in Brazil; writer; beatified, 1980. June 9.

Joseph, first century. Husband of the Blessed Virgin Mary, described in Matthew's Gospel as "an upright man" (1:19) and identified as a carpenter (13:55); devotion to him existed in the eighth century in the East and in the 11th in the West; proclaimed protector and patron of the universal Church, 1870; also patron of workers and the dying. Mar. 19* (Solemnity); May 1* (the Worker).

Joseph Benedict Cottolengo, 1786-1842. Italian priest; established the Little House of Divine Providence (Piccola Casa) in Valdocca just outside Turin to care for the aged and those with physical, emotional or mental handicaps; also founded a religious congregation to staff the facility; canonized, 1934. Apr. 30.

Joseph Cafasso, 1811-60. Italian priest; renowned confessor; promoted devotion to the Blessed Sacrament; canonized, 1947; June 23.

Joseph Calasanz, 1556-1648. Spanish priest; went to Rome in 1592; started a free school in a poor district, 1597; founded the Order of Pious Schools (Piarists), 1617, for educational work; canonized, 1767. Aug. 25*.

Joseph of Cupertino, 1603-63. Italian Franciscan; noted for remarkable incidents of levitation; canonized, 1767. Sept. 18.

Joseph Pignatelli, 1737-1811. Spanish Jesuit; left Spain when Jesuits were banished in 1767, going first to Corsica and then to Italy; worked for revival of the Order after its suppression by Pope Clement XIV in 1773; named the first superior when the Jesuits were reestablished in the Kingdom of Naples in 1804; canonized, 1954. Nov. 28.

Jude Thaddeus, first century. Apostle. One of the Catholic Letters, the shortest, bears his name; referred to as one of the brothers of the Lord in the Gospels; according to tradition he preached the Gospel in Mesopotamia, Persia and elsewhere, and was martyred; invoked as the patron of desperate cases. Oct. 28* (with St. Simon).

Julia Billiart, 1751-1816. French foundress of the Sisters of Notre Dame de Namur, a teaching and missionary congregation, 1804, the year she was miraculously cured of a crippling paralysis from which she had suffered for 22 years; canonized, 1969. Apr. 8.

Justin de Jacobis, 1800-60. Italian Vincentian; missionary in Ethiopia from 1839 until his death there; established missions and a native clergy; named vicar apostolic and ordained bishop, 1849; canonized, 1975. July 31.

Justin Martyr, 100-65. Early ecclesiastical writer of *Apologia for the Christian Religion, Dialogue with the Jew Tryphon*; martyred at Rome. June 1*.

Kateri Tekakwitha, Blessed, 1656-80. Lily of the Mohawks. Indian maiden born at Ossernenon (Auriesville), New York; baptized a Christian, Easter, 1676, by the Jesuit Father Jacques de Lambertville; was devoted to prayer, penitential practices and care of sick and aged in a Christian village near Montreal; buried at Caughnawaga, Ontario; beatified, June 22, 1980. July 14* (U.S.).

Korean Martyrs. See Andrew Kim, Paul Chong and Companions.

Ladislaus, 1040-95. King of Hungary; supported Pope Gregory VII in his investiture struggle against Henry IV; one of the great national heroes of Hungary, where he is known as Lazlo; canonized, 1192. June 27.

Lawrence, d. 258. One of the seven deacons of Rome; widely venerated martyr who suffered death, according to long-standing but unverifiable legend, by fire on a gridiron. Aug. 10*.

Lawrence of Brindisi, 1559-1619. Doctor of the Church. Born in Brindisi, Italy; jointed the Capuchin Franciscans; vigorous and influential preacher in the post-Reformation period; entrusted with diplomatic and political missions; his collected works include scriptural commentaries, sermons, homilies and doctrinal writings; canonized, 1881; proclaimed doctor, 1959. July 21*.

Leo I, the Great, c. 400-61. Pope, Doctor of the Church. Born in Tuscany, Italy; pope, 440-61; wrote a doctrinal letter explaining the two natures and one Person of Christ, against the background of the Nestorian and Monophysite heresies; other works include sermons, letters and writings against the errors of Manichaeism and Pelagianism; was instrumental in dissuading Attila from sacking Rome, 452; proclaimed doctor, 1574. Nov. 10*

Leonard Murialdo, 1828-1900. Italian priest; educator; active in work for social reform; founded the Pious Society of St. Joseph of Turin, 1873; canonized, 1970. Mar. 30.

Leonard of Port Maurice, 1676-1751. Italian Franciscan; ascetical writer; preached missions throughout Italy; spread devotion of the Stations of the Cross; canonized, 1867; patron of parish missions. Nov. 26.

Leopold Mandic, 1866-1942. Croatian-born Capuchin priest; spent most of his priestly life in Padua, Italy; described by John Paul II as "nothing but a poor monk, small and sickly," whose pastoral mission and gift was hearing confessions; canonized, 1983. July 30.

Louis IX, 1215-70. King of France, 1226-70; a just ruler; participated in the Sixth Crusade; a patron of the Secular Franciscan Order; canonized, 1297. Aug. 25*.

Louis Bertrán, 1526-81. Spanish Dominican; missionary in Colombia and Caribbean countries, 1562-69; canonized, 1671. Oct. 9.

Louis de Montfort (Louis Mary Grignon), 1673-1716. French priest; founder of the Sisters of Divine Wisdom, 1703, and Missionaries of the Company of Mary, 1715; promoted devotion to Mary; wrote *True Devotion to the Blessed Virgin*; canonized, 1947. Apr. 28.

Louise de Marillac, 1591-1660. French foundress, with St. Vincent de Paul, of the Sisters of Charity, 1633, for care of the poor, sick and neglected; canonized, 1934; patroness of social workers. Mar. 15.

Lucy, d. 304. Sicilian maiden; martyred during Diocletian's persecution; one of the most widely venerated of the early virgin-martyrs; patroness of Syracuse, Sicily; invoked by those suffering from eye diseases (based on a legend that she offered her eyes to a suitor who admired them). Dec. 13*.

Lucy Filippini, 1672-1732. Italian educator, helped improve the status of women through education; founded educational institutions throughout Italy; considered a founder of the Religious Teachers Filippini, 1692; canonized, 1930. Mar. 25.

Luke, first century. Evangelist. A Greek convert to the Christian community, called "Our Most Dear Physician" by Paul, of whom he was a missionary companion; author of the third Gospel and Acts of the Apostles; the place (Achaia, Bithynia, Egypt) and circumstances of his death are not certain; patron of physicians and artists. Oct. 18*.

Madeleine Sophie Barat, 1779-1865. French foundress of the Society of the Sacred Heart of Jesus; canonized, 1925. May 25.

Malachy, 1095-1148. Irish bishop; appointed archbishop of Armagh in 1129 but was prevented from taking possession of the see for several years; worked to restore discipline; instrumental in establishing the first Cistercian house in Ireland, 1142; died at Clairvaux in St. Bernard's arms on his return from a pilgrimage to Rome; canonized, 1190; so-called papal prophecies attributed to him are forgeries which came to light only in the last decade of the 16th century. Nov. 3.

Marcellinus and Peter, d. 304. Roman martyrs during Diocletian's persecution; Marcellinus was a priest; their names were placed in the Canon of the Mass. June 2*.

Margaret Clitherow, 1556-86. English martyr; convert shortly after her marriage to John Clitherow, a Catholic; imprisoned for sheltering priests in her home; condemned to be pressed to death; one of Forty Martyrs of England and Wales; canonized, 1970. Mar. 25.

Margaret Mary Alacoque, 1647-90. French nun; joined the Visitation convent at Paray-le Monial, 1671; spread devotion to the Sacred Heart in accordance with revelations made to her in 1675; canonized, 1920. Oct. 16*.

Margaret of Cortona, 1247-97. Franciscan tertiary; reformed in 1273 after the death of her lover by violence; lived a penitential life; became a Franciscan tertiary, 1276; canonized, 1728. Feb. 22.

Margaret of Hungary, 1242-70. Daughter of King Bela IV of Hungary; refused to marry; lived a life of self-imposed penances; canonized, 1943. Jan. 18.

Margaret of Scotland, 1050-93. Queen of Scotland; noted for solicitude for the poor and promotion of justice; canonized, 1250. Nov. 16*.

Marguerite Bourgeoys, 1620-1700. French foundress, missionary; settled in Canada, 1653; founded the Congregation of Notre Dame de Montreal, 1658; beatified, 1950; canonized, 1982. Jan. 19.

Maria Goretti, 1890-1902. Italian virgin-martyr; a model of purity; canonized, 1950. July 6*.

Mariana Paredes of Jesus, 1618-45. Called the Lily of Quito; lived as a solitary; canonized, 1950. May 26.

Marie-Leonie Paradis, Blessed, 1840-1912. Canadian Religious; joined the Holy Cross Sisters in Indiana, 1870; founded the Little Sisters of the Holy Family, dedicated to domestic service, 1880 in Sherbrooke; beatified, 1984, by John Paul II on his visit to Canada.

Marie Marguerite d'Youville, Blessed, 1701-71. Canadian widow; foundress of the Sisters of Charity (Grey Nuns), 1738 at Montreal; beatified, 1959. Dec. 23.

Marie of the Incarnation, Blessed (Marie Guyard Martin), 1599-1672. French widow; joined the Ursuline Nuns; arrived in Canada, 1639; first superior of the Ursulines in Quebec; missionary to Indians; writer; beatified, 1980. Apr. 30.

Marie-Rose Durocher, Blessed, 1811-49. Canadian Religious; foundress of the Sisters of the Holy Names of Jesus and Mary; beatified, May 23, 1982. Oct. 6* (U.S.).

Mark, first century. Evangelist. A cousin of Barnabas and member of the first Christian community at Jerusalem; missionary companion of Paul and Barnabas, then of Peter; author of the Gospel which bears his name; according to legend, founded the Church at Alexandria, was bishop there and was martyred in the streets of the city. Apr. 25*.

Martha, first century. Sister of Lazarus and Mary of Bethany; Gospel accounts record her concern for details of hospitality, symbolic of the active life in contrast to Mary's contemplative bent; patron of cooks. July 29*.

Martin I, d. 655. Pope, 649-55; banished from Rome, 653, by the emperor because of his condemnation of Monothelitism; considered a martyr. Apr. 13*.

Martin de Porres, 1579-1639. Peruvian Dominican oblate; his father was a Spanish soldier and his mother a black freedwoman from Panama; called the Wonder Worker of Peru; beatified, 1837; canonized, 1962. Nov. 3*.

Martin of Tours, 316-97. Bishop of Tours; was a young soldier stationed in Amiens when he gave half of his cloak to a naked beggar who approached him for alms one winter night; later, in a vision, he saw Christ wearing the cloak; he was baptized, left the army and eventually came under the direction of St. Hilary of Poitiers; lived as a recluse and established a community of monk-hermits; was made bishop of Tours, 371; was a pioneer of monasticism in the West before St. Benedict; one of the first non-martyrs venerated as a saint; patron of soldiers. Nov. 11*.

Mary Domenica Mazzarello, 1837-81. Italian foundress, with St. John Bosco, of the Daughters of Mary Help of Christians, 1872; canonized, 1951. May 14.

Mary Josepha Rossello, 1811-80. Italian-born foundress of the Daughters of Our Lady of Mercy; canonized, 1949. Dec. 7.

Mary Magdalen (Magdalene), first century. Gospels record her as a devoted follower of Christ to whom He appeared after the resurrection; her identification with Mary of Bethany (sister of Martha and Lazarus) and the woman sinner (Lk. 7:36-50) has been questioned. July 22*.

Mary Magdalen dei Pazzi, 1566-1607. Italian Carmelite nun; mystic; canonized, 1669. May 25*.

Mary Magdalen Postel, 1756-1846. French foundress of the Sisters of Christian Schools of Mercy, 1807; canonized, 1925. July 16.

Mary Michaela Desmaisières, 1809-65. Spanish-born foundress of the Institute of the Handmaids of the Blessed Sacrament, 1848; canonized, 1934. Aug. 24.

Matthew, first century. Apostle and Evangelist. A Galilean, called Levi by Luke and John, and the Son of Alphaeus by Mark; a tax collector; the first Gospel bears his name; according to various accounts, preached the Gospel in Judea, Ethiopia and Parthia, and was martyred; patron of accountants, bankers, bookkeepers, tax collectors. Sept. 21*.

Matthias, first century. Apostle. A disciple of Jesus whom the faithful Eleven chose to replace Judas; uncertain traditions report that he preached the Gospel in Palestine, Cappadocia or Ethiopia, and was martyred. May 14*.

Maximilian Kolbe, 1894-1941. Polish Conventual Franciscan; prisoner of Auschwitz who heroically offered his life in place of a fellow prisoner; beatified, 1971; canonized, 1982. Aug. 14*.

Methodius. See Cyril and Methodius.

Michael. Archangel, one of the three mentioned by name in Scripture; described as protector of God's people (Dan. 10:13, 21; 12:1) and leader of the heavenly armies against the devil and his forces (Rev. 12:7-9); the first angel to be given a liturgical feast. Sept. 29* (with Gabriel and Raphael).

Miguel Febres Cordero, 1854-1910. Ecuadorean Christian Brother; educator; taught in Ecuador for 32 years; canonized, 1984.

Monica, 332-87. Mother of St. Augustine of Hippo; model of a patient mother; died at Ostia in the year of Augustine's conversion, while accompanying him back to Africa. Aug 27* (the day before the commemoration of Augustine).

Nereus and Achilleus, d. c. 100. Early martyrs; soldiers who, according to legend, were baptized by St. Peter. May 12*.

Nicholas of Flüe, 1417-87. Swiss layman; a successful farmer and active in public life when, at the age of 50 with the consent of his wife and 10 children, he retreated from the world to live as a hermit; known as Brother Claus by the Swiss; canonized, 1947. Mar. 21.

Nicholas of Myra, fourth century. Bishop of Myra in Asia Minor; one of the most popular saints in both East and West; most of the incidents of his life are based on legend; patron of Russia and of children, merchants, pawnbrokers. Dec. 6*.

Nicholas of Tolentino, 1245-1305. Italian hermit; famed preacher; canonized, 1446. Sept. 10.

Nicholas Tavelic, d. 1391. Franciscan priest; born in Dalmatia; joined the Franciscans in Italy; missionary in Bosnia for 20 years before going to the Middle East where he and three other friars — Deodatus of Aquitaine, Peter of Narbonne and Stephen of Cuneo — were martyred by Moslems; canonized, 1970. Nov. 14.

Noel Chabanel, 1613-49. French Jesuit; missionary among Huron Indians in Canada; murdered by a renegade Huron, Dec. 8, 1649; canonized, 1930; one of the Jesuit North American Martyrs. Oct. 19* (U.S.).

Norbert, 1080-1134. German bishop; founder of the Canons Regular of Premontré (Premonstratensians or Norbertines), 1120; promoted reform of the clergy, devotion to the Blessed Sacrament; canonized, 1582. June 6*.

Odilia, d. c. 720. Benedictine abbess; according to legend, was born blind, abandoned by her family and adopted by a convent of nuns where her sight was miraculously restored; patroness of the blind. Dec. 13.

Oliver Plunket, 1629-81. Irish martyr; theologian; archbishop of Armagh and primate of Ireland; worked to restore the Church in Ireland; arrested and charged falsely with plotting to overthrow the government; martyred at Tyburn; beatified, 1920; canonized, 1975. July 1.

Pancras, d. c. 304. Roman martyr; nothing is known of his life. May 12*.

Paola Frassinetti, 1809-82. Italian nun; foundress, 1834, of the Sisters of St. Dorothy; canonized, 1984. June 11.

Paschal Baylon, 1540-92. Spanish Franciscan lay brother; spent his life as a doorkeeper in various Franciscan friaries; defended doctrine of the Real Presence of Christ in the Blessed Sacrament; canonized, 1690; patron of all Eucharistic confraternities and congresses, 1897. May 17.

Patrick, 389-461. Famous missionary of Ireland; place of birth unknown, but he was a Romano-Briton who was taken as a captive to Ireland about 405; he escaped about six years later, studied on the Continent, was ordained to the priesthood, consecrated bishop, and returned to Ireland as a missionary; organized the Church and established it on a firm foundation; patron of Ireland, with Sts. Bridget and Columba. Mar. 17*.

Paul, first century. Apostle of the Gentiles. Born at Tarsus, of the tribe of Benjamin, a Roman citizen; participated in the persecution of Christians until the time of his miraculous conversion on the way to Damascus; did most of his preaching among the Gentiles in the course of three major missionary journeys; 14 New Testament Letters bear his name; two years of imprisonment at Rome, following initial arrest in Jerusalem and confinement at Caesarea, ended with martyrdom, by beheading, outside the walls of the city during the Neronian persecution. June 29* (with St. Peter); Jan. 25* (Conversion).

Paul Miki and Companions, d. 1597. Martyrs of Japan. Paul Miki, a Jesuit, and 25 other priests and laymen were martyred at Nagasaki; canonized, 1982, the first canonized martyrs of the Far East. Feb. 6*.

Paul of the Cross, 1694-1775. Italian Religious; founder of the Passionists; canonized, 1867. Oct. 19*.

Pauline von Mallinckrodt, Blessed, 1817-81. German foundress of the Sisters of Christian Charity, 1849; beatified, 1985. Apr. 30.

Paulinus of Nola, d. 451. Bishop; born in Bordeaux; a Roman official, he went to Spain about 390 to live as a hermit, became a priest and was chosen bishop by the people of Nola; was also a poet and prose writer. June 22*.

Pedro de San José Betancur, Blessed, 1626-67. Secular Franciscan; born in the Canary Islands; arrived in Guatemala, 1651, where he established a hospital and school and homes for the poor; beatified, 1980. Apr. 25.

Peregrine, 1260-1347. Italian Servite; invoked against cancer (he was miraculously cured of cancer of the foot after a vision); canonized, 1726. May 1.

Perpetua and Felicity, d. 202 or 203. Martyrs; Perpetua was a young married woman, Felicity was a slave girl; both were martyred at Carthage. Mar. 7*.

Peter, first century. Chief of the Apostles. Simon, son of Jona, born in Bethsaida, brother of Andrew, a fisherman; called Cephas or Peter by Christ, who made him the chief of the Apostles and head of the Church as His vicar; named first in the listings of the Apostles in the Synoptic Gospels and the Acts of the Apostles; with James the Greater and John, witnessed the raising of Jairus' daughter to life, the Transfiguration, the agony of Jesus in the Garden of Gethsemani; was the first to preach the Gospel in and around Jerusalem and was the leader of the first Christian community there; established a local church in Antioch; presided over the Council of Jerusalem in 51; wrote two Catholic Letters to the Christians in Asia Minor; established his see in Rome, where he spent his last years and was martyred by crucifixion during the Neronian persecution. June 29* (with St. Paul); Feb. 22* (Chair of Peter).

Peter Canisius, 1521-97. Doctor of the Church. Born in Nijmegen, Holland; Jesuit; wrote popular expositions of the Catholic faith in several catechisms which were widely circulated in 20 editions in his lifetime alone; was one of the moving figures in the Counter-Reformation period, especially in southern and western Germany; canonized and proclaimed doctor, 1925. Dec. 21*.

Peter Chanel, 1803-41. French Marist; missionary to Oceania, where he was martyred; canonized, 1954. Apr. 28*.

Peter Chrysologus, c. 400-50. Doctor of the Church. Born in Imola, Italy; served as archbishop of Ravenna, c. 433-50; his sermons and writings, many of which were designed to counteract Monophysitism, were pastoral and practical; proclaimed doctor, 1729. July 30*.

Peter Claver, 1581-1654. Spanish Jesuit; missionary among blacks of South America and West Indies; canonized, 1888; patron of Catholic missions among black people. Sept. 9* (U.S.).

Peter Damian, 1007-72. Doctor of the Church. Born in Ravenna, Italy; Benedictine; cardinal; his writings and sermons, many of which concerned ecclesiastical and clerical reform, were pastoral and practical; proclaimed doctor, 1828. Feb. 21*.

Peter Fourier, 1565-1640. French priest; co-founder with Alice LeClercq (Mother Teresa of Jesus) of the Augustinian Canonesses of Our Lady, 1598; canonized, 1897. Dec. 9.

Peter González, 1190-1246. Spanish Dominican; worked among seamen; court chaplain and confessor of King St. Ferdinand of Castile; patron of sailors. Apr. 14.

Peter Julian Eymard, 1811-68. French priest; founder of the Congregation of the Blessed Sacrament (men), 1856, and Servants of the Blessed Sacrament (women), 1864; dedicated to Eucharistic apostolate; canonized, 1962. Aug. 1.

Peter Nolasco, c. 1189-1258. Spent much of his life rescuing captives from the Moors; founded the Mercedarians (Order of Our Lady of Mercy), 1218, in Spain; canonized, 1628. Jan. 31.

Peter of Alcantara, 1499-1562. Spanish Franciscan; mystic; initiated a Franciscan reform; confessor of St. Teresa of Jesus (Avila); canonized, 1669. Oct. 19.

Philip, first century. Apostle. Born in Bethsaida; according to legend, preached the Gospel in Phrygia, where he suffered martyrdom by crucifixion. May 3* (with St. James the Less).

Philip Benizi, 1233-85. Italian Servite; noted preacher; peacemaker; general of the Servites in 1267; canonized, 1671. Aug. 23.

Philip Neri, 1515-95. Italian Religious; founded the Congregation of the Oratory; considered a second apostle of Rome because of his mission activities there; canonized, 1622. May 26*.

Philip of Jesus, 1571-97. Mexican Franciscan; martyred at Nagasaki, Japan; canonized, 1862; patron of Mexico City. Feb. 6*.

Pius V, 1504-72. Pope, 1566-72; enforced decrees of the Council of Trent; organized an expedition against the Turks, resulting in victory at Lepanto; canonized, 1712. Apr. 30*.

Pius X. See Twentieth Century Popes.

Polycarp, second century. Bishop of Smyrna; ecclesiastical writer; martyr. Feb. 23*.

Pontian, d. c. 235. Pope, 230-35; exiled to Sardinia by the emperor; regarded as a martyr. Aug. 13* (with Hippolytus).

Rafaela María Porras y Ayllón, 1850-1925. Spanish Religious; founded the Handmaids of the Sacred Heart, 1877; canonized, 1977. Jan. 6.

Raphael. Archangel, one of the three mentioned by name in Scripture; his mission is described in Tobit (chapters 5-12), where he described himself as "one of the seven angels who enter and serve before the Glory of the Lord" (Tobit 12:15); patron of the blind, happy meetings, travelers. Sept. 29* (with Michael and Gabriel).

Raymond Nonnatus, d. 1240. Spanish Mercedarian; cardinal; devoted his life to ransoming captives from the Moors; Aug. 31.

Raymond of Peñafort, 1175-1275. Spanish Dominican; confessor of Pope Gregory IX; systematized and codified canon law, in effect until 1917; master general of the Dominicans, 1238; canonized, 1601. Jan. 7*.

René Goupil, 1607-42. French lay missionary; had studied surgery at Orleans, France; missionary companion of St. Isaac Jogues among the Hurons; martyred, 1642; canonized, 1930; one of the Jesuit North American Martyrs. Oct. 19* (U.S.).

Rita of Cascia, 1301-1457. Widow; joined the cloistered Augustinian Religious of Umbria, 1413; canonized, 1900; invoked in impossible and desperate cases. May 22.

Robert Bellarmine, 1542-1621. Doctor of the Church. Born in Tuscany, Italy; Jesuit; archbishop of Capua, 1602-05; wrote *Controversies*, a three-volume exposition of doctrine under attack during and after the Reformation, two catechisms and the spiritual work, *The Art of Dying Well*; was an authority on ecclesiology and Church-state relations; canonized, 1930; proclaimed doctor, 1931. Sept. 17*.

Robert Southwell, 1561-95. English Jesuit; poet; martyred at Tyburn; canonized, 1970; one of the Forty English and Welsh Martyrs. Feb. 21.

Roch, 1350-79. French layman; pilgrim; devoted his life to the care of plague-stricken; widely venerated; invoked against pestilence. Aug. 17.

Romuald, 951-1027. Italian monk; founded the Camaldolese Benedictines. June 19*.

Roque Gonzalez, Blessed, 1576-1628. Paraguayan Jesuit; worked in Indian mission settlements (Reductions); martyred; beatified, 1934. Nov. 17.

Rose of Lima, 1586-1617. Peruvian Dominican tertiary; first native-born saint of the New World; canonized, 1671; patroness of South America. Aug. 23*.

Rose Philippine Duchesne, Blessed, 1769-1852. French nun; educator and missionary in the U.S.; established the first convent of the Society of the Sacred Heart in the United States; founded schools for girls; did missionary work among Indians; beatified, 1940. Nov. 17.

Scholastica, d. c. 559. Sister of St. Benedict; regarded as the first nun of the Benedictine Order. Feb. 10*.

Sebastian, third century. Roman martyr; traditionally pictured as a handsome youth with arrows; martyred; patron of athletes, archers. Jan. 20*.

Sebastián de Aparicio, Blessed, 1502-1600. Franciscan brother; born in Spain; settled in Mexico, about 1533; worked as a road builder and farmer before becoming a Franciscan at about the age of 70; beatified, 1787. Feb. 25.

Seven Holy Founders of the Servants of Mary (Buonfiglio Monaldo, Alexis Falconieri, Benedict dell'Antello, Bartholomew Amidei, Ricovero Uguccione, Gerardino Sostegni, John Buonagiunta Monetti). Florentine youths who founded the Servites (Order of Friar Servants of Mary), 1233, in obedience to a vision; canonized, 1888. Feb. 17*.

Sharbel Makhlouf, 1828-98. Lebanese Maronite monk-hermit; canonized, 1977. Dec. 24.

Simon, first century. Apostle. Called the Cananean, or the Zealot;

according to legend, preached in various places in the Middle East and suffered martyrdom by being sawed in two. Oct. 28* (with Jude).

Sixtus II, d. 258. Pope, 257-58; was martyred during the persecution of Valerian. Aug. 7* (with four deacons martyred on the same day).

Stanislaus, 1030-79. Polish bishop; martyr; elected bishop of Cracow in 1072; when he excommunicated King Boleslav II because of his evil life, the king killed him while he was celebrating Mass; greatly venerated in Poland; canonized, 1253. Apr. 11*.

Stephen, d. c. 33. Deacon; first Christian martyr; chosen by the Apostles as the first of the first seven deacons; stoned to death. Dec. 26*.

Stephen, 975-1038. King; apostle of Hungary; welded the Magyars into national unity; organized dioceses and founded monasteries; canonized, 1083. Aug. 16*.

Sylvester I, d. 335. Pope, 314-35; the first ecumenical council, Nicaea I, was held during his pontificate. Dec. 31*.

Tarcisius, d. third century. Early martyr; according to tradition, was martyred while carrying the Blessed Sacrament to Christians in prison; patron of first communicants. Aug. 15.

Teresa Margaret Redi, 1747-70. Italian Carmelite; lived a life of prayer and austere penance; canonized, 1934. Mar. 11.

Teresa of Jesus (Avila), 1515-82. Doctor of the Church. Born in Avila, Spain; entered the Carmelite Order, 1535; in the early 1560s, initiated a primitive Carmelite, discalced-Alcantarine reform which greatly influenced men and women Religious, especially in Spain; wrote extensively on spiritual and mystical subjects; principal works included her *Autobiography, Way of Perfection, The Interior Castle, Meditations on the Canticle, The Foundations, Visitation of the Discalced Nuns*; canonized, 1614; proclaimed first woman doctor, Sept. 27, 1970. Oct. 15*.

Teresa of Jesus Jornet e Ibars, 1843-97. Spanish nun; founded the Little Sisters of the Abandoned Aged, 1873; canonized, 1974. Aug. 26.

Théophane Venard, Blessed, 1829-61. French missionary priest; martyr; entered the Society of Foreign Missions in Paris, 1851; sent as a missionary to Hong Kong and then to West Tonkin, French Indochina; martyred in the persecution which broke out in 1860; beatified, 1900. Feb. 2.

Thérèse Couderc, 1805-85. French Religious; foundress of the Religious of Our Lady of Retreat in the Cenacle, 1826; canonized, 1970. Sept. 26.

Thérèse of Lisieux (Thérèse Martin, "Little Flower"), 1873-97. French Carmelite nun; allowed to enter Carmel at 15, died nine years later of tuberculosis; her "little way" of spiritual perfection became widely known through her spiritual autobiography; despite her obscure life, became one of the most popular saints; canonized, 1925; patron of foreign missions. Oct. 1*.

Thomas (Didymus), first century. Apostle. Notable for his initial incredulity regarding the Resurrection and his subsequent forthright confession of the divinity of Christ risen from the dead; according to legend, preached the Gospel in places from the Caspian Sea to the Persian Gulf and eventually reached India where he was martyred near Madras; Thomas Christians trace their origin to him. July 3*.

Thomas Aquinas, 1225-74. Doctor of the Church. Born near Naples, Italy; Dominican; teacher and writer on virtually the whole range of philosophy and theology; principal works were *Summa contra Gentiles*, a manual and systematic defense of Christian doctrine, and *Summa Theologiae*, a new (at that time) exposition of theology on philosophical principles; canonized, 1323; proclaimed doctor, 1567; called Doctor Communis, Doctor Angelicus, the Great Synthesizer because of the way in which he related faith and reason, theology and philosophy (especially that of Aristotle), and systematized the presentation of Christian doctrine; named patron of Catholic schools and education, 1880. Jan. 28*.

Thomas Becket, 1118-70. English martyr; archbishop of Canterbury; chancellor under Henry II; murdered for upholding the rights of the Church; canonized, 1173. Dec. 29*.

Thomas More, 1478-1535. English martyr; statesman, chancellor under Henry VIII; author of *Utopia*; opposed Henry's divorce; refused to renounce the authority of the papacy; beheaded; canonized, 1935. June 22* (with St. John Fisher).

Thorlac, 1133-93. Icelandic bishop; instituted reforms in his diocese; although his cult was never officially approved, he was declared patron of Iceland, Jan. 14, 1984. Dec. 23.

Timothy, d. c. 97. Bishop of Ephesus; disciple and companion of St. Paul; martyr. Jan. 26*.

Titus, d. c. 96. Bishop; companion of St. Paul. Jan. 26*.

Titus Brandsma, Blessed, 1881-1942. Dutch Carmelite priest; professor, scholar and journalist; denounced Nazi persecution of Jews; defender of Catholic education and a free press; arrested by Nazis, Jan. 19, 1942; executed by lethal injection at Dachau, July 26, 1942; beatified, 1985. July 26.

Turibius de Mogrovejo, 1538-1606. Spanish-born archbishop of Lima, Peru, 1580-1606; as a layman was chief judge of the court of Inquisition in Granada; ordained a priest, 1578, and bishop, 1580, when he left Spain for Lima; vigorous reformer; evangelizer of Indians; canonized, 1726. Mar. 23*.

Uganda Martyrs. See Charles Lwanga and Companions.

Valentine, d. 269. Priest; physician; martyred at Rome; legendary patron of lovers. Feb. 14.

Vicenta María López y Vicuña, 1847-96. Spanish foundress of the Daughters of Mary Immaculate, for domestic service; canonized, 1975. Dec. 26.

Vincent, d. 304. Spanish deacon; martyred at Valencia during Diocletian's persecution. Jan. 22*.

Vincent de Paul, 1580?-1660. French priest; noted for his dedication and service of the poor; founder of the Congregation of the Mission (Vincentians, Lazarists), 1625, and co-founder of the Sisters of Charity; canonized, 1737; declared patron of all charitable organizations and works by Pope Leo XIII. Sept. 27*.

Vincent Ferrer, 1350-1419. Spanish Dominican; famed preacher; contributed to ending of the Western Schism when he withdrew his support of antipope Benedict XIII in 1416; canonized, 1455. Apr. 5*.

Vincent Pallotti, 1795-1850. Italian priest; founded the Society of the Catholic Apostolate (Pallottines), 1835. Jan. 22.

Vincent Strambi, 1745-1824. Italian Passionist; bishop of Macera and Tolentino; reformer; adviser to Pope Leo XII, 1823; canonized, 1950. Sept. 25.

Vincenza Gerosa, 1784-1847. Italian co-foundress of the Sisters of Charity of Lovere; canonized, 1950. June 28.

Vitus, d. c. 300. Martyr; died in Lucania, southern Italy; regarded as protector of epileptics and those suffering from St. Vitus' Dance (chorea); patron of actors and dancers; because of lack of historical evidence, his memorial was relegated to particular calendars in the calendar reform of 1970. June 15.

Walburga, d. 779. English-born Benedictine Religious; belonged to the group of nuns who established convents in Germany at the invitation of St. Boniface; abbess of Heidenheim. Feb. 25.

Wenceslaus, d. 935. Duke of Bohemia; murdered by his brother; acclaimed as a martyr; patron of Czechoslovakia. Sept. 28*.

Zita, 1218-78. Italian maid; noted for her charity to the poor; canonized, 1696; patroness of domestics. Apr. 27.

SAINTS — PATRONS AND INTERCESSORS

A patron is the Blessed Virgin Mary (under various titles), an angel or saint who is venerated as a special intercessor or protector before God. Liturgical veneration may be accorded only to those officially designated or approved by the Church. The Congregation for Divine Worship handles procedures for the choice and approval of liturgical veneration for patrons. Popular devotions to patrons are lawful if they accord with the laws and norms of the Holy See and are subordinate to and in harmony with the liturgy.

Most patrons have been so designated as the result of popular devotion and long-standing custom. The Church has made official designation of relatively few patrons; in such cases, the dates of designation are given in parentheses in the lists that follow.

Patrons of Places

Alsace: Odilia.

Americas: Our Lady of Guadalupe, Rose of Lima.

Angola: Immaculate Heart of Mary (Nov. 21, 1984).

Argentina: Our Lady of Lujan.

Armenia: Gregory the Illuminator.

Asia Minor: John, Evangelist.

Australia: Our Lady Help of Christians.

Belgium: Joseph.

Bohemia: Wenceslaus, Ludmilla.

Borneo: Francis Xavier.

Brazil: Nossa Senhora de Aparecida, Immaculate Conception, Peter of Alcántara.

Canada: Joseph, Anne.

Chile: James the Greater, Our Lady of Mt. Carmel.

China: Joseph.

Colombia: Peter Claver, Louis Bertrán.

Corsica: Immaculate Conception.

Czechoslovakia: Wenceslaus, John Nepomucene, Procopius.

Denmark: Ansgar, Canute.

Dominican Republic: Our Lady of High Grace, Dominic.

East Indies: Thomas, Apostle.

Ecuador: Sacred Heart.

El Salvador: Our Lady of Peace (Oct. 10, 1966).

England: George.

Europe: Benedict (1964), Cyril and Methodius, co-patrons (Dec. 31, 1980).

Finland: Henry.

France: Our Lady of the Assumption, Joan of Arc, Thérèse of Lisieux (May 3, 1944).

Germany: Boniface, Michael.

Gibraltar: Blessed Virgin Mary under title "Our Lady of Europe" (May 31, 1979).

Greece: Nicholas, Andrew.

Holland: Willibrord.

Hungary: Blessed Virgin Mary under title "Great Lady of Hungary," Stephen, King.

Iceland: Thorlac (Jan. 14, 1984).

India: Our Lady of the Assumption.

Ireland: Patrick, Brigid and Columba.

Italy: Francis of Assisi, Catherine of Siena.

Japan: Peter Baptist.

Korea: Joseph and Mary, Mother of the Church.

Lesotho: Immaculate Heart of Mary.

Lithuania: Casimir, Bl. Cunegunda.

Luxembourg: Willibrord.

Malta: Paul, Our Lady of the Assumption.

Mexico: Our Lady of Guadalupe.

Monaco: Devota.

Moravia: Cyril and Methodius.

New Zealand: Our Lady Help of Christians.

Norway: Olaf.

Papua New Guinea (including northern Solomon Islands): Michael the Archangel (May 31, 1979).

Paraguay: Our Lady of the Assumption (July 13, 1951).

Peru: Joseph (Mar. 19, 1957).

Philippines: Sacred Heart of Mary.

Poland: Casimir, Bl. Cunegunda, Stanislaus of Cracow, Our Lady of Czestochowa.

Portugal: Immaculate Conception, Francis Borgia, Anthony of Padua, Vincent of Saragossa, George.

Russia: Andrew, Nicholas of Myra, Thérèse of Lisieux.

Scandinavia: Ansgar.

Scotland: Andrew, Columba.

Silesia: Hedwig.

Slovakia: Our Lady of Sorrows.

South Africa: Our Lady of the Assumption (Mar. 15, 1952).

South America: Rose of Lima.

Spain: James the Greater, Teresa of Jesus (Avila).

Sri Lanka (Ceylon): Lawrence.

Sweden: Bridget, Eric.

Tanzania: Immaculate Conception (Dec. 8, 1984).

United States: Immaculate Conception (1846).

Uruguay: Blessed Virgin Mary under title "La Virgen de los Treinte y Tres" (Nov. 21, 1962).

Venezuela: Our Lady of Coromoto.

Wales: David.

West Indies: Gertrude.

Special Patrons

Accountants: Matthew.

Actors: Genesius.

Advertisers: Bernardine of Siena (May 20, 1960).

Alpinists: Bernard of Montjoux (or Menthon) (Aug. 20, 1923).

Altar boys: John Berchmans.

Anesthetists: René Goupil.

Animals: Francis of Assisi.

Archers: Sebastian.

Architects: Thomas, Apostle.

Armorers: Dunstan.

Art: Catherine of Bologna.

Artists: Luke, Catherine of Bologna, Bl. Angelico (Feb. 21, 1984).

Astronomers: Dominic.

Athletes: Sebastian.

Authors: Francis de Sales.

Aviators: Our Lady of Loreto (1920), Thérèse of Lisieux, Joseph of Cupertino.

Bakers: Elizabeth of Hungary, Nicholas.

Bankers: Matthew.

Barbers: Cosmas and Damian, Louis.

Barren women: Anthony of Padua, Felicity.

Basketmakers: Anthony, Abbot.

Beggars: Martin of Tours.

Blacksmiths: Dunstan.
Blind: Odilia, Raphael.
Blood banks: Januarius.
Bodily ills: Our Lady of
Lourdes.
Bookbinders: Peter Celestine.
Bookkeepers: Matthew.
Booksellers: John of God.
Boy Scouts: George.
Brewers: Augustine of Hippo,
Luke, Nicholas of Myra.
Bricklayers: Stephen.
Brides: Nicholas of Myra.
Brushmakers: Anthony, Abbot.
Builders: Vincent Ferrer.
Butchers: Anthony (Abbot),
Luke.

Cabdrivers: Fiacre.
Cabinetmakers: Anne.
Cancer patients: Peregrine.
Canonists: Raymond of
Peñafort.
Carpenters: Joseph.
Catechists: Viator, Charles
Borromeo, Robert
Bellarmine.
Catholic Action: Francis of
Assisi (1916).
Chandlers: Ambrose, Bernard of
Clairvaux.
Charitable societies: Vincent de
Paul (May 12, 1885).
Children: Nicholas of Myra.
Children of Mary: Agnes, Maria
Goretti.
Choirboys: Dominic Savio (June
8, 1956), Holy Innocents.
Church: Joseph (Dec. 8, 1870).
Clerics: Gabriel of the
Sorrowful Mother.
Communications personnel:
Bernardine.
Confessors: Alphonsus Liguori
(Apr. 26, 1950), John
Nepomucene.

Convulsive children:
Scholastica.
Cooks: Lawrence, Martha.
Coopers: Nicholas of Myra.
Coppersmiths: Maurus.

Dairy workers: Brigid.
Deaf: Francis de Sales.
Dentists: Apollonia.
Desperate situations: Gregory
of Neocaesarea, Jude
Thaddeus, Rita of Cascia.
Dietitians (in hospitals):
Martha.
Dyers: Maurice, Lydia.
Dying: Joseph.

Ecologists: Francis of Assisi
(Nov. 29, 1979).
Editors: John Bosco.
Emigrants: Frances Xavier
Cabrini (Sept. 8, 1950).
Engineers: Ferdinand III.
Epilepsy, motor diseases: Vitus,
Willibrord.
Eucharistic congresses and
societies: Paschal Baylon
(Nov. 28, 1897).
Expectant mothers: Raymund
Nonnatus, Gerard Majella.
Eye diseases: Lucy.

Falsely accused: Raymund
Nonnatus.
Farmers: George, Isidore.
Farriers: John the Baptist.
Firemen: Florian.
Fire prevention: Catherine of
Siena.
First communicants: Tarcisius.
Fishermen: Andrew.
Florists: Thérèse of Lisieux.
Forest workers: John Gualbert.
Foundlings: Holy Innocents.
Fullers: Anastasius the Fuller,
James the Less.

Funeral directors: Joseph of Arimathea, Dismas.

Gardeners: Adelard, Tryphon, Fiacre, Phocas.
Glassworkers: Luke.
Goldsmiths: Dunstan, Anastasius.
Gravediggers: Anthony, Abbot.
Greetings: Valentine.
Grocers: Michael.

Hairdressers: Martin de Porres.
Happy meetings: Raphael.
Hatters: Severus of Ravenna, James the Less.
Headache sufferers: Teresa of Jesus (Avila).
Heart patients: John of God.
Hospital administrators: Basil the Great, Frances X. Cabrini.
Hospitals: Camillus de Lellis and John of God (June 22, 1886), Jude Thaddeus.
Housewives: Anne.
Hunters: Hubert, Eustachius.

Infantrymen: Maurice.
Innkeepers: Amand, Martha.
Invalids: Roch.

Jewelers: Eligius, Dunstan.
Journalists: Francis de Sales (Apr. 26, 1923).
Jurists: John Capistran.

Laborers: Isidore, James, John Bosco.
Lawyers: Ivo (Yves Helory), Genesius, Thomas More.
Learning: Ambrose.
Librarians: Jerome.
Lighthouse keepers: Venerius.
Locksmiths: Dunstan.

Maids: Zita.
Marble workers: Clement I.
Mariners: Michael, Nicholas of Tolentino.
Medical record librarians: Raymond of Peñafort.
Medical social workers, John Regis.
Medical technicians: Albert the Great.
Mentally ill: Dymphna.
Merchants: Francis of Assisi, Nicholas of Myra.
Messengers: Gabriel.
Metalworkers: Eligius.
Military chaplains: John Capistran (Feb. 10, 1984).
Millers: Arnulph, Victor.
Missions, Foreign: Francis Xavier (Mar. 25, 1904), Thérèse of Lisieux (Dec. 14, 1927).
Missions, Black: Peter Claver (1896, Leo XIII), Benedict the Black.
Missions, Parish: Leonard of Port Maurice (Mar. 17, 1923).
Mothers: Monica.
Motorcyclists: Our Lady of Grace.
Motorists: Christopher, Frances of Rome.
Mountaineers: Bernard of Montjoux (or Menthon).
Musicians: Gregory the Great, Cecilia, Dunstan.

Notaries: Luke, Mark.
Nurses: Camillus de Lellis and John of God (1930), Agatha, Raphael.
Nursing and nursing service: Elizabeth of Hungary, Catherine of Siena.

Orators: John Chrysostom (July 8, 1908).

Organ builders: Cecilia.
Orphans: Jerome Emiliani.

Painters: Luke.
Paratroopers: Michael.
Pawnbrokers: Nicholas.
Pharmacists: Cosmas and Damian, James the Greater.
Pharmacists (in hospitals): Gemma Galgani.
Philosophers: Justin.
Physicians: Pantaleon, Cosmas and Damian, Luke, Raphael.
Pilgrims: James the Greater.
Plasterers: Bartholomew.
Poets: David, Cecilia.
Poison sufferers: Benedict.
Policemen: Michael.
Poor: Lawrence, Anthony of Padua.
Poor souls: Nicholas of Tolentino.
Porters: Christopher.
Possessed: Bruno, Denis.
Postal employees: Gabriel.
Priests: John Vianney (Apr. 23, 1929).
Printers: John of God, Augustine of Hippo, Genesius.
Prisoners: Dismas, Joseph Cafasso.
Protector of crops: Ansovinus.
Public relations: Bernardine of Siena (May 20, 1960).
Public relations (of hospitals): Paul, Apostle.

Radiologists: Michael (Jan. 15, 1941).
Radio workers: Gabriel.
Retreats: Ignatius Loyola (July 25, 1922).
Rheumatism: James the Greater.
Saddlers: Crispin and Crispinian.

Sailors: Cuthbert, Brendan, Eulalia, Christopher, Peter Gonzales, Erasmus, Nicholas.
Scholars: Brigid.
Schools, Catholic: Thomas Aquinas (Aug. 4, 1880), Joseph Calasanz (Aug. 13, 1948).
Scientists: Albert (Aug. 13, 1948).
Sculptors: Claude.
Seamen: Francis of Paola.
Searchers of lost articles: Anthony of Padua.
Secretaries: Genesius.
Seminarians: Charles Borromeo.
Servants: Martha, Zita.
Shoemakers: Crispin and Crispinian.
Sick: Michael, John of God and Camillus de Lellis (June 22, 1886).
Silversmiths: Andronicus.
Singers: Gregory, Cecilia.
Skaters: Lidwina.
Skiers: Bernard of Montjoux (or Menthon)
Social workers: Louise de Marillac (Feb. 12, 1960).
Soldiers: Hadrian, George, Ignatius, Sebastian, Martin of Tours, Joan of Arc.
Speleologists: Benedict.
Stenographers: Genesius, Cassian.
Stonecutters: Clement.
Stonemasons: Stephen.
Students: Thomas Aquinas.
Surgeons: Cosmas and Damian, Luke.
Swordsmiths: Maurice.

Tailors: Homobonus.
Tanners: Crispin and Crispinian, Simon.

Tax collectors: Matthew.

Teachers: Gregory the Great, John Baptist de la Salle (May 15, 1950).

Telecommunications workers: Gabriel (Jan. 12, 1951).

Television: Clare of Assisi (Feb. 14, 1958).

Tertiaries (Secular Franciscans): Louis of France, Elizabeth of Hungary.

Theologians: Augustine, Alphonsus Liguori.

Throat ailments: Blase.

Travelers: Anthony of Padua, Nicholas of Myra, Christopher, Raphael.

Travel hostesses: Bona (Mar. 2, 1962).

Universities: Blessed Contardo Ferrini.

Vocations: Alphonsus.

Watchmen: Peter of Alcantara.

Weavers: Paul the Hermit, Anastasius the Fuller, Anastasia.

Wine merchants: Amand.

Women in labor: Anne.

Workingmen: Joseph.

Writers: Francis de Sales (Apr. 26, 1923), Lucy.

Yachtsmen: Adjutor.

Young girls: Agnes.

Youth: Aloysius Gonzaga (1729, Benedict XIII; 1926, Pius XI), John Berchmans, Gabriel of the Sorrowful Mother.

Emblems, Portrayals of Saints

Portrayals of saints sometimes include the instrument of martyrdom (e.g., transverse cross, St. Andrew), incidents in the legendary or historical life of the saint (e.g., dragon, St. George), or a symbol denoting some characteristic of the saint (e.g., bee/beehive, diligence, great eloquence; shell, pilgrim; book and pen, writer).

Agatha: Tongs, veil.

Agnes: Lamb.

Ambrose: Bees, dove, ox, pen.

Andrew: Transverse cross.

Anne, Mother of the Blessed Virgin: Door.

Anthony, Abbot: Bell, hog.

Anthony of Padua: Infant Jesus, bread, book, lily.

Augustine of Hippo: Dove, child, shell, pen.

Barnabas: Stones, ax, lance.

Bartholomew: Knife, flayed and holding his skin.

Benedict: Broken cup, raven, bell, crosier, bush.

Bernard of Clairvaux: Pen, bees, instruments of the Passion.

Bernardine of Siena: Tablet or sun inscribed with IHS.

Blase: Wax, taper, iron comb.

Bonaventure: Communion, ciborium, cardinal's hat.

Boniface: Oak, ax, book, fox, scourge, fountain, raven, sword.

Bridget of Kildare: Cross, flame over her head, candle.

Bridget of Sweden: Book, pilgrim's staff.

Catherine of Ricci: Ring, crown, crucifix.

Catherine of Siena: Stigmata, cross, ring, lily.

Cecilia: Organ.

Charles Borromeo: Communion, coat of arms with word *Humilitas*.

Christopher: Giant, torrent, tree, Child Jesus on his shoulders.

Clare of Assisi: Monstrance.

Cosmas and Damian: A phial, box of ointment.

Cyril of Alexandria: Blessed Virgin holding the Child Jesus, pen.

Cyril of Jerusalem: Purse, book.

Dominic: Rosary, star.

Edmund the Martyr: Arrow, sword.

Elizabeth of Hungary: Alms, flowers, bread, the poor, a pitcher.

Francis of Assisi: Wolf, birds, fish, skull, the Stigmata.

Francis Xavier: Crucifix, bell, vessel.

Genevieve: Bread, keys, herd, candle.

George: Dragon.

Gertrude: Crown, taper, lily.

Gregory I (the Great): Tiara, crosier, dove.

Helena: Cross.

Hilary: Stick, pen, child.

Ignatius of Loyola: Communion, chasuble, book, apparition of Our Lord.

Isidore: Bees, pen.

James the Greater: Pilgrim's staff, shell, key, sword.

James the Less: Square rule, halberd, club.

Jerome: Lion.

John Berchmans: Rule of St. Ignatius, cross, rosary.

John Chrysostom: Bees, dove, pen.

John of God: Alms, a heart, crown of thorns.

John the Baptist: Lamb, head cut off on platter, skin of an animal.

John the Evangelist: Eagle, chalice, kettle, armor.

Josaphat Kuncevye: Chalice, crown, winged deacon.

Joseph, Spouse of the Blessed Virgin: Infant Jesus, lily, rod, plane, carpenter's square.

Jude: Sword, square rule, club.

Justin Martyr: Ax, sword.

Lawrence: Cross, book of the Gospels, gridiron.

Leander of Seville: A pen.

Liborius: Pebbles, peacock.

Longinus: In arms at foot of the cross.

Louis IX of France: Crown of thorns, nails.

Lucy: Cord, eyes on a dish.

Luke: Ox, book, brush, palette.

Mark: Lion, book.

Martha: Holy water sprinkler, dragon.

Mary Magdalene: Alabaster box of ointment.

Matthew: Winged man, purse, lance.

Matthias: Lance.

Maurus: Scales, spade, crutch.

Meinrad: Two ravens.

Michael: Scales, banner, sword, dragon.

Monica: Girdle, tears.

Nicholas: Three purses or balls, anchor or boat, child.

Patrick: Cross, harp, serpent, baptismal font, demons, shamrock.

Paul: Sword, book or scroll.

Peter: Keys, boat, cock.

Philip, Apostle: Column.

Philip Neri: Altar, chasuble, vial.

Rita of Cascia: Rose, crucifix, thorn.

Roch: Angel, dog, bread.

Rose of Lima: Crown of thorns, anchor, city.

Sebastian: Arrows, crown.

Simon Stock: Scapular.

Teresa of Jesus (Avila): Heart, arrow, book.

Thérèse of Lisieux: Roses entwining a crucifix.

Thomas, Apostle: Lance, ax.

Thomas Aquinas: Chalice, monstrance, dove, ox, person trampled under foot.

Vincent (Deacon): Gridiron, boat.

Vincent de Paul: Children.

Vincent Ferrer: Pulpit, cardinal's hat, trumpet, captives.

Chapter Six

Holy Days and Feast Days

The history as well as the present experience of worship in the Church is expressed in the annual observance of sacred times and feasts. The nature and purposes of these observances in the Roman Calendar were described by the Second Vatican Council in the *Constitution on the Sacred Liturgy*.

"Within the cycle of a year . . . (the Church) unfolds the whole mystery of Christ, not only from His incarnation and birth until His ascension, but also as reflected in the day of Pentecost, and the expectation of a blessed, hoped-for return of the Lord.

"Recalling thus the mysteries of redemption, the Church opens to the faithful the riches of her Lord's powers and merits, so that these are in some way made present at all times, and the faithful are enabled to lay hold of them and become filled with saving grace" (No. 102).

"The Church has also included in the annual cycle days devoted to the memory of the martyrs and the other saints . . . (who) sing God's perfect praise in heaven and offer prayers for us. By celebrating the passage of these saints from earth to heaven the Church proclaims the paschal mystery as achieved in the saints who have suffered and been glorified with Christ; she proposes them to the faithful as examples who draw all to the Father through Christ, and through their merits she pleads for God's favors" (No. 104).

Seasons and Saints

Advent: The Church calendar begins with the first Sunday of Advent, a season of four weeks or slightly less duration with the theme of expectation of and preparation for the celebration of the birth of Jesus at Christmas.

Christmas: This season begins with the vigil of Christmas and lasts until the Sunday after January 6, inclusive.

Lent: The penitential season of Lent begins on Ash Wednesday, which occurs between February 4 and March 11, depending on the date of Easter, and lasts until the Mass of the Lord's Supper (Holy Thursday). It has six Sundays. The sixth Sunday marks the beginning of Holy Week and is known as Passion (formerly called Palm) Sunday. The origin of Lenten observances dates back to the fourth century or earlier.

Easter Triduum: The Easter Triduum begins with evening Mass of the Lord's Supper and ends with Evening Prayer on Easter Sunday.

Easter Season: The Easter season, whose theme is resurrection from sin to the life of grace, lasts for 50 days, from Easter to Pentecost. Easter, the first Sunday after the first full moon following the vernal equinox, occurs between March 22 and April 25.

Ordinary Time: The season of Ordinary Time begins on the Monday after the Sunday following January 6 and continues until the day before Ash Wednesday, inclusive. It begins again on the Monday after Pentecost and ends on the Saturday before the first Sunday of Advent. It consists of 33 or 34 weeks.

The commemorations of saints are celebrated concurrently with the liturgical seasons and feasts of our Lord. Their purpose is to illustrate the paschal mysteries as reflected in the lives of saints, to honor them as heroes of holiness, and to appeal for their intercession.

Sundays and Other Holy Days

Sunday is the original Christian feast day and holy day of obligation because of the unusually significant events of salvation history which took place and are commemorated on the first day of the week — viz., the resurrection of Christ, the key event of His life and the fundamental fact of Christianity; and the descent of the Holy Spirit upon the Apostles on Pentecost, the birthday of the Church.

Holy days of obligation are special occasions on which Catholics who have reached the age of reason are seriously obliged, as on Sundays, to assist at Mass; they are also to refrain from work and involvement with business which impede participation in divine worship and the enjoyment of appropriate rest and relaxation.

The holy days of obligation observed in the United States are: Christmas, the Nativity of Jesus, December 25; Solemnity of Mary the Mother of God, January 1; Ascension of the Lord; Assumption of Blessed Mary the Virgin, August 15; All Saints' Day, November 1; Immaculate Conception of Blessed Mary the Virgin, December 8.

In addition to these, there are four other holy days of obligation prescribed in the general law of the Church which are not so observed in the U.S.: Epiphany, January 6; St. Joseph, March 19; Corpus Christi; Sts. Peter and Paul, June 29. The solemnities of Epiphany and Corpus Christi are transferred to a Sunday in countries where they are not observed as holy days of obligation.

Feasts

The following list of feast days is representative rather than all-inclusive of liturgical celebrations throughout the year. (For several feasts of Mary, see Chapter 4.)

All Saints, November 1, holy day of obligation, solemnity. Commemorates all the blessed in heaven, and is intended particularly to honor the blessed who have no special feasts. The background of the feast dates to the fourth century when groups of martyrs, and later other saints, were honored on a common day in various places. In 609 or 610, the Pantheon, a pagan temple at Rome, was consecrated as a Christian church for the honor of Our Lady and the martyrs (later All Saints). In 835, Gregory IV fixed November 1 as the date of observance.

All Souls, Commemoration of the Faithful Departed, November 2. The dead were prayed for from the earliest days of Christianity. By the sixth century it was customary in Benedictine monasteries to hold a commemoration of deceased members of the order at Pentecost. A common commemoration of all the faithful departed on the day after All Saints was instituted in 998 by St. Odilo, of the Abbey of Cluny, and an observance of this kind was accepted in Rome in the 14th century. In 1915, Benedict XV granted priests throughout the world permission to celebrate three Masses for this commemoration. He also granted a special indulgence for the occasion.

Annunciation of the Lord (formerly, Annunciation of the Blessed Virgin Mary), March 25, solemnity. A feast of the incarnation which commemorates the announcement by the Archangel Gabriel to the Virgin Mary that she was to become the Mother of Christ (Lk. 1:26-38), and the miraculous conception of Christ by her. The feast was instituted about 430 in the East. The Roman observance dates from the seventh century, when celebration was said to be universal.

Ascension of the Lord, movable observance held 40 days after Easter, holy day of obligation, solemnity. Commemorates the ascension of Christ into heaven 40 days after His resurrection from the dead (Mk. 16:19; Lk. 24:51; Acts 1:2). The feast recalls the completion of Christ's mission on earth for the salvation of all people and His entry into heaven with glorified human nature. The ascension is a pledge of the final glorification of all who achieve salvation. Documentary evidence of the feast dates from early in the fifth century, but it was observed long before that time in connection with Pentecost and Easter.

Ash Wednesday, movable observance, six and one-half weeks before Easter. It was set as the first day of Lent by Pope St. Gregory the Great (590-604) with the extension of an earlier and shorter penitential season to a total period including 40 weekdays of fasting before Easter. It is a day of fast and abstinence. Ashes, symbolic of penance, are blessed and distributed among the faithful during the day. They are used to mark the forehead with the Sign of the Cross, with the reminder: "Remember, man, that you are dust, and unto dust you shall return," or: "Repent, and believe the Good News."

Baptism of the Lord, movable, usually celebrated on the Sunday after January 6, feast. Recalls the baptism of Christ by John the Baptist (Mk. 1:9-11), an event associated with the liturgy of the Epiphany. This baptism was the occasion for Christ's manifestation of himself at the beginning of His public life.

Candlemas Day, February 2. See Presentation of the Lord.

Chair of Peter, February 22. This feast, which has been in the Roman calendar since 336, is6 liturgical expression of belief in the episcopacy and hierarchy of the Church.

Christmas, Birth of Our Lord Jesus Christ, December 25, holy day of obligation, solemnity. Commemorates the birth of Christ (Lk. 2:1-20). This event was originally commemorated in the East on the feast of Epiphany or Theophany. The Christmas feast itself originated in the West; by 354 it was certainly kept on December 25. This date may have been set for the observance to offset pagan ceremonies held at about the same time to commemorate the birth of the sun at the winter solstice. There are texts for three Christmas Masses — at midnight, dawn and during the day.

Christ the King, movable, celebrated on the last Sunday of the liturgical year, solemnity. Commemorates the royal prerogatives of Christ and is equivalent to a declaration of His rights to the homage, service and fidelity of men in all phases of individual and social life. Pius XI instituted the feast December 11, 1925.

Conversion of St. Paul, January 25, feast. An observance mentioned in some calendars from the eighth and ninth centuries. Pope Innocent III (1198-1216) ordered its observance with great solemnity.

Corpus Christi, movable, celebrated on the Thursday (or Sunday, as in the U.S.) following Trinity Sunday, solemnity. Commemorates the institution of the Holy Eucharist (Mt. 26:26-28). The feast originated at Liege in 1246 and was extended throughout the Church in the West by Urban IV in 1264. St. Thomas Aquinas composed the Liturgy of the Hours for the feast.

Dedication of St. John Lateran, November 9, feast. Commemorates the first public consecration of a church, that of the Basilica of the Most Holy Savior by Pope St. Sylvester November 9, 324. The church, as well as the Lateran Palace, was the gift of Emperor Constantine. Since the 12th century it has been known as St. John Lateran, in honor of John the Baptist after whom the adjoining baptistery was named. It was rebuilt by Innocent X (1644-55), reconsecrated by Benedict XIII in 1726, and enlarged by Leo XIII (1878-1903). This basilica is regarded as the church of highest dignity in Rome and throughout the Roman Rite.

Easter, movable celebration held on the first Sunday after the full moon following the vernal equinox (between March 22 and April 25), solemnity with an octave. Commemorates the Resurrection of Christ from the dead (Mk. 16:1-7). The observance of this mystery, kept since the first days of the Church, extends throughout the Easter season, which lasts until the feast of Pentecost, a period of 50 days. Every Sunday in the year is regarded as a "little" Easter. The date of Easter determines the dates of movable feasts, such as Ascension and Pentecost, and the number of weeks before Lent and after Pentecost.

Easter Vigil, called by St. Augustine the "Mother of All Vigils," the night before Easter. Ceremonies are all related to the resurrection and renewal-in-grace theme of Easter: blessing of the new fire, procession with the Easter Candle, singing of the Easter Proclamation (Exsultet), Liturgy of the Word with at least three Old Testament readings, the Litany of Saints, blessing of water, baptism of converts and infants, renewal of baptismal promises, Liturgy of the Eucharist. The vigil ceremonies are held after sundown.

Epiphany of Our Lord, January 6 or (in the U.S.) a Sunday between January 2 and 8. Commemorates the manifestations of the divinity of Christ. It is one of the oldest Christian feasts, with an Eastern origin traceable to the beginning of the third century and antedating the Western feast of Christmas. Originally, it commemorated the manifestations of Christ's divinity — or Theophany — in His birth, the homage of the Magi, and baptism by John the Baptist. Later, the first two of these commemorations were transferred to Christmas when the Eastern Church adopted that feast between 380 and 430. The central feature of the Eastern observance now is the manifestation or declaration of Christ's divinity in His baptism and at the beginning of His public life. The Epiphany was adopted by the Western Church during the same period in which the Eastern Church accepted Christmas. In the Roman Rite, commemoration is made in the Mass of the homage of the wise men from the East (Mt. 2:1-12).

Good Friday, the Friday before Easter, the second day of the Easter Triduum. Liturgical elements of the observance are commemoration of the Passion and Death of Christ in the reading of the Passion (according to John), special prayers for the Church and people of all ranks, the veneration of the Cross, and a Communion service. The celebration takes place in the afternoon, preferably at 3:00 p.m.

Guardian Angels, October 2, memorial. Commemorates the angels who protect people from spiritual and physical dangers and assist them in doing good. A feast in their honor celebrated in Spain in the 16th century was extended to the whole Church by Paul V in 1608. In 1670, Clement X set October 2 as the date of observance. Earlier, guardian angels were honored liturgically in conjunction with the feast of St. Michael.

Holy Family, movable observance on the Sunday after Christmas, feast. Commemorates the Holy Family of Jesus, Mary and Joseph as the model of domestic society, holiness and virtue. The devotional background of the feast was very strong in the 17th century. In the 18th century, in prayers composed for a special Mass, a Canadian bishop likened the Christian family to the Holy Family. Leo XIII consecrated families to the Holy Family. In 1921, Benedict XV extended the Divine Office and Mass of the feast to the whole Church.

Holy Innocents, December 28, feast. Commemorates the infants who suffered death at the hands of Herod's soldiers seeking to kill the child Jesus (Mt. 2:13-18). A feast in their honor has been observed since the fifth century.

Holy Saturday, the day before Easter. The Sacrifice of the Mass is not celebrated, and Holy Communion may be given only as Viaticum. If possible, the Easter fast should be observed until the Easter Vigil.

Holy Thursday, the Thursday before Easter. Commemorates the institution of the sacraments of the Eucharist and Holy Orders, and the washing of the feet of the Apostles by Jesus at the Last Supper. The Mass of the Lord's Supper in the evening marks the beginning of the Easter Triduum. Following the Mass, there is a procession of the Blessed Sacrament to a place of reposition for adoration by the faithful. At an earlier Mass of Chrism, bishops bless oils (of catechumens, chrism, the sick) for use during the year. (For pastoral reasons, diocesan bishops may permit additional Masses, but these should not overshadow the principal Mass of the Lord's Supper.)

Joachim and Ann, July 26, memorial. Commemorates the parents of Mary. A joint feast, celebrated September 9, originated in the East near the end of the sixth century. Devotion to Ann, introduced in the eighth century at Rome, became widespread in Europe in the 14th century; her feast was extended throughout the Latin Church in 1584. A feast of Joachim was introduced in the West in the 15th century.

John the Baptist, Birth, June 24, solemnity. The precursor of Christ, whose cousin he was, was commemorated universally in the liturgy by the fourth century. He is the only saint, except the Blessed Virgin Mary, whose birthday is observed as a feast. Another feast, on August 29, commemorates his passion and death at the order of Herod (Mk. 6:14-29).

Joseph, March 19, solemnity. Joseph is honored as the husband of the Blessed Virgin Mary, the patron and protector of the universal Church and workman. Devotion to him already existed in the eighth century in the East, and in the 11th in the West. Various feasts were celebrated before the 15th century when March 19 was fixed for his commemoration; this feast was extended to the whole Church in 1621 by Gregory V. In 1955, Pius XII instituted the feast of St. Joseph the Workman for observance May 1; this feast, which may be celebrated by local option, supplanted the Solemnity or Patronage of St. Joseph formerly observed on the third Wednesday after Easter. St. Joseph was proclaimed protector and patron of the universal Church in 1870 by Pius IX.

Michael, Gabriel and Raphael, Archangels, September 29, feast. A feast bearing the title of Dedication of St. Michael the Archangel formerly commemorated on this date the consecration in 530 of a church near Rome in honor of Michael, the first angel given a liturgical feast. For a while, this feast was combined with a commemoration of the Guardian Angels. The separate feasts of Gabriel (March 24) and

Raphael (October 24) were suppressed by the calendar in effect since 1970 and this joint feast of the three archangels was instituted.

Passion Sunday (formerly called Palm Sunday), the Sunday before Easter. Marks the start of Holy Week by recalling the triumphal entry of Christ into Jerusalem at the beginning of the last week of His life (Mt. 21:1-9). A procession and other ceremonies commemorating this event were held in Jerusalem from very early Christian times and were adopted in Rome by the ninth century, when the blessing of palms for the occasion was introduced. Full liturgical observance includes the blessing of palms and a procession before the principal Mass of the day. The Passion, by Matthew, Mark or Luke, is read during the Mass.

Pentecost, also called Whitsunday, movable celebration held 50 days after Easter, solemnity. Commemorates the descent of the Holy Spirit upon the Apostles, the preaching of Peter and the other Apostles to Jews in Jerusalem, the baptism and aggregation of some 3,000 persons in the Christian community (Acts 2:1-41). It is regarded as the birthday of the Catholic Church. The original observance of the feast antedated the earliest extant documentary evidence from the third century.

Peter and Paul, Sts., June 29, solemnity. Commemorates the martyrdoms of Peter by crucifixion and Paul by beheading during the Neronian persecution. This joint commemoration of the chief Apostles dates at least from 258 at Rome.

Presentation of the Lord (formerly called Purification of the Blessed Virgin Mary, also Candlemas), February 2, feast. Commemorates the presentation of Jesus in the Temple — according to prescriptions of Mosaic Law (Lv. 12:2-8; Ex. 13:2; Lk. 2:22-32) — and the purification of Mary 40 days after His birth. In the East, where the feast antedated fourth-century testimony regarding its existence, it was observed primarily as a feast of Our Lord; in the West, where it was adopted later, it was regarded more as a feast of Mary until the calendar in effect since 1970. Its date was set for February 2 after the celebration of Christmas was fixed for December 25, late in the fourth century. The blessing of candles, probably in commemoration of Christ who was the Light to enlighten the Gentiles, became common about the 11th century and gave the feast the secondary name of Candlemas.

Resurrection. See Easter.

Sacred Heart of Jesus, movable observance held on the Friday after the second Sunday after Pentecost (Corpus Christi, in the U.S.), solemnity. The object of the devotion is the divine Person of Christ, whose heart is the symbol of His love for men — for whom He accomplished the work of redemption. The Mass and Office now used on the feast were prescribed by Pius XI in 1929. Devotion to the Sacred Heart was introduced into the liturgy in the 17th century through the efforts of St. John Eudes, who composed an Office and Mass for the feast. It was furthered as the result of the revelations of St. Margaret Mary Alacoque after 1675 and by the work of Claude de la Colombière, S.J. In 1765, Clement XIII approved a Mass and Office for the feast, and in 1856 Pius IX extended the observance throughout the Roman Rite.

Transfiguration of the Lord, August 6, feast. Commemorates the revelation of His divinity by Christ to Peter, James and John on Mt. Tabor (Mt. 17:1-9). The feast, which is very old, was extended throughout the universal Church in 1457 by Callistus III.

Trinity, Most Holy, movable observance held on the Sunday after Pentecost, solemnity. Commemorates the most sublime mystery of the Christian faith, i.e., that there are Three Divine Persons — Father, Son and Holy Spirit — in one God (Mt. 28:18-20). A votive Mass of the Most Holy Trinity dates from the seventh century; an Office was composed in the 10th century; in 1334, John XXII extended the feast to the universal Church.

Triumph of the Cross, September 14, feast. Commemorates the finding of the cross on which Christ was crucified, in 326 through the efforts of St. Helena, mother of Constantine; the consecration of the Basilica of the Holy Sepulchre nearly 10 years later; and the recovery in 628 or 629 by Emperor Heraclius of a major portion of the cross which had been removed by the Persians from its place of veneration at Jerusalem. The feast originated in Jerusalem and spread through the East before being adopted in the West. General adoption followed the building at Rome of the Basilica of the Holy Cross "in Jerusalem," so called because it was the place of enshrinement of a major portion of the cross of crucifixion.

Chapter Seven

A Selective Glossary of Terms

Additional terms have been described in appropriate contexts in "A Concise Guide to the Catholic Church."

A

Abbacy: A non-diocesan territory whose people are under the pastoral care of an abbot acting in general in the manner of a bishop.

Abbess: The female superior of a monastic community of nuns; e.g., Benedictines, Poor Clares, some others. Elected by members of the community, an abbess has general authority over her community but no sacramental jurisdiction.

Abbey: See Monastery.

Abbot: The male superior of a monastic community of men Religious; e.g., Benedictines, Cistercians, some others. Elected by members of the community, an abbot has ordinary jurisdiction and general authority over his community. Eastern-Rite equivalents of an abbot are a *hegumen* and an *archimandrite*. A regular abbot is the head of an abbey or monastery. An abbot general or archabbot is the head of a congregation consisting of several monasteries. An abbot primate is the head of the modern Benedictine Confederation.

Abjuration: Renunciation of apostasy, heresy or schism by a solemn oath.

Ablution: A term derived from Latin, meaning washing or cleansing, and referring to the cleansing of the hands of a priest celebrating Mass, after the offering of gifts.

Abortion: The expulsion of a non-viable human fetus from the womb of the mother, with moral implications stemming from the humanity of the fetus from the moment of conception and its consequent right to life. Accidental expulsion, as in cases of miscarriage, is without moral fault.

Direct abortion, in which a fetus is intentionally removed from the womb, constitutes a direct attack on an innocent human being, a violation of the Fifth Commandment. All who are involved in the deliberate and successful act of abortion are automatically excommunicated (Canon 1398 of the Code of Canon Law). Direct abortion is not justifiable for any reason, e.g.: therapeutic, for the physical and/or psychological welfare of the mother; preventive, to avoid the birth of a defective or unwanted child; social, in the interests of family and/or community. Indirect abortion, which occurs when a fetus is expelled during medical or other treatment of the mother for a reason other than procuring expulsion, is permissible under the principle of double effect for a proportionately serious reason; e.g., when a medical or surgical procedure is necessary to save the life of the mother.

Absolution: The act by which an authorized priest, acting as the agent of Christ and minister of the Church, grants forgiveness of sins in the Sacrament of Penance. The essential formula of absolution is: "I absolve you from your sins; in the name of the Father, and of the Son, and of the Holy Spirit. Amen." Priests receive the power to absolve in virtue of their ordination and the right to exercise this power in virtue of faculties of jurisdiction given them by their bishop, their religious superior, or by canon law. The faculties of jurisdiction can be limited or restricted regarding certain sins and penalties or censures. In cases of necessity, and also in cases of the absence of their own confessors, Eastern- and Roman-

Rite Catholics may ask for and receive sacramental absolution from a priest of a separated Eastern Church. Separated Eastern Christians may similarly ask for and receive sacramental absolution from an Eastern- or Roman-Rite priest. Any priest can absolve a person in danger of death; in the absence of a priest with the usual faculties, this includes a laicized priest or a priest under censure.

Absolution, General: (1) Sacramental absolution without prior individual confession can be given in these extraordinary circumstances: (a) danger of death, when there is neither time nor priests available for hearing confessions; (b) grave necessity of a number of penitents who, because of a shortage of confessors, would be deprived of sacramental grace or Communion for a lengthy period of time through no fault of their own. Persons receiving general absolution are obliged to be properly instructed, disposed and resolved to make an individual confession of the grave sins from which they have been absolved; this confession should be made as soon as the opportunity to confess presents itself and before any second reception of general absolution. Staging events for the giving of general absolution is forbidden. (2) A blessing of the Church with the grant of a plenary indulgence to properly disposed persons.

Accessory to Another's Sin: One who culpably assists another in the performance of an evil action. This may be done by counsel, command, provocation, consent, praise, flattery, concealment, participation, silence, defense of the evil done.

Adoration: The highest act and purpose of religious worship, which is directed in love and reverence to God alone in acknowledgment of His infinite perfection and goodness, and of His total dominion over creatures. Adoration, which is also called *latria*, consists of internal and external elements, private and social prayer, liturgical acts and ceremonies, and, especially, sacrifice.

Adultery: (1) Sexual intercourse between a married person and another to whom one is not married; a violation of the obligations of chastity and justice. The Sixth Commandment prohibition against adultery also prohibits all external sins of a sexual nature. (2) Any sin of impurity (thought, desire, word, action) involving a married person who is not one's husband or wife has the nature of adultery.

Advent Wreath: A wreath of laurel, spruce, or similar foliage with four candles which are lighted successively in the weeks of Advent to symbolize the approaching celebration of the birth of Christ, the Light of the World, at Christmas. The wreath originated among German Protestants.

Agapē: A Greek word, meaning love, love feast, designating the meal of fellowship eaten at some gatherings of early Christians. Although held in some places in connection with the Mass, the agapē was not part of the Mass, nor was it of universal institution and observance. It was infrequently observed by the fifth century and disappeared altogether between the sixth and eighth centuries.

Age of Reason: (1) The time of life when one begins to distinguish between right and wrong, to understand an obligation and take on moral responsibility; seven years of age is the presumption in Church law. (2) Historically, the 18th-century period of Enlightenment in England and France, the age of the Encyclopedists and Deists. According to a basic thesis of the Enlightenment, human experience and reason are the only sources of certain knowledge of truth; consequently, faith and revelation are discounted as valid sources of knowledge, and the reality of supernatural truth is called into doubt and/or denied.

Aggiornamento: An Italian word having the general meaning of bringing up to date, renewal, revitalization, descriptive of the processes of spiritual renewal and institutional reform and change in the Church;

fostered by the Second Vatican Council.

Agnosticism: A theory which holds that a person cannot have certain knowledge of immaterial reality, especially the existence of God and things pertaining to Him. Immanuel Kant, one of the philosophical fathers of agnosticism, stood for the position that God, as well as the human soul, is unknowable on speculative grounds; nevertheless, he found practical imperatives for acknowledging God's existence, a view shared by many agnostics. The First Vatican Council declared that the existence of God and some of His attributes can be known with certainty by human reason, even without divine revelation. The word "agnosticism" was first used, in the sense given here, by T.H. Huxley in 1869.

Alms: An act, gift or service of compassion, motivated by love of God and neighbor, for the help of persons in need; an obligation of charity, which is measurable by the ability of one person to give assistance and by the degree of another's need. Almsgiving, along with prayer and fasting, is regarded as a work of penance as well as a corporal work of mercy.

Alpha and Omega: The first and last letters of the Greek alphabet, used to symbolize the eternity of God (Rv. 1:8) and the divinity and eternity of Christ, the beginning and end of all things (Rv. 21:6; 22:13). Use of the letters as a monogram of Christ originated in the fourth century or earlier.

Anathema: A Greek word with the root meaning of cursed or separated and the adapted meaning of excommunication, used in Church documents, especially the canons of ecumenical councils, for the condemnation of heretical doctrines and of practices opposed to proper discipline.

Anchorite: A kind of hermit living in complete isolation and devoting himself exclusively to exercises of religion and severe penance. The closest contemporary approach to the life of an anchorite is that of

Carthusian and Camaldolese hermits.

Angels: Purely spiritual beings with intelligence and free will, whose name indicates their mission as ministers of God and ministering spirits to men. They were created before the creation of the visible universe; the devil and bad angels, who were created good, fell from glory through their own fault. In addition to these essentials of defined doctrine, it is held that angels are personal beings; they can intercede for persons; fallen angels were banished from God's glory in heaven to hell; bad angels can tempt persons to commit sin. The doctrine of guardian angels, although not explicitly defined as a matter of faith, is rooted in long-standing tradition. No authoritative declaration has ever been issued regarding choirs or various categories of angels: according to theorists, there are nine choirs, consisting of seraphim, cherubim, thrones, dominations, principalities, powers, virtues, archangels and angels. In line with scriptural usage, only three angels can be named — Michael, Raphael and Gabriel.

Anger: Passionate displeasure arising from some kind of offense suffered at the hands of another person, frustration or other cause, combined with a tendency to strike back at the cause of the displeasure; a violation of the Fifth Commandment and one of the capital sins if the displeasure is out of proportion to the cause and/or if the retaliation is unjust.

Anglican Orders: Holy orders conferred according to the rite of the Anglican Church, which Leo XIII declared null and void in the bull *Apostolicae Curae*, Sept. 13, 1896. The orders were declared null because they were conferred according to a rite that was substantially defective in form and intent, and because of a break in apostolic succession that occurred when Matthew Parker became head of the Anglican hierarchy in 1559. In making his declaration, Pope Leo cited earlier arguments against validity made by Julius III in 1553 and 1554 and by Paul IV in 1555. He also noted related directives requiring absolute ordination, according to the Catholic ritual, of convert ministers who had been ordained according to the Anglican Ordinal.

Antichrist: The man of sin, the lawless and wicked antagonist of Christ and the work of God; a mysterious figure of prophecy mentioned in the New Testament. Supported by Satan, submitting to no moral restraints, and armed with tremendous power, Antichrist will set himself up in opposition to God, work false miracles, persecute the people of God, and employ unimaginable means to lead people into error and evil during a period of widespread defection from the Christian faith before the end of time; he will be overcome by Christ. Catholic thinkers have regarded Antichrist as a person, a caricature of Christ, who will lead a final violent struggle against God and His people; they have also applied the title to personal and impersonal forces in history hostile to God and the Church. Official teaching has said little about Antichrist. In 1318, it labeled as partly heretical, senseless, and fanciful the assertions made by the Fraticelli about his coming; in 1415, the Council of Constance condemned the Wycliff thesis that excommunications made by the pope and other prelates were the actions of Antichrist.

Antiphon: (1) A short verse or text, generally from Scripture, recited in the Liturgy of the Hours before and after psalms and canticles. (2) Any verse sung or recited by one part of a choir or congregation in response to the other part, as in antiphonal or alternate chanting.

Apologetics: The science and art of developing and presenting the case for the reasonableness of the Christian faith, by a wide variety of means including facts of experience, history, science, philosophy. The constant objective of apologetics, as well as of the total process of pre-evangelization, is preparation for response to God in faith; its ways and means,

however, are subject to change in accordance with the various needs of people and different sets of circumstances.

Apostasy: (1) Total repudiation of the Christian faith. An apostate automatically incurs a penalty of excommunication. (2) Apostasy from orders is the unlawful withdrawal from or rejection of the obligations of the clerical state by a man who has received major orders. An apostate from orders is subject to a canonical penalty. (3) Apostasy from the religious life occurs when a Religious with perpetual vows unlawfully leaves the community with the intention of not returning, or actually remains outside the community without permission. An apostate from religious life is subject to a canonical penalty.

Apostolate: The ministry or work of an apostle. In Catholic usage, the word is an umbrella-like term covering all kinds and areas of work and endeavor for the service of God and the Church and the good of people. Thus, the apostolate of bishops is to carry on the mission of the Apostles as pastors of the people of God; of priests, to preach the word of God and to carry out the sacramental and pastoral ministry for which they are ordained; of Religious, to follow and do the work of Christ in conformity with the evangelical counsels and their rule of life; of lay persons, as individuals and/or in groups, to give witness to Christ and build up the kingdom of God through practice of their faith, professional competence and the performance of good works in the concrete circumstances of daily life. Apostolic works are not limited to those done within the Church or by specifically Catholic groups, although some apostolates are officially assigned to certain persons or groups and are under the direction of church authorities. Apostolate derives from the commitment and obligation of baptism, confirmation, holy orders, matrimony, the duties of one's state in life, etc.

Apostolic Succession: Bishops of the Church, who form a collective body or college, are successors to the Apostles by ordination and divine right; as such they carry on the mission entrusted by Christ to the Apostles as guardians and teachers of the deposit of faith, principal pastors and spiritual authorities of the faithful. The doctrine of apostolic succession is based on New Testament evidence and the constant teaching of the Church, reflected as early as the end of the first century in a letter of Pope St. Clement to the Corinthians. A significant facet of the doctrine is the role of the pope as the successor of St. Peter, the vicar of Christ and head of the college of bishops. The doctrine of apostolic succession means more than continuity of apostolic faith and doctrine; its basic requisite is ordination by the laying on of hands in apostolic succession.

Archangel: An angel who carries out special missions for God in His dealings with persons. Three of them are named in the Bible: Michael, leader of the angelic host and protector of the synagogue; Raphael, guide of Tobiah and healer of his father, who is regarded as the patron of travelers; Gabriel, called the angel of the incarnation because of his announcement to Mary that she was to be the Mother of Christ.

Archives: Documentary records, and the place where they are kept, of the spiritual and temporal government and affairs of the Church, a diocese, church agencies like the departments of the Roman Curia, bodies like religious institutes, and individual parishes. The strictest secrecy is always in effect for confidential records concerning matters of conscience, and documents of this kind are destroyed as soon as circumstances permit.

Ark of the Covenant: The sacred chest of the Israelites in which were placed and carried the tablets of stone inscribed with the Ten Commandments, the basic moral precepts of the Old Covenant (Ex. 25:10-22; 37:1-9). The Ark was also a symbol of God's presence. The Ark was probably destroyed with the Temple in 587 B.C.

Asceticism: The practice of self-discipline. In the spiritual life, asceticism — by personal prayer, meditation, self-denial, works of mortification, and outgoing interpersonal works — is motivated by love of God and contributes to growth in holiness.

Ashes: Religious significance has been associated with their use as symbolic of penance since Old Testament times. Thus, ashes of palms, blessed on the previous Sunday of the Passion, are placed on the foreheads of the faithful on Ash Wednesday to remind them to do works of penance, especially during the season of Lent, and that they are dust and will return to dust. Ashes are a sacramental.

Aspiration: Short exclamatory prayer: e.g., My Jesus, mercy.

Atheism: Denial of the existence of God, finding expression in a system of thought (speculative atheism) or a manner of acting (practical atheism) as though there were no God. The Second Vatican Council, in its *Pastoral Constitution on the Church in the Modern World* (Nos. 19 to 21), noted that a profession of atheism may represent an explicit denial of God, the rejection of a wrong notion of God, an affirmation of man rather than of God, an extreme protest against evil. It said that such a profession might result from acceptance of such propositions as: there is no absolute truth; man can assert nothing, absolutely nothing, about God; everything can be explained by scientific reasoning alone; the whole question of God is devoid of meaning. The constitution also cited two opinions of influence in atheistic thought. One of them regards recognition of dependence on God as incompatible with human freedom and independence. The other views belief in God and religion as a kind of opiate which sedates man on earth, reconciling him to the acceptance of suffering, injustice, shortcomings, etc., because of hope for greater things after death, and thereby hindering him from seeking and working for improvement and change for the better here and now. All of these views, in one way or another, have been involved in the No-God and Death-of-God schools of thought in recent and remote history.

Atonement: The redemptive activity of Christ, who reconciled man with God through His incarnation and entire life, and especially by His suffering and resurrection. The word also applies to prayer and good works by which persons join themselves with and take part in Christ's work of reconciliation and reparation for sin.

Attributes of God: Perfections of God. God possesses — and is — all the perfections of being, without limitation. Because He is infinite, all of these perfections are one, perfectly united in Him. Man, however, because of the limited power of understanding, views these perfections separately, as distinct characteristics — even though they are not actually distinct in God. God is: almighty, eternal, holy, immortal, immense, immutable, incomprehensible, ineffable, infinite, invisible, just, loving, merciful, most high, most wise, omnipotent, omniscient, omnipresent, patient, perfect, provident, supreme, true.

Avarice (Covetousness): A disorderly and unreasonable attachment to and desire for material things; called a capital sin because it involves preoccupation with material things to the neglect of spiritual goods and obligations of justice and charity.

B

Baldachino: A canopy over an altar.

Beatification: A preliminary step toward canonization of a saint. It begins with an investigation of the candidate's life, writings and heroic practice of virtue, and the certification of at least two miracles worked by God through his or her intercession. If the findings of the investigation so indicate, the pope decrees that the Servant of God may be called Blessed and may be honored locally or in a limited way in the liturgy. Additional procedures lead to canonization.

Beatific Vision: The intuitive, immediate and direct vision and experience of God enjoyed in the light of glory by all the blessed in heaven. The vision is a supernatural mystery.

Beatitude: A literary form of the Old and New Testaments in which blessings are promised to persons for various reasons. Beatitudes are mentioned 26 times in the Psalms, and in other books of the Old Testament. The best-known beatitudes — identifying blessedness with participation in the kingdom of God and His righteousness, and descriptive of the qualities of Christian perfection — are those recounted in Mt. 5:3-11 and Lk. 6:20-22.

Benedictus: The canticle or hymn of Zechariah at the circumcision of St. John the Baptist (Lk. 1:68-79). It is an expression of praise and thanks to God for sending John as a precursor of the Messiah. The *Benedictus* is recited in the Liturgy of the Hours as part of the Morning Prayer.

Blasphemy: Any expression of insult or contempt with respect to God, principally, and to holy persons and things, secondarily; a violation of the honor due to God in the context of the First and Second Commandments.

Blasphemy of the Spirit: Deliberate resistance to the Holy Spirit, called the unforgivable sin (Mt. 12:31) because it makes His saving action impossible. Thus, the only unforgivable sin is the one for which a person will not seek pardon from God.

Blessing: Invocation of God's favor, by official ministers of the Church or by private individuals. Blessings are recounted in the Old Testament and New Testament, and are common in the Christian tradition. Many types of blessings are listed in the *Roman Ritual.* Private blessings, as well as those of an official kind, are efficacious. Blessings are imparted with the Sign of the Cross and appropriate prayer.

Brief, Apostolic: A papal letter, less formal than a bull, signed for the pope by a secretary and impressed with the seal of the Fisherman's Ring. Simple apostolic letters of this kind are issued for beatifications and with respect to other matters.

Bull, Apostolic: The most solemn form of papal document, beginning with the name and title of the pope (e.g., John Paul II, Servant of the Servants of God), dealing with an important subject, and having attached to it either a seal called a *bulla* or a red-ink imprint of the device on the seal.

Burial, Ecclesiastical: Interment with ecclesiastical rites, a right of the Christian faithful. The Church recommends burial of the bodies of the dead, but cremation is permissible if it does not involve reasons against Church teaching. Ecclesiastical burial is in order for catechumens; for unbaptized children whose parents intended to have them baptized before death; and even — in the absence of their own ministers — for baptized non-Catholics unless it would be considered against their will.

C

Calumny: Harming the name and good reputation of a person by lies; a violation of obligations of justice and truth. Restitution is due for calumny.

Calvary: A knoll about 15 feet high just outside the western wall of Jerusalem where Christ was crucified, so called from the Latin *calvaria* (skull) which described its shape.

Canon: A Greek word meaning rule, norm, standard, measure. (1) The word designates the Canon of Sacred Scripture, which is the list of books recognized by the Church as inspired by the Holy Spirit. (2) In the sense of regulating norms, the word designates the Code of Canon Law enacted and promulgated by ecclesiastical authority for the orderly and pastoral administration and government of the Church. A revised Code, effective November 27, 1983, consists of 1,752 canons in seven books under the titles of General Norms, the People of God, the Teaching Mission of the Church, the Sanctifying Mission of the Church, Temporal Goods of the Church, Penal Law and Procedural Law. The antecedent of this code was promulgated in 1917 and became effective in 1918; it consisted of 2,414 canons in five books covering General Rules, Ecclesiastical Persons, Sacred Things, Trials, Crimes and Punishments. Eastern-Rite Churches have their own canon law. (3) The term also designates the Eucharistic Prayers, anaphoras of the Mass, the core of the liturgy. (4) Certain dignitaries of the Church have the title of Canon, and some Religious are known as Canons.

Canonization: An infallible declaration by the pope that a person, who died as a martyr, and/or practiced Christian virtue to a heroic degree, is now in heaven and is worthy of honor and imitation by all the faithful. Such a declaration is preceded by the process of beatification and another detailed investigation concerning the person's reputation for holiness, writings, and (except in the case of martyrs) miracles ascribed to his or her intercession after death. Miracles are not required for martyrs. The pope can dispense from some of the formalities ordinarily required in canonization procedures (equivalent canonization), as Pope John XXIII did in the canonization of St. Gregory Barbarigo on May 26, 1960. A saint is worthy of honor in liturgical worship throughout the universal Church. From its earliest years the Church has venerated saints. Public official honor always required the approval of the bishop of the place. Martyrs were the first to be honored. St. Martin of Tours, who died in 397, was an early non-martyr venerated as a saint. The first official canonization by a pope for the universal Church was that of St. Ulrich by John XV in 993. Alexander III reserved the process of canonization to the Holy See in 1171. In 1588 Sixtus V established the Sacred Congregation of Rites for the principal purpose of handling causes for beatification and canonization: this function is now the work of the Congregation for the Causes of Saints.

Canticle: A scriptural chant or prayer differing from the psalms. Three of the canticles prescribed for use in the Liturgy of the Hours are: the *Magnificat* (Lk. 1:46-55), the *Benedictus* (Lk. 1:68-79), and the *Nunc Dimittis* (Lk. 2:29-32).

Capital Sins: Moral faults which, if habitual, give rise to many more sins. They are pride, covetousness, lust, anger, gluttony, envy, sloth. The opposite virtues are: humility, liberality, chastity, meekness, temperance, brotherly love, diligence.

Cardinal Virtues: The four principal moral virtues are prudence, justice, temperance and fortitude.

Catacombs: Underground Christian cemeteries in various cities of the Roman Empire and Italy, especially in the vicinity of Rome; the burial sites of many martyrs and other Christians.

Catechesis: Religious instruction and formation not only for persons preparing for baptism but also for the faithful in various stages of their spiritual development.

Catechism: A summary of Christian doctrine in question-and-answer form, used for purposes of instruction.

Catechumen: A person preparing in a program of instruction and spiritual formation for baptism and reception into the Church. The Church has a special relationship with catechumens. It invites them to lead the life of the Gospel, introduces them to the celebration of the sacred rites, and grants them various prerogatives that are proper to the faithful (one of which is the right to ecclesiastical burial).

Cathedraticum: The tax paid to a bishop by all churches and benefices subject to him for the support of episcopal administration and for works of charity.

Catholic: A Greek word, meaning universal, first used in the title, Catholic Church, in a letter written by St. Ignatius of Antioch about 107 to the Christians of Smyrna.

Celebret: A Latin word, meaning Let him celebrate, the name of a letter of recommendation issued by a bishop or other superior stating that a priest is in good standing and therefore eligible to celebrate Mass or perform other priestly functions.

Celibacy: The unmarried state of life, required in the Roman Church of candidates for holy orders and of men already ordained to holy orders, for the practice of perfect chastity and total dedication to the service of people in the ministry of the Church. Celibacy is enjoined as a condition for ordination by church discipline and law, not by dogmatic necessity. In the Roman Church, a consensus in favor of celibacy developed in the early centuries while the clergy included both celibates and men who had been married once. The first local legislation on the subject was enacted by a local council held in Elvira, Spain, about 306; it forbade bishops, priests, deacons and other ministers to have wives. Similar enactments were passed by other local councils from that time on, and by the 12th century particular laws regarded marriage by clerics in major orders to be not only unlawful but also null and void. The latter view was translated by the Second Lateran Council in 1139 into what seems to be the first written universal law making holy orders an invalidating impediment to marriage. In 1563 the Council of Trent ruled definitely on the matter and established the discipline in force in the Roman Church. Some exceptions to this discipline have been made in recent years. Several married Protestant and Episcopalian (Anglican) clergymen who became converts and were subsequently ordained to the priesthood have been permitted to continue in marriage. Married men over the age of 35 can be ordained to the permanent diaconate. Eastern Church discipline on celibacy differs from that of the Roman Church. In line with legislation enacted by the Synod of Trullo in 692 and still in force, candidates for holy orders may marry before becoming deacons and may continue in marriage thereafter, but marriage after ordination is forbidden. Eastern-Rite bishops in the U.S., however, do not ordain married candidates for the priesthood. Eastern-Rite bishops are unmarried.

Cenacle: The upper room in Jerusalem where Christ ate the Last Supper with His Apostles.

Censer: A metal vessel with a perforated cover and suspended by chains, in which incense is burned. It is used at some Masses, Benediction of the Blessed Sacrament and other liturgical functions.

Censorship of Books: An exercise of vigilance by the Church for safeguarding authentic religious teaching. Pertinent legislation in a decree issued by the Congregation for the Doctrine of the Faith April 9, 1975, is embodied in the Code of Canon Law (Book III, Title IV).

Censures: Spiritual penalties inflicted by the Church on its members for committing certain serious offenses and for being or remaining obstinate therein. Excommunication (exclusion from the community of the faithful, barring a person from sacramental and other participation in the goods and offices of the community of the Church), suspension (prohibition of a cleric to exercise orders) and interdict (personal deprivation of the sacraments and of ministerial participation) have been the censures in force since the time of Innocent III (1214). Their intended purposes are to deter persons from committing sins which, more seriously and openly than others, threaten the common good of the Church and its members; to punish and correct offenders; and to provide for the making of reparation for harm done to the community of the Church. Censures may be in-

curred automatically (*ipso facto*) on the commission of certain offenses for which fixed penalties have been laid down in church law (*latae sententiae*); or they may be inflicted by sentence of a judge (*ferendae sententiae*). Automatic excommunication, for example, is incurred for the offenses of abortion, apostasy, heresy and schism. Obstinacy in crime — also called contumacy, disregard of a penalty, defiance of church authority — is presumed by law in the commission of offenses for which automatic censures are decreed. The presence and degree of contumacy in other cases, for which judicial sentence is required, is subject to determination by a judge. Absolution can be obtained from any censure, provided the person repents and desists from obstinacy. Absolution may be reserved to the pope, the bishop of a place, or the major superior of an exempt clerical religious institute. Any priest can absolve a person in danger of death from all censures; in other cases, faculties to absolve from reserved censures can be exercised by competent authorities or given to other priests. The penal law of the Church is contained in Book VI of the Code of Canon Law.

Chamberlain: (1) The Chamberlain of the Holy Roman Church is a cardinal who administers the property and revenues of the Holy See. On the death of the pope he becomes head of the College of Cardinals and summons and directs the conclave until a new pope is elected. (2) The Chamberlain of the Sacred College of Cardinals has charge of the property and revenues of the college and keeps the record of business transacted in consistories. (3) The Chamberlain of the Roman Clergy is the president of the secular clergy of Rome.

Chancellor: Notary of a diocese, who draws up written documents in the government of the diocese; takes care of, arranges and indexes diocesan archives, records of dispensations and ecclesiastical trials.

Chancery: (1) A branch of

church administration that handles written documents used in the government of a diocese. (2) The administrative office of a diocese, a bishop's office.

Chapel: A building or part of a building used for divine worship; a portion of a church set aside for the celebration of Mass or for some special devotion.

Chaplain: A priest appointed for the pastoral service of any division of the armed forces, religious communities, institutions, various groups of the faithful.

Chaplet: A term, meaning little crown, applied to a rosary or, more commonly, to a small string of beads used for devotional purposes; e.g., the Infant of Prague chaplet.

Chapter: A general meeting of delegates of religious orders for elections and the handling of other important affairs of their communities.

Charisms: Gifts or graces given by God to persons for the good of others and the Church. Examples are special gifts for apostolic work, prophecy, healing, discernment of spirits, the life of evangelical poverty, here-and-now witness to faith in various circumstances of life. The Second Vatican Council made the following statement about charisms in the *Dogmatic Constitution on the Church* (No. 12): "It is not only through the sacraments and church ministries that the same Holy Spirit sanctifies and leads the people of God and enriches it with virtues. Allotting His gifts 'to everyone according as He will' (1 Cor. 12:11), He distributes special graces among the faithful of every rank. By these gifts He makes them fit and ready to undertake the various tasks or offices advantageous for the renewal and upbuilding of the Church, according to the words of the Apostle: 'The manifestation of the Spirit is given to everyone for profit' (1 Cor. 12:7). These charismatic gifts, whether they be the most outstanding or the more simple and widely diffused, are to be received with thanksgiving and consolation, for they are exceedingly suitable and useful for the needs of the Church. Still, extraordinary gifts are not to be rashly sought after, nor are the fruits of apostolic labor to be presumptuously expected from them. In any case, judgment as to their genuineness and proper use belongs to those who preside over the Church, and to whose special competence it belongs, not indeed to extinguish the Spirit, but to test all things and hold fast to that which is good" (cf. 1 Thes. 5:12, 19-21).

Charity: Love of God above all things for His own sake, and love of one's neighbor as oneself because and as an expression of one's love for God; the greatest of the three theological virtues. The term is sometimes also used to designate sanctifying grace.

Chastity: Properly ordered behavior with respect to sex. In marriage, the exercise of the procreative power is integrated with the norms and purposes of marriage. Outside of marriage, the rule is self-denial of the voluntary exercise and enjoyment of the procreative faculty in thought, word or action. The vow of chastity, which reinforces the virtue of chastity with the virtue of religion, is an evangelical counsel and one of the three vows professed by Religious.

Christ: The title of Jesus, derived from the Greek translation *Christos* of the Hebrew term *Messiah*, meaning the Anointed of God, the Savior and Deliverer of His people. Christian use of the title is a confession of belief that Jesus is the Savior.

Christianity: The sum total of things related to belief in Christ — the Christian religion, Christian churches, Christians themselves, society based on and expressive of Christian beliefs, culture reflecting Christian values.

Christians: The name first applied about the year 43 to followers of Christ at Antioch, the capital of Syria. It was used by the pagans as a contemptuous term. The word applies to persons who profess belief in the divinity and teachings of Christ and who give witness to Him in life.

Church: (1) Regarding the Catholic Church, the Second Vatican Council declared in the *Dogmatic Constitution on the Church*: "They are fully incorporated into the society of the Church who, possessing the Spirit of Christ, accept her entire system and all the means of salvation given to her, and through union with her visible structure are joined to Christ, who rules her through the Supreme Pontiff and the bishops. This joining is effected by the bonds of professed faith, of the sacraments, of ecclesiastical government, and of communion" (No. 14). (2) In general, any religious body. (3) A building set aside and dedicated for divine worship.

Circumcision: A ceremonial practice symbolic of initiation and participation in the covenant between God and Abraham.

Circumincession: The indwelling of each divine Person of the Holy Trinity in the others.

Clergy: Men ordained for sacred ministries and assigned to pastoral and other duties for the service of the people and the Church. (1) Diocesan or secular clergy are committed to pastoral ministry in parishes and in other capacities in a particular church (diocese) under the direction of their bishop, to whom they are bound by a promise of obedience. (2) Regular clergy belong to religious institutes (orders, congregations, societies — institutes of consecrated life) and are so-called because they observe the rule (*regula* in Latin) of their respective institutes. They are committed to the ways of life and apostolates of their institutes. In ordinary pastoral ministry, they are under the direction of local bishops as well as their own superiors.

Clericalism: A term generally used in a derogatory sense to mean action, influence and interference by the Church and the clergy in matters with which they allegedly should not be concerned. Anticlericalism is a reaction of antipathy, hostility, distrust and opposition to the Church and clergy arising from real and/or alleged faults of the clergy, overextension of the role of the laity, or for other reasons.

Cloister: Part of a monastery, convent or other house of Religious reserved for use by members of the institute.

Code: A digest of rules or regulations, such as the Code of Canon Law.

Collegiality: The bishops of the Church, in union with and subordinate to the pope — who has full, supreme and universal power over the Church which he can exercise independently — have supreme teaching and pastoral authority over the whole Church. In addition to their proper authority of office for the good of the faithful in their respective dioceses or other jurisdictions, the bishops have authority to act for the good of the universal Church. This collegial authority is exercised in a solemn manner in an ecumenical council and can also be exercised in other ways sanctioned by the pope. Doctrine on collegiality was set forth by the Second Vatican Council in the *Dogmatic Constitution on the Church*. By extension, the concept of collegiality is applied to other forms of participation and co-responsibility by members of a community.

Commissariat of the Holy Land: A special jurisdiction within the Order of Friars Minor whose main purposes are the collecting of funds for support of the Holy Places in Palestine and staffing of the Holy Places and missions in the Middle East with priests and brothers. There are about 70 such commissariats in more than 30 countries. One of them has headquarters at Mt. St. Sepulchre, Washington, D.C. Franciscans have had custody of the Holy Places since 1342.

Communion of Faithful, Saints: The communion of all the people of God — on earth, in heavenly glory, in purgatory — with Christ and each other in faith, grace, prayer and good works.

Concelebration: The liturgical act in which several priests, led by one member of the group, offer Mass together, all consecrating the bread and wine. Concelebration has always been common in churches of the Eastern Rite. In the Roman Rite, it was long restricted, taking place only at the ordination of bishops and the ordination of priests. The *Constitution on the Sacred Liturgy* issued by the Second Vatican Council set new norms for concelebration, which is now relatively common in the Roman Rite.

Concordance, Biblical: An alphabetical verbal index enabling a user knowing one or more words of a scriptural passage to locate the entire text.

Concordat: A Church-state treaty with the force of law concerning matters of mutual concern — e.g., rights of the Church, arrangement of ecclesiastical jurisdictions, marriage laws, education. The Concordat of Worms (1122) was the first treaty of this kind.

Concupiscence: Any tendency of the sensitive appetite. The term is most frequently used in reference to desires and tendencies for sinful sense pleasure.

Confession: Sacramental confession is the act by which a person tells or confesses sins to a priest who is authorized to give absolution in the sacrament of penance.

Confessor: A priest who administers the sacrament of penance. The title of confessor, formerly given to a category of male saints, was suppressed in the calendar in effect since 1970.

Confraternity: An association whose members practice a particular form of religious devotion and/or are engaged in some kind of apostolic work.

Conscience: Practical judgment concerning the moral goodness or sinfulness of an action. In the Catholic view, this judgment is made by reference of the action, its attendant circumstances and the intentions of the person to the requirements of moral law as expressed in the Ten Commandments, the summary law of love for God and neighbor, the life and teaching of Christ, and the authoritative teaching and practice of the Church with respect to the total demands of divine revelation. A person is obliged: (1) to obey a certain and correct conscience; (2) to obey a certain conscience even if it is inculpably erroneous; (3) not to obey, but to correct, a conscience known to be erroneous or lax; (4) to rectify a scrupulous conscience by following the advice of a confessor and by other measures; (5) to resolve doubts of conscience before acting. It is legitimate to act for solid and probable reasons when a question of moral responsibility admits of argument.

Consistory: An assembly of cardinals presided over by the pope.

Constitution: (1) An apostolic or papal constitution is a document in which a pope enacts and promulgates law. (2) A formal and solemn document issued by an ecumenical council on a doctrinal or pastoral subject, with binding force in the whole Church; e.g., the four constitutions issued by the Second Vatican Council on the Church, liturgy, revelation, and the Church in the modern world. (3) The constitutions of institutes of consecrated life and societies of apostolic life spell out details of and norms drawn from the various rules for the guidance and direction of the life and work of their members.

Consubstantiation: A theory which holds that the Body and Blood of Christ coexist with the substance of bread and wine in the Holy Eucharist. This theory, also called impanation, is incompatible with the doctrine of transubstantiation.

Contraception: Anything done by positive interference to prevent sexual intercourse from resulting in conception. Direct contraception is against the order of nature and is seriously sinful. Indirect contraception — as a secondary effect of medical treatment or other action having a necessary, good, non-contraceptive purpose — is permissible under the principle of the double effect. The practice of periodic continence is not contraception because it does not involve positive interference with the order of nature.

Contrition: Sorrow for sin coupled with a purpose of amendment. Contrition arising from a supernatural motive is necessary for the forgiveness of sin. (1) Perfect contrition is total sorrow for and renunciation of attachment to sin, arising from the motive of pure love of God. Perfect contrition, which implies the intention of doing all God wants done for the forgiveness of sin (including confession in a reasonable period of time), is sufficient for the forgiveness of serious sin and the remission of all temporal punishment due for sin. (The intention to receive the sacrament of penance is implicit — even if unrealized, as in the case of some persons — in perfect contrition.) (2) Imperfect contrition or attrition is sorrow arising from a quasi-selfish supernatural motive; e.g., the fear of losing heaven, suffering the pains of hell, etc. Imperfect contrition is sufficient for the forgiveness of serious sin when joined with absolution in confession, and sufficient for the forgiveness of venial sin even outside of confession.

Contumely: Personal insult, reviling a person in his presence by accusation of moral faults, by refusal of recognition or due respect; a violation of obligations of justice and charity.

Corporal Works of Mercy: Feeding the hungry, giving drink to the thirsty, clothing the naked, visiting the imprisoned, sheltering the homeless, visiting the sick, burying the dead.

Council, Ecumenical: An assembly of the college of bishops, with and under the presidency of the pope, which has supreme authority over the Church in matters pertaining to faith, morals, worship and discipline. The Second Vatican Council was the 21st of its kind in the history of the Church.

Council, Plenary: A council held for the particular churches belonging to the same episcopal conference. Such a council can be convoked to take action related to the pastoral activity and mission of the Church in the territory. The membership of such councils is fixed by canon law; their decrees, when approved by the Holy See, are binding in the territory.

Councils: Bodies representative of various categories of members of the Church which participate with bishops and other church authorities in making decisions and carrying out action programs for the good of the Church and the accomplishment of its mission to its own members and society in general. Examples are priests' senates or councils, councils of Religious and lay persons, parish councils, diocesan pastoral councils.

Councils, Provincial: Meetings of the bishops of a province. The metropolitan, or ranking archbishop, of an ecclesiastical province convenes and presides over such councils in a manner prescribed by canon law to take action related to the life and mission of the Church in the province. Acts and decrees must be approved by the Holy See before being promulgated.

Counsels, Evangelical: Gospel counsels of perfection, especially voluntary poverty, perfect chastity and obedience, which were recommended by Christ to those who would devote themselves exclusively and completely to the immediate service of God. Religious (members of institutes of consecrated life) bind themselves by public vows to observe these counsels in a life of total consecration to God and service to people through various kinds of apostolic works.

Counter-Reformation: The period of approximately 100 years following the Council of Trent, which witnessed a reform within the Church to stimulate genuine Catholic life and to counteract effects of the Reformation.

Covenant: A bond of relationship between parties pledged to each other. God-initiated covenants in the Old Testament included those with Abraham, Noah, Moses, Levi, David. The Mosaic (Sinai) covenant made Israel God's Chosen People on terms of fidelity to true faith, true worship, and righteous conduct according to the Decalogue. The New Testament covenant, prefigured in the Old Testament, is the bond persons have with God through Christ. All persons are called to be parties to this perfect and everlasting covenant, which was mediated and ratified by Christ. The marriage covenant seals the closest possible relationship between a man and a woman.

Creation: The production by God of something out of nothing. The biblical account of creation is contained in the first two chapters of Genesis.

Creator: God, the supreme, self-existing Being, the absolute and infinite First Cause of all things.

Creature: Everything in the realm of being is a creature, except God.

Cremation: The reduction of a human corpse to ashes by means of fire. Cremation is not in line with Catholic tradition and practice, even though it is not opposed to any article of faith. The Congregation for the Doctrine of the Faith, under date of May 8, 1963, circulated among bishops an instruction which upheld the traditional practices of Christian burial but modified anti-cremation legislation. Cremation may be permitted for serious reasons, of a private as well as public nature, provided it does not involve any contempt of the Church or of religion, or any attempt to deny, question, or belittle the doctrine of the resurrection of the body. The person who chooses cremation may receive the last rites and be given ecclesiastical burial. A priest may say prayers for the deceased at the crematorium, but full liturgical ceremonies may not take place there. The principal reason behind an earlier prohibition against cremation was the fact that, historically, the practice had represented an attempt to deny the doctrine of the resurrection of the body.

Crib or Crèche: A devotional representation of the birth of Jesus. The custom of erecting cribs is generally attributed to St. Francis of Assisi who in 1223 obtained from Pope Honorius III permission to use a crib and figures of the Christ Child, Mary, St. Joseph, and others, to represent the mystery of the Nativity.

Crosier: The bishop's staff, symbolic of his pastoral office, responsibility and authority.

Crypt: An underground or partly underground chamber; e.g., the lower part of a church used for worship and/or burial.

Cura Animarum: A Latin phrase, meaning care of souls, designating the pastoral ministry and responsibility of bishops and priests.

Curia: The personnel and offices through which (1) the pope administers the affairs of the universal Church, the Roman Curia, or (2) a bishop the affairs of a diocese, diocesan curia. The principal officials of a diocesan curia are the vicar general of the diocese, the chancellor, officials of the diocesan tribunal or court, examiners, consultors, auditors, notaries.

Custos: A religious superior who presides over a number of convents collectively called a custody. In some institutes of consecrated life a custos may be the deputy of a higher superior.

D

Deaconess: A woman officially appointed and charged by the Church to carry out service-like functions. Phoebe apparently was one (Rom. 16:1-2); a second probable reference to the office is in 1 Tm. 3:11. The office — for assistance at the baptism of women, for pastoral service to women and for works of charity — had considerable development in the third and also in the fourth century when the actual term came into use (in place of such designations as *diacona, vidua, virgo canonica*). Its importance declined subsequently with the substitution of infusion in place of immersion as the common method of baptism in the West, and with the increase of the practice of infant baptism. There is no record of the ministry of deaconess in the West after the beginning of the 11th century. The office continued, however, for a longer time in the East. The Vatican's Theological Commission, in a paper prepared in 1971, noted that there had been in the past a form of diaconal ordination for women. With a rite and purpose distinctive to women, it differed essentially from the ordination of deacons, which had sacramental effects.

Dean: (1) A priest with supervisory responsibility over a section of a diocese known as a deanery. The post-Vatican II counterpart of a dean is an episcopal vicar. (2) The senior or ranking member of a group.

Decree: An edict or ordinance issued by a pope and/or by an ecumenical council, with binding force in the whole Church; by a department of the Roman Curia, with binding force for concerned parties; by a territorial body of bishops, with binding force for persons in the area; by individual bishops, with binding force for concerned parties until revocation or the death of the bishop. The nine decrees issued by the Second Vatican Council were combinations of doctrinal and pastoral statements with executive orders for action and movement toward renewal and reform in the Church.

Dedication of a Church: The ceremony whereby a church is solemnly set apart for the worship of God. The custom of dedicating churches had an antecedent in Old Testament ceremonies for the dedication of the Temple, as in the times of Solomon and the Maccabees. The earliest extant record of the dedication of a Christian church dates from early in the fourth century, when it was done simply by the celebration of Mass. Other ceremonies developed later. A church can be dedicated by a simple blessing or a solemn consecration. The rite of consecration is generally performed by a bishop.

Deism: A system of natural religion which acknowledges the existence of God but regards Him as so transcendent and remote from man and the universe that divine revelation and the supernatural order of things are irrelevant and unacceptable. It developed from rationalistic principles in England in the 17th and 18th centuries, and had Voltaire, Rousseau and the Encyclopedists among its advocates in France.

Despair: Abandonment of hope for salvation arising from the conviction that God will not provide the necessary means for attaining it, that following God's way of life for salvation is impossible, or that one's sins are unforgivable; a serious sin against the Holy Spirit and the theological virtues of hope and faith, involving distrust in the mercy and goodness of God and a denial of the truths that God wills the salvation of all persons and provides sufficient grace for it. Real despair is distinguished from unreasonable fear with respect to the difficulties of attaining salvation, from morbid anxiety over the demands of divine justice, and from feelings of despair.

Detachment: Control of affection for creatures by two principles: (1) supreme love and devotion belong to God; (2) love and service of creatures should be an expression of love for God.

Detraction: Revelation of true but hidden faults of a person without sufficient and justifying reason; a violation of requirements of justice and charity, involving the obligation to make restitution when this is possible without doing more harm to the good name of the offended party. In some cases, e.g., to prevent evil, secret faults may and should be disclosed.

Devil: (1) Lucifer, Satan, chief

of the fallen angels who sinned and were banished from heaven. Still possessing angelic powers, he can cause such diabolical phenomena as possession and obsession, and can tempt men to sin. (2) Any fallen angel.

Devotion: (1) Religious fervor, piety; dedication. (2) The consolation experienced at times during prayer; a reverent manner of praying. (3) A particular form of prayer or religious practice.

Disciple: A term used sometimes in reference to the Apostles but more often to a larger number of followers (72) of Christ mentioned in Lk. 10:1.

Disciplina Arcani: A Latin phrase, meaning discipline of the secret and referring to a practice of the early Church, especially during the Roman persecutions, to: (1) conceal Christian truths from those who, it was feared, would misinterpret, ridicule and profane the teachings, and persecute Christians for believing them; (2) instruct catechumens in a gradual manner, withholding the teaching of certain doctrines until the catechumens proved themselves of good faith and sufficient understanding.

Dispensation: The relaxation of a law in a particular case. Laws made for the common good sometimes work undue hardship in particular cases. In such cases, where sufficient reasons are present, dispensations may be granted by proper authorities. Bishops, religious superiors and others may dispense from certain laws; the pope can dispense from all ecclesiastical laws. No one has authority to dispense from obligations of the divine law.

Divination: Attempting to foretell future or hidden things by means of things like dreams, necromancy, spiritism, examination of entrails, astrology, augury, omens, palmistry, drawing straws, dice, cards, etc. Practices like these attribute to creatural things a power which belongs to God alone and are violations of the First Commandment.

Divine Praises: Fourteen praises recited or sung at Benediction of the Blessed Sacrament in reparation for sins of sacrilege, blasphemy and profanity (some of these praises date from the end of the 18th century): Blessed be God. / Blessed be His holy Name. / Blessed be Jesus Christ, true God and true Man. / Blessed be the Name of Jesus. / Blessed be His most Sacred Heart. / Blessed be His most Precious Blood. / Blessed be Jesus in the most holy Sacrament of the Altar. / Blessed be the Holy Spirit, the Paraclete. / Blessed be the great Mother of God, Mary most holy. / Blessed be her holy and Immaculate Conception. / Blessed be her glorious Assumption. / Blessed be the name of Mary, Virgin and Mother. / Blessed be St. Joseph, her most chaste Spouse. / Blessed be God in His Angels and in His Saints.

Double Effect Principle: Actions sometimes have two effects closely related to each other, one good and the other bad, and a difficult moral question can arise: Is it permissible to place an action from which two such results follow? It is permissible to place the action, if: the action is good in itself and is directly productive of the good effect; the circumstances are good; the intention of the person is good; the reason for placing the action is proportionately serious to the seriousness of the indirect bad effect. For example: Is it morally permissible for a pregnant woman to undergo medical or surgical treatment for a pathological condition if the indirect and secondary effect of the treatment will be the loss of the child? The reply is affirmative, for these reasons: The action, i.e., the treatment, is good in itself, cannot be deferred until a later time without very serious consequences, and is ordered directly to the cure of critically grave pathology. By means of the treatment, the woman intends to save her life, which she has a right to do. The loss of the child is not directly sought as a means for the cure of the mother, but results indirectly and in a secondary manner from the placing of the action, i.e., the treatment, which is good in itself. The double effect principle does not support the principle that the end justifies the means.

Doxology: (1) The lesser doxology, or ascription of glory to the Trinity, is the Glory be to the Father. The first part dates back to the third or fourth century, and came from the form of baptism. The concluding words, "As it was in the beginning," etc., are of later origin. (2) The greater doxology, "Glory to God in the highest," begins with the words of angelic praise at the birth of Christ recounted in the Infancy Narrative (Lk. 2:14). It is often recited at Mass. Of early Eastern origin, it is found in the *Apostolic Constitutions* in a form much like the present. (3) The formula of praise at the end of the Eucharistic Prayer at Mass, sung or said by the celebrant while he holds aloft the paten containing the consecrated host in one hand and the chalice containing the consecrated wine in the other.

Dulia: A Greek term meaning the veneration or homage, different in nature and degree from that given to God, paid to the saints. It includes honoring the saints and seeking their intercession with God.

Duty: A moral obligation deriving from the binding force of law, the exigencies of one's state in life, and other sources.

E

Easter Controversy: A three-phase controversy over the time for the celebration of Easter. Some early Christians in the Near East, called Quartodecimans, favored the observance of Easter on the 14th day of Nisan, the spring month of the Hebrew calendar, whenever it occurred. Against this practice, Pope St. Victor I, about 190, ordered a Sunday observance of the feast. The Council of Nicaea, in line with usages of the Church at Rome and Alexandria, decreed in 325 that Easter should be observed on the first Sunday following the first full moon of spring. Uniformity of practice in the West was not achieved until several centuries later, when the British Isles, in delayed compliance with measures enacted by the Synod of Whitby in 664, accepted the Roman date of observance. Unrelated to the controversy is the fact that some Eastern Christians, in accordance with traditional calendar practices, celebrate Easter at a different time than the Roman- and Eastern-Rite churches.

Easter Duty, Season: The serious obligation binding Catholics of the Roman Rite to receive the Eucharist during the Easter season (in the U.S., from the first Sunday of Lent to Trinity Sunday).

Easter Water: Holy water blessed with special ceremonies and distributed on the Easter Vigil; used during Easter Week for blessing the faithful and homes.

Ecclesiology: Study of the nature, constitution, members, mission, functions, etc., of the Church.

Ecstasy: An extraordinary state of mystical experience in which a person is so absorbed in God that the activity of the exterior senses is suspended.

Ecumenism: The movement of Christians and their churches toward the unity willed by Christ. The Second Vatican Council called the movement "those activities and enterprises which, according to various needs of the Church and opportune occasions, are started and organized for the fostering of unity among Christians" (*Decree on Ecumenism,* No. 4). Spiritual ecumenism, i.e., prayer for unity, is the heart of the movement. The movement also involves scholarly and pew-level efforts for the development of mutual understanding and better interfaith relations in general, and collaboration by the churches and their members in the social area.

Elevation: The raising of the host after consecration at Mass for adoration by the faithful. The custom was introduced in the Diocese of Paris about the close of the 12th century to offset an erroneous teaching of the time which held that transubstantiation of the bread did not take place until after the consecration of the wine in the chalice. The elevation of the chalice following the consecration of the wine was introduced in the 15th century.

End Justifies the Means: An unacceptable ethical principle which states that evil means may be used to produce good effects.

Envy: Sadness over another's good fortune because it is considered a loss to oneself or a detraction from one's own excellence; one of the seven capital sins, a violation of the obligations of charity.

Episcopal Conferences: Official bodies — organized and operating under general norms and particular statutes approved by the Holy See — in and through which the bishops of a given country or territory act together as pastors of the Church. The U.S. conference is the National Conference of Catholic Bishops.

Episcopate: (1) The office, dignity and sacramental powers bestowed upon a bishop at his ordination. (2) The body of bishops collectively.

Equivocation: (1) The use of words, phrases, or gestures having more than one meaning in order to conceal information which a questioner has no strict right to know. It is permissible to equivocate (have a broad mental reservation) in some circumstances. (2) A lie, i.e., a statement of untruth. Lying is intrinsically wrong. A lie told in joking, evident as such, is not wrong.

Eschatology: Doctrine concerning the last things: death, judgment, heaven and hell, and the final state of perfection of the people and kingdom of God at the end of time.

Eternity: The interminable, perfect possession of life in its totality without beginning or end; an attribute of God, who has no past or future but always is. Man's existence has a beginning but no end and is, accordingly, called immortal.

Euthanasia: Mercy killing, the direct causing of death for the purpose of ending human suffering. Euthanasia is murder and is totally illicit, for the natural law forbids the direct taking of one's own life or that of an innocent person. The use of drugs to relieve suffering in serious cases, even when this results in a shortening of life as an indirect and secondary effect, is permissible under conditions of the double-effect principle. It is also permissible for a seriously ill person to refuse to follow — or for other responsible persons to refuse to permit — extraordinary medical procedures even though the refusal might entail shortening of life.

Evolution: Scientific theory concerning the development of the physical universe from unorganized matter (inorganic evolution) and, especially, the development of existing forms of vegetable, animal and human life from earlier and more primitive organisms (organic evolution). Various ideas about evolution were advanced for some centuries before scientific evidence in support of the main-line theory of organic evolution, which has several formulations, was discovered and verified in the second half of the 19th century and afterwards. This evidence — from the findings of comparative anatomy and other sciences — confirmed evolution within species and cleared the way to further investigation of questions regarding the processes of its accomplishment. While a number of such questions remain open with respect to human evolution, a point of doctrine not open to question is the immediate creation of the human soul by God. For some time, theologians regarded the theory with hostility, considering it to be in opposition to the account of creation in the early chapters of Genesis and subversive of belief in such doctrines as creation, the early state of man in grace, and the fall of man from grace. This state of affairs and the tension it generated led to considerable controversy regarding an alleged conflict between religion and science. Gradually, however, the tension was diminished with the development of biblical studies from the latter part of the 19th century onwards, with clarification of the distinctive features of religious truth and scientific truth, and with the refinement of evolutionary concepts. So far as the Genesis account of creation is concerned, the Catholic view is that the writer(s) did not write as a scientist but as the communicator of religious truth in a manner adapted to the understanding of the people of his time. He used anthropomorphic language, the figure of days and other literary devices to state the salvation truths of creation, the fall of man from grace, and the promise of redemption. It was beyond the competency and purpose of the writer(s) to describe creation and related events in a scientific manner.

Exposition of the Blessed Sacrament: "In churches where the Eucharist is regularly reserved, it is recommended that solemn exposition of the Blessed Sacrament for an extended period of time should take place once a year, even though the period is not strictly continuous. . . . Shorter expositions of the Eucharist (Benediction) are to be arranged in such a way that the blessing with the Eucharist is preceded by a reasonable time for readings of the word of God, songs, prayers and a period for silent prayer." So stated Vatican directives issued in 1973.

Existentialism: A philosophy with radical concern for the problems of individual existence and identity viewed in particular here-and-now patterns of thought which presuppose irrationality and absurdity in human life and the whole universe. It is preoccupied with questions about freedom, moral decision and responsibility against a background of denial of objective truth and universal norms of conduct; is characterized by prevailing anguish, dread, fear, pessimism, despair; is generally atheistic, although its modern originator, Soren Kierkegaard (d. 1855), and Gabriel Marcel (d. 1973) attempted to give it a Christian orien-

tation. Pius XII called it "the new erroneous philosophy which, opposing itself to idealism, immanentism and pragmatism, has assumed the name of existentialism, since it concerns itself only with the existence of individual things and neglects all consideration of their immutable essences" (Encyclical *Humani Generis,* August 12, 1950).

Exorcism: (1) Driving out evil' spirits; a rite in which evil spirits are charged and commanded on the authority of God and with the prayer of the Church to depart from a person or to cease causing harm to a person suffering from diabolical possession or obsession. The sacramental is officially administered by a priest delegated for the purpose by the bishop of the place. Elements of the rite include the Litany of Saints; recitation of the Our Father, one or more creeds, and other prayers; specific prayers of exorcism; the reading of Gospel passages and use of the Sign of the Cross. Private exorcism for the liberation of a person from the strong influence of evil spirits, through prayer and the use of sacramentals like holy water, can be done by anyone. (2) Exorcisms which do not imply the conditions of either diabolical possession or obsession form part of the ceremony of baptism, and are also included in formulas for various blessings; e.g., of water.

F

Faculties: Grants of jurisdiction or authority by the law of the Church or superiors (pope, bishop, religious superior) for exercise of the powers of holy orders; e.g., priests are given faculties to hear confessions, officiate at weddings; bishops are given faculties to grant dispensations, etc.

Faith: In religion, faith has several aspects. Catholic doctrine calls faith the assent of the mind to truths revealed by God, the assent being made with the help of grace and by command of the will on account of the authority and trustworthiness of God revealing. The term faith also refers to the truths that are believed (content of faith) and to the way in which a person, in response to Christ, gives witness to and expresses belief in daily life (living faith). All of these elements, and more, are included in the following statement: " 'The obedience of faith' (Rom. 16:26; 1:5; 2 Cor. 10:5-6) must be given to God who reveals, an obedience by which man entrusts his whole self freely to God, offering 'the full submission of intellect and will to God who reveals' (First Vatican Council, *Dogmatic Constitution on the Catholic Faith,* Chap. 3), and freely assenting to the truth revealed by Him. If this faith is to be shown, the grace of God and the interior help of the Holy Spirit must precede and assist, moving the heart and turning it to God, opening the eyes of the mind, and giving 'joy and ease to everyone in assenting to the truth and believing it' " (Second Council of Orange, Canon 7) (Second Vatican Council, *Constitution on Revelation,* No. 5). Faith is necessary for salvation.

Faith, Rule of: The norm or standard of religious belief. The Catholic doctrine is that belief must be professed in the divinely revealed truths in the Bible and tradition as interpreted and proposed by the infallible teaching authority of the Church.

Fast, Eucharistic: Abstinence from food and drink, except water and medicine, is required for one hour before the reception of the Eucharist. Persons who are advanced in age or suffer from infirmity or illness, together with those who care for them, can receive Holy Communion even if they have not abstained from food and drink for an hour. A priest celebrating two or three Masses on the same day can eat and drink something before the second or third Mass without regard for the hour limit.

Father: A title of priests, who are regarded as spiritual fathers because they are the ordinary ministers of baptism, by which persons are born to supernatural life, and because of

their pastoral service to their people.

Fear: A mental state caused by the apprehension of present or future danger. Grave fear does not necessarily remove moral responsibility for an act, but may lessen it.

Fisherman's Ring: A signet ring engraved with the image of St. Peter fishing from a boat, and encircled with the name of the reigning pope. It is not worn by the pope. It is used to seal briefs, and is destroyed after each pope's death.

Forgiveness of Sin: Catholics believe that sins are forgiven by God through the mediation of Christ in view of the repentance of the sinner and by means of the sacrament of penance.

Fortitude: Courage to face dangers or hardships for the sake of what is good; one of the four cardinal virtues and one of the seven gifts of the Holy Spirit.

Fortune Telling: Attempting to predict the future or the occult by means of cards, palm reading, etc.; a form of divination, prohibited by the First Commandment.

Forum: The sphere in which ecclesiastical authority or jurisdiction is exercised. (1) External: Authority is exercised in the external forum to deal with matters affecting the public welfare of the Church and its members. Those who have such authority because of their office (e.g., diocesan bishops) are called *ordinaries.* (2) Internal: Authority is exercised in the internal forum to deal with matters affecting the private spiritual good of individuals. The sacramental forum is the sphere in which the sacrament of penance is administered; other exercises of jurisdiction in the internal forum take place in the non-sacramental forum.

Freedom, Religious: The Second Vatican Council declared that the right to religious freedom in civil society "means that all men are to be immune from coercion on the part of individuals or of social groups and of any human power, in such wise that in matters religious no one is to be forced to act in a manner contrary to his own beliefs. Nor is anyone to be restrained from acting in accordance with his own beliefs, whether privately or publicly, whether alone or in association with others, within due limits" of requirements for the common good. The foundation of this right in civil society is the "very dignity of the human person" (*Declaration on Religious Freedom,* No. 2). The conciliar statement did not deal with the subject of freedom within the Church. It noted the responsibility of the faithful "carefully to attend to the sacred and certain doctrine of the Church" (No. 14).

Freemasons: A fraternal order which originated in London in 1717 with the formation of the first Grand Lodge of Freemasons. From England, the order spread to Europe and elsewhere. Its principles and basic rituals embody a naturalistic religion, active participation in which is incompatible with Christian faith and practice. For serious doctrinal and pastoral reasons, Catholics were forbidden to join the Freemasons under penalty of excommunication, according to church law before 1983. The prohibition remains in force but without the penalty of excommunication, according to the revised Code of Canon Law in force since November 27, 1983.

Free Will: The faculty or capability of making a reasonable choice among several alternatives. Freedom of will underlies the possibility and fact of moral responsibility.

Friar: Term applied to members of mendicant orders to distinguish them from members of monastic orders.

Fruits of the Holy Spirit: Charity, joy, peace, patience, benignity, goodness, longanimity, mildness, faith, modesty, continence, chastity.

G

Gehenna: Greek form of a Jewish name, *Gehinnom,* for a valley near Jerusalem, the site of Moloch worship; used as a synonym for hell.

Genuflection: Bending of the knee, a natural sign of adoration or reverence, as when persons genuflect with the right knee in passing before the tabernacle to acknowledge the Eucharistic presence of Christ.

Gethsemani: A Hebrew word meaning oil press, designating the place on the Mount of Olives where Christ prayed and suffered in agony the night before He died.

Gifts of the Holy Spirit: Supernatural habits disposing a person to respond promptly to the inspiration of grace; promised by Christ and communicated through the Holy Spirit, especially in the sacrament of confirmation. They are: wisdom, understanding, counsel, fortitude, knowledge, piety, fear of the Lord.

Gluttony: An inordinate appetite for food and drink; one of the seven capital sins.

God: The infinitely perfect Supreme Being, uncaused and absolutely self-sufficient, eternal; the Creator and final end of all things. The one God subsists in three equal Persons: the Father and the Son and the Holy Spirit. God, although transcendent and distinct from the universe, is present and active in the world in realization of His plan for the salvation of men, principally through revelation, the operations of the Holy Spirit, the life and ministry of Christ, and the continuation of Christ's ministry in the Church. The existence of God is an article of faith, clearly communicated in divine revelation. Even without this revelation, however, the Church teaches, in a declaration by the First Vatican Council, that men can acquire certain knowledge of the existence of God and some of His attributes. This can be done on the bases of principles of reason and reflection on human experience. Nonrevealed arguments or demonstrations for the existence of God have been developed from the principle of causality; the contingency of man and the universe; the existence of design, change and movement in the universe; human awareness of moral responsibility; widespread human testimony to the existence of God.

Grace: A free gift of God to men (and angels), grace is a created sharing or participation in the life of God. It is given to men through the merits of Christ and is communicated by the Holy Spirit. It is necessary for salvation. The principal means of grace are the sacraments (especially the Eucharist), prayer and good works. Sanctifying or habitual grace makes men holy and pleasing to God, adopted children of God, members of Christ, temples of the Holy Spirit, heirs of heaven capable of supernaturally meritorious acts. With grace, God gives men the supernatural virtues and gifts of the Holy Spirit. The sacraments of baptism and penance were instituted to give grace to those who do not have it; the other sacraments, to increase it in those already in the state of grace. The means for growth in holiness, or the increase of grace, are prayer, the sacraments, and good works. Sanctifying grace is lost by the commission of serious sin. Each sacrament confers sanctifying grace for the special purpose of the sacrament; in this context, grace is called sacramental grace. Actual grace is a supernatural help of God which enlightens and strengthens a person to do good and to avoid evil. It is not a permanent quality, like sanctifying grace. It is necessary for the performance of supernatural acts. It can be resisted and refused. Persons in the state of serious sin are given actual grace to lead them to repentance.

Grace at Meals: Prayers said before meals, asking a blessing of God, and after meals, giving thanks to God. In addition to traditional prayers for these purposes, many variations suitable for different occasions are possible, at personal option.

H

Habit: (1) A disposition to do things easily, given with grace (and therefore supernatural) and/or acquired by repetition of similar acts. (2) The distinctive garb worn by Religious.

Hagiography: Writings or documents about saints and other holy persons.

Heaven: The state of those who, having achieved salvation, are in glory with God and enjoy the beatific vision. The phrase, kingdom of heaven, refers to the order or kingdom of God, grace, salvation.

Hell: The state of punishment of the damned — i.e., those who die in mortal sin, in a condition of self-alienation from God and of opposition to the divine plan of salvation. The punishment of hell begins immediately after death and lasts forever.

Heresy: The formal and obstinate denial or doubt by a baptized person, who remains a nominal Christian, of any truth which must be believed as a matter of divine and Catholic faith. Formal heresy involves deliberate resistance to the authority of God, who communicates revelation through Scripture and tradition and the teaching authority of the Church. Obstinate refusal to accept the infallible teaching of the Church constitutes the canonical crime of heresy. Formal heretics automatically incur the penalty of excommunication (Canon 1364 of the Code of Canon Law). Material heretics are those who, in good faith and without formal obstinacy, do not accept articles or matters of divine and Catholic faith. Heresies have been significant not only as disruptions of unity of faith but also as occasions for the clarification and development of doctrine.

Heterodoxy: False doctrine, teaching or belief; a departure from truth.

Holy See: (1) The diocese of the pope, Rome. (2) The pope himself and/or the various officials and bodies of the Church's central administration at Vatican City — the Roman Curia — which act in the name and by authority of the pope.

Holy Spirit: God the Holy Spirit, third Person of the Holy Trinity, who proceeds from the Father and the Son and with whom He is equal in every respect; inspirer of the prophets and writers of sacred Scripture; promised by Christ to the Apostles as their advocate and strengthener; appeared in the form of a dove at the baptism of Christ and as tongues of fire at His descent upon the Apostles; soul of the Church and guarantor, by His abiding presence and action, of truth in doctrine; communicator of grace to men, for which reason He is called the sanctifier.

Holy Water: Water blessed by the Church and used as a sacramental, a practice which originated in apostolic times.

Homosexuality: The condition of a person whose sexual orientation is toward persons of the same rather than the opposite sex. The condition, usually discovered during adolescence rather than deliberately caused, is not sinful in itself. Homosexual acts are seriously sinful in themselves; subjective responsibility for such acts, however, may be conditioned and diminished by compulsion and related factors.

Hope: One of the three theological virtues, by which one firmly trusts that God wills his salvation and will give him the means to attain it.

Host, The Sacred: The bread under whose appearances Christ is and remains present in a unique, sacramental manner after the consecration which takes place during Mass.

Humility: A virtue which induces a person to evaluate himself at his true worth, to recognize his dependence on God, and to give glory to God for the good he has and can do.

Hypostatic Union: The union of the human and divine natures in the one divine Person of Christ.

I

Icons: Byzantine-style paintings or representations of Christ, the Blessed Virgin and other saints, venerated in the Eastern Churches where they take the place of statues.

Idolatry: Worship of any but the true God; a violation of the First Commandment.

I H S: In Greek, the first three letters of the name of Jesus — Iota, Eta, Sigma.

Immortality: The survival and continuing existence of the human soul after death.

Impurity: Unlawful indulgence in sexual pleasure.

Incardination: The affiliation of a priest to his diocese. Every secular priest must belong to a certain diocese. Similarly, every priest of a religious institute must belong to some jurisdiction of his institute; this affiliation, however, is not called incardination.

Incarnation: (1) The coming-into-flesh or taking of human nature by the Second Person of the Trinity. He became human as the Son of Mary, being miraculously conceived by the power of the Holy Spirit, without ceasing to be divine. His divine Person hypostatically unites His divine and human natures. (2) The supernatural mystery coextensive with Christ from the moment of His human conception and continuing through His life on earth; His sufferings and death; His resurrection from the dead and ascension to glory with the Father; His sending, with the Father, of the Holy Spirit upon the Apostles and the Church; and His unending mediation with the Father for the salvation of men.

Incest: Sexual intercourse with relatives by blood or marriage; a sin of impurity and also a grave violation of the natural reverence due to relatives. Other sins of impurity (desire, etc.) concerning relatives have the nature of incest.

Inculturation: This was one of the subjects of an address delivered by Pope John Paul II February 15, 1982, at a meeting in Lagos with the bishops of Nigeria. "An important aspect of your own evangelizing role is the whole dimension of the inculturation of the Gospel into the lives of your people. The Church truly respects the culture of each people. In offering the Gospel message, the Church does not intend to destroy or to abolish what is good and beautiful. In fact, she recognizes many cultural values and, through the power of the Gospel, purifies and takes into Christian worship certain elements of a people's customs. The Church comes to bring Christ; she does not come to bring the culture of another race. Evangelization aims at penetrating and elevating culture by the power of the Gospel. It is through the Providence of God that the divine message is made incarnate and is communicated through the culture of each people. It is forever true that the path of culture is the path of man, and it is on this path that man encounters the one who embodies the values of all cultures and fully reveals the man of each culture to himself. The Gospel of Christ, the Incarnate Word, finds its home along the path of culture, and from this path it continues to offer its message of salvation and eternal life."

Index of Prohibited Books: A list of books which Catholics were formerly forbidden to read, possess or sell, under penalty of excommunication. The books were banned by the Holy See after publication because their treatment of matters of faith and morals and related subjects were judged to be erroneous or serious occasions of doctrinal error. The Congregation for the Doctrine of the Faith declared June 14, 1966, that the Index and its related penalties of excommunication no longer had the force of law in the Church. Persons are still obliged, however, to take normal precautions against occasions of doctrinal error.

Indifferentism: A theory that any one religion is as true and good — or false — as any other religion, and that it makes no difference, objectively, what religion one professes, if any. The theory is completely subjective, finding its justification entirely in personal choice without reference to or respect for objective validity. It is also self-contradictory, since it regards as equally acceptable — or unacceptable — the beliefs of all religions, which in fact are not only not all the same but are in some cases opposed to each other.

Indulgence: The remission before God of the temporal punishment due for sins already forgiven as far as their guilt is concerned, which a follower of Christ — with the proper dispositions and under certain determined conditions — acquires through the intervention of the Church. The Church grants indulgences in accordance with doctrine concerning the superabundant merits of Christ and the saints, the Power of the Keys, and the sharing of spiritual goods in the communion of saints. (1) Partial Indulgence: Properly disposed faithful who perform an action to which a partial indulgence is attached obtain, in addition to the remission of temporal punishment acquired by the action itself, an equal remission of punishment through the intervention of the Church. (This grant was formerly designated in terms of days and years.) The proper dispositions for gaining a partial indulgence are sorrow for sin and freedom from serious sin, performance of the required good work, and the intention (which can be general or immediate) to gain the indulgence. 2) Plenary Indulgence: To gain a plenary indulgence, it is necessary for a person to be free of all attachment to sin, to perform the work to which the indulgence is attached, and to fulfill the three conditions of sacramental confession, Eucharistic Communion and prayer for the intention of the pope.

Indult: A favor or privilege granted by competent ecclesiastical authority, giving permission to do something not allowed by the common law of the Church.

Infant Jesus of Prague: An 18-inch-high wooden statue of the Child Jesus which has figured in a form of devotion to the Holy Childhood and Kingship of Christ since the 17th century. Of uncertain origin, the statue was presented by Princess Polixena to the Carmelites of Our Lady of Victory Church, Prague, in 1628.

Infused Virtues: The theological virtues of faith, hope and charity; principles or capabilities of supernatural action, they are given with sanctifying grace by God rather than acquired by repeated acts of a person. They can be increased by practice; they are lost by contrary acts. Natural-acquired moral virtues, like the cardinal virtues of prudence, justice, temperance and fortitude, can be considered infused in a person whose state of grace gives that person supernatural orientation.

I N R I: The first letters of words in the Latin inscription atop the cross on which Christ was crucified: (I)esus (N)azaraenus, (R)ex (I)udaeorum — Jesus of Nazareth, King of the Jews.

Insemination, Artificial: The implanting of human semen by some means other than consummation of natural marital intercourse. In view of the principle that procreation should result only from marital intercourse, donor insemination is not permissible. The use of legitimate artificial means to further the fruitfulness of marital intercourse is permissible.

In Sin: The condition of a person called spiritually dead because he does not possess sanctifying grace, the principle of supernatural life, action and merit. Such grace can be regained through repentance.

Intercommunion: The common celebration and reception of the Eucharist by members of different Christian churches; a pivotal issue in ecumenical theory and practice. Catholic participation and intercommunion in the eucharistic liturgy of another church without a valid priesthood and with a variant eucharistic belief is out of order. Under certain conditions, other Christians may receive the Eucharist in the Catholic Church. Intercommunion is acceptable to some Protestant churches and unacceptable to others.

Interregnum: The period of time between the death of a pope and the election of his successor. Another term applied to the period is *Sede vacante,* meaning the See (of Rome) being vacant. The main concerns during an interregnum are matters connected with the death and burial of the pope, the election of his successor, and the maintenance of ordinary routine for the proper functioning of the Roman Curia and the Diocese of Rome.

Intinction: A method of administering Holy Communion under the dual appearances of bread and wine, in which the consecrated host is dipped in the consecrated wine before being given to the communicant. The administering of Holy Communion in this manner, which has been traditional in Eastern-Rite liturgies, was authorized in the Roman Rite for various occasions by the *Constitution on the Sacred Liturgy* promulgated by the Second Vatican Council.

Irenicism: Peace-seeking, conciliation, as opposed to polemics; an important element in ecumenism, provided it furthers pursuit of the Christian unity willed by Christ without degenerating into a peace-at-any-price disregard for religious truth.

Irregularity: An impediment to the lawful reception or exercise of holy orders. The Church instituted irregularities — which include apostasy, heresy, homicide, attempted suicide — out of reverence for the dignity of the sacraments.

Itinerarium: Prayers for a spiritually profitable journey.

J

Jesus: The name of Jesus, meaning Savior in Christian usage, derived from the Aramaic and Hebrew *Yeshua* and *Joshua,* meaning *Yahweh* is salvation.

Judgment: (1) Last or final judgment: Final judgment by Christ, at the end of the world and the general resurrection. (2) Particular judgment: The judgment that takes place immediately after a person's death, portending heaven, hell or purgatory.

Jurisdiction: Right, power, authority to rule. Jurisdiction in the Church is of divine institution; has pastoral service for its purpose; includes legislative, judicial and executive authority; can be exercised only by persons with the power of orders. (1) Ordinary jurisdiction is attached to ecclesiastical offices by law; the officeholders, called Ordinaries, have authority over those who are subject to them. (2) Delegated jurisdiction is that which is granted to persons rather than attached to offices. Its extent depends on the terms of the delegation.

Justice: One of the four cardinal virtues by which a person gives to others what is due to them as a matter of right.

Justification: The act by which God makes a person just, and the consequent change in the spiritual status of a person, from sin to grace; the remission of sin and the infusion of sanctifying grace through the merits of Christ and the action of the Holy Spirit.

K

Kerygma: Proclaiming the word of God, in the manner of the Apostles, as here and now effective for salvation. This method of preaching or instruction, centered on Christ and geared to the facts and themes of salvation history, is designed to dispose people to faith in Christ and/or to intensify the experience and practice of that faith in those who have it.

Keys, Power of the: Spiritual authority and jurisdiction in the Church, symbolized by the keys of the kingdom of heaven. Christ promised the keys to St. Peter, as head-to-be of the Church (Mt. 16:19), and commissioned him with full pastoral responsibility to feed His lambs and sheep (Jn. 21:15-17). The pope, as the successor of St. Peter, has this power in a primary and supreme manner. The bishops of the Church also have the power, in union with and subordinate to the pope. Priests share in it through holy orders and the delega-

tion of authority. Examples of the application of the Power of the Keys are the exercise of teaching and pastoral authority by the pope and bishops, the absolving of sins in the sacrament of penance, the granting of indulgences, the imposing of spiritual penalties on persons who commit certain serious sins.

L

Laicization: The process by which a man ordained to holy orders is relieved of the obligations of orders and the ministry and is returned to the status of a lay person.

Languages of the Church: The first language in church use, for divine worship and the conduct of ecclesiastical affairs, was Aramaic, the language of the first Christians in and around Jerusalem. As the Church spread westward, Greek was adopted and prevailed until the third century when it was supplanted by Latin for official use in the West. According to traditions established very early in churches of the Eastern Rites, many different languages were adopted for use in divine worship and for the conduct of ecclesiastical affairs. The practice was, and still is, to use the vernacular or a language closely related to the common tongue of the people. In the Western Church, Latin prevailed as the general official language until the promulgation on December 4, 1963, of the *Constitution on the Sacred Liturgy* by the second session of the Second Vatican Council. Since that time, vernacular languages have come into use in the Mass, administration of the sacraments, and the Liturgy of the Hours. The change was introduced in order to make the prayers and ceremonies of divine worship more informative and meaningful to all. Latin, however, remains the official language for documents of the Holy See, administrative and procedural matters.

Law: An ordinance or rule governing the activity of things. (1) Natural law: Moral norms corresponding to man's nature by which he orders his conduct toward God, neighbor, society and himself. This law, which is rooted in human nature, is of divine origin, can be known by the use of reason, and binds all men having the use of reason. The Ten Commandments are declarations and amplifications of natural law. The primary precepts of natural law, to do good and to avoid evil, are universally recognized, despite differences with respect to understanding and application resulting from different philosophies of good and evil. (2) Divine positive law: That which has been revealed by God. Among its essentials are the twin precepts of love of God and love of neighbor, and the Ten Commandments. (3) Ecclesiastical law: That which is established by the Church for the spiritual welfare of the faithful and the orderly conduct of ecclesiastical affairs. (4) Civil law: That which is established by a socio-political community for the common good.

Life in Outer Space: Whether rational life exists on other bodies in the universe, besides earth, is a question for scientific investigation to settle. The possibility can be granted, without prejudice to the body of revealed truth.

Limbo: The limbo of the fathers was the state of rest and natural happiness after death enjoyed by the just of pre-Christian times until they were admitted to heaven following the ascension of Christ. Belief in this matter is stated in the Apostles' Creed. The existence of a limbo for unbaptized persons of infant status — a state of rest and natural happiness — has never been formally defined.

Litany: A prayer in the form of responsive petition; e.g., St. Joseph, pray for us, etc. Examples are the litanies of Loreto (Litany of the Blessed Mother), the Holy Name, All Saints, the Sacred Heart, the Precious Blood, St. Joseph, Litany for the Dying.

Loreto, House of: A Marian shrine in Loreto, Italy, consisting of the home of the Holy Family which, according to an old tradition, was transported in a miraculous manner from Nazareth to Dalmatia and finally to Loreto between 1291 and 1294. Investigations conducted shortly after the appearance of the structure in Loreto revealed that its dimensions matched those of the house of the Holy Family missing from its place of enshrinement in a basilica at Nazareth. Among the many popes who regarded it with high honor was John XXIII, who went there on pilgrimage October 4, 1962. The house of the Holy Family is enshrined in the Basilica of Our Lady.

Lust: A disorderly desire for sexual pleasure; one of the seven capital sins.

M

Magi: In the Infancy Narrative of St. Matthew's Gospel (2:1-12), three wise men from the East whose visit and homage to the Child Jesus at Bethlehem indicated Christ's manifestation of himself to non-Jewish people. The narrative teaches the universality of salvation. The traditional names of the Magi are Caspar, Melchior and Balthasar.

Magnificat: The canticle or hymn of the Virgin Mary on the occasion of her visitation to her cousin Elizabeth (Lk. 1:46-55). It is an expression of praise, thanksgiving and acknowledgment of the great blessings given by God to Mary, the Mother of the Second Person of the Blessed Trinity made Man. The *Magnificat* is recited in the Liturgy of the Hours as part of the Evening Prayer.

Martyr: A Greek word, meaning witness, denoting one who voluntarily suffered death for the faith or some Christian virtue.

Martyrology: A catalogue of martyrs and other saints, arranged according to the calendar. The *Roman Martyrology* contains the official list of saints venerated by the Church. Additions to the list are made in beatification and canonization decrees of the Congregation for the Causes of Saints.

Mass for the People: On Sundays

and certain feasts throughout the year, pastors are required to offer Mass for the faithful committed to their care. If they cannot offer the Mass on these days, they must do so at a later date or provide that another priest offer the Mass.

Master of Novices: The person in charge of the training and formation of candidates for an institute of consecrated life during novitiate.

Materialism: Theory which holds that matter is the only reality and everything in existence is merely a manifestation of matter; there is no such thing as spirit, and the supernatural does not exist. Materialism is incompatible with Christian doctrine.

Meditation: Mental, as distinguished from vocal, prayer, in which thoughts, affections and resolutions of the will predominate. There is a meditative element to all forms of prayer, which always involves the raising of the heart and mind to God.

Mendicants: A term derived from Latin and meaning beggars, applied to members of religious orders without property rights; the members, accordingly, worked or begged for their support. The original mendicants were Franciscans and Dominicans in the early 13th century; later, the Carmelites, Augustinians, Servites and others were given the mendicant title and privileges, with respect to exemption from episcopal jurisdiction and wide faculties for preaching and administering the sacrament of penance. The practice of begging is limited at the present time, although it is still allowed with the permission of competent superiors and bishops. Mendicants are supported by free-will offerings and income received for spiritual services and other work.

Mercy, Divine: The love and goodness of God, manifested particularly in a time of need.

Merit: In religion, the right to a supernatural reward for good works freely done for a supernatural motive by a person in the state of and with the assistance of grace. The right to

such reward is from God, who binds himself to give it. Accordingly, good works, as described, are meritorious for salvation.

Metempsychosis: Theory of the passage or migration of the human soul after death from one body to another for the purpose of purification from guilt. The theory denies the unity of the soul and human personality, and the doctrine of individual moral responsibility.

Millennium: A thousand-year reign of Christ and the just upon earth before the end of the world. This belief of the Millenarians, Chiliasts, and some sects of modern times is based on an erroneous interpretation of Rv. 20.

Miracles: Observable events or effects in the physical or moral order of things, with reference to salvation, which cannot be explained by the ordinary operation of laws of nature and which, therefore, are attributed to the direct action of God. They make known, in an unusual way, the concern and intervention of God in human affairs for the salvation of men. The most striking examples are the miracles worked by Christ. Numbering about 35, they included His own resurrection; the raising of three persons to life (Lazarus, the daughter of Jairus, the son of the widow of Naim); the healing of blind, leprous and other persons; nature miracles; and prophecies, or miracles of the intellectual order. The Church believes it is reasonable to accept miracles as manifestations of divine power for purposes of salvation. God, who created the laws of nature, is their master; hence, without disturbing the ordinary course of things, He can — and has in the course of history before and after Christ — occasionally set aside these laws and has also produced effects beyond their power of operation. The Church does not call miraculous anything which does not admit of easy explanation; on the contrary, miracles are admitted only when the events have a bearing on the order of grace and every possible natural explanation has been tried and found wanting.

Missal: A liturgical book of Roman Rite also called the *Sacramentary,* containing the celebrant's prayers of the Mass, along with general instructions and ceremonial directives. The Latin text of the new *Roman Missal,* replacing the one authorized by the Council of Trent in the 16th century, was published by the Vatican Polyglot Press in 1970. Its use in English was made mandatory in the U.S. from December 1, 1974. Readings and scriptural responsories formerly in the missal are contained in the *Lectionary*.

Missiology: Study of the missionary nature, constitution and activity of the Church in all aspects: theological reasons for missionary activity, laws and instructions of the Holy See, history of the missions, social and cultural background, methods, norms for carrying on missionary work.

Mission: (1) Strictly, it means being sent to perform a certain work, such as the mission of Christ to redeem mankind, the mission of the Apostles and the Church and its members to perpetuate the prophetic, priestly and royal mission of Christ. (2) A place where: the Gospel has not been proclaimed; the Church has not been firmly established; the Church, although established, is weak. (3) An ecclesiastical territory with the simplest kind of canonical organization, under the jurisdiction of the Congregation for the Evangelization of Peoples. (4) A church or chapel without a resident priest. (5) A special course of sermons and spiritual exercises conducted in parishes for the purpose of renewing and deepening the spiritual life of the faithful and for the conversion of lapsed Catholics.

Modernism: The "synthesis of all heresies," which appeared near the beginning of the 20th century. It undermines the objective validity of religious beliefs and practices which, it contends, are products of the subconscious developed by mankind un-

der the stimulus of a religious sense. It holds that the existence of a personal God cannot be demonstrated, the Bible is not inspired, Christ is not divine, nor did He establish the Church or institute the sacraments. A special danger lies in Modernism, which is still influential, because it uses Catholic terms with perverted meanings. St. Pius X condemned 65 propositions of Modernism in 1907 in the decree *Lamentabili* and issued the encyclical *Pascendi* to explain and analyze its errors.

Monastery: The dwelling place, as well as the community thereof, of monks belonging to the Benedictine and Benedictine-related orders like the Cistercians and Carthusians. Distinctive of monasteries are: their separation from the world; the enclosure or cloister; the permanence or stability of attachment characteristic of their members, wherever they might be; autonomous government in accordance with a monastic rule, like that of St. Benedict in the West or of St. Basil in the East; the special dedication of its members to the community celebration of the liturgy as well as to work that is suitable to the surrounding area and the needs of its people. Monastic superiors of men have such titles as abbot and prior; of women, abbess and prioress. In most essentials, an abbey is the same as a monastery.

Monk: A member of a monastic order — e.g., the Benedictines, the Benedictine-related Cistercians and Carthusians, and the Basilians, who bind themselves by religious profession to stable attachment to a monastery, the contemplative life and the work of their community. In popular use, the title is wrongly applied to many men Religious who really are not monks.

Monotheism: Belief in and worship of one God.

Morality: Conformity or difformity of behavior to standards of right conduct.

Mortification: Acts of self-discipline, including prayer, hardship, austerities and penances undertaken for the sake of progress in virtue.

Motu Proprio: A Latin phrase designating a document issued by a pope on his own initiative. Documents of this kind often concern administrative matters.

Mysteries of Faith: Supernatural truths whose existence cannot be known without revelation by God and whose intrinsic truth, while not contrary to reason, can never be wholly understood even after revelation. These mysteries are above reason, not against reason. Among them are the divine mysteries of the Trinity, Incarnation and Eucharist. Some mysteries — e.g., concerning God's attributes — can be known by reason without revelation, although they cannot be fully understood.

N

Necromancy: Supposed communication with the dead; a form of divination.

Non-Expedit: A Latin expression, meaning it is not expedient (fitting, proper), used to state a prohibition or refusal of permission.

Novena: A term designating public or private devotional practices over a period of nine consecutive days; or, by extension, over a period of nine weeks, in which one day a week is set aside for the devotions.

Novice: A man or woman preparing, in a formal period of trial and formation called a *novitiate*, for membership in an institute of consecrated religious life. The novitiate lasts a minimum of 12 and a maximum of 24 months; at its conclusion, the novice professes temporary vows of poverty, chastity and obedience. The period of novitiate must include 12 months in the novitiate community and can include one or more periods of apostolic engagement outside the novitiate community.

Nun: (1) Strictly, a member of a religious order of women with solemn vows (*moniales*). (2) In general, all women Religious, even those in sim-

ple vows who are more properly called sisters.

Nunc Dimittis: The canticle or hymn of Simeon at the sight of Jesus at the Temple on the occasion of His presentation (Lk. 2:29-32). It is an expression of joy and thanksgiving for the blessing of having lived to see the Messiah. It is prescribed for use in the Night Prayer of the Liturgy of the Hours.

O

Oath: Calling upon God to witness the truth of a statement. Violating an oath, e.g., by perjury in court, or taking an oath without sufficient reason, is a violation of the honor due to God.

Obedience: Submission to one in authority. General obligations of obedience fall under the Fourth Commandment. The vow of obedience professed by Religious is one of the evangelical counsels.

Obsession, Diabolical: The extraordinary state of one who is seriously molested by evil spirits in an external manner. Obsession is more than just temptation.

Occultism: Practices involving ceremonies, rituals, chants, incantations, other cult-related activities intended to affect the course of nature, the lives of practitioners and others, through esoteric powers of magic, diabolical or other forces; one of many forms of superstition.

Octave: A period of eight days given over to the celebration of a major feast such as Easter.

Oils, Holy: The oils consecrated by bishops on Holy Thursday or another suitable day, and by priests under certain conditions for use in certain sacraments and consecrations. (1) The oil of catechumens (olive or vegetable oil), used at baptism; also, poured with chrism into the baptismal water blessed in Easter Vigil ceremonies. (2) Chrism (olive or vegetable oil mixed with balm), used at baptism, in confirmation, at the ordination of a priest and bishop, in the dedication of churches and altars. (3)

Oil of the sick (olive or vegetable oil) used in anointing the sick.

Oratory: A chapel.

Ordinariate: An ecclesiastical jurisdiction for special purposes and people. Examples are Eastern-Rite ordinariates in places where Eastern-Rite dioceses do not exist.

Ordinary: One who has the jurisdiction of an office: the pope, diocesan bishops, vicars general, prelates of missionary territories, vicars apostolic, prefects apostolic, vicars capitular during the vacancy of a see, superiors general, abbots primate and other major superiors of men Religious.

Ordination: The consecration of sacred ministers for divine worship and the service of people in things pertaining to God. The power of ordination comes from Christ and the Church, and must be conferred by a minister capable of communicating it.

Organ Transplants: The transplanting of organs from one person to another is permissible provided it is done with the consent of the concerned parties and does not result in the death or essential mutilation of the donor. Advances in methods and technology have increased the range of transplant possibilities in recent years.

Original Sin: The sin of Adam (Gen. 2:8 to 3:24), personal to him and passed on to all persons as a state of privation of grace. Despite this privation and the related wounding of human nature and weakening of natural powers, original sin leaves unchanged all that man himself is by nature. The scriptural basis of the doctrine was stated especially by St. Paul in 1 Cor. 15:21, ff., and Rom. 5:12-21. Original sin is remitted by baptism and incorporation in Christ, through whom grace is given to persons.

P

Paganism: A term referring to religions other than Christianity, Judaism and Mohammedanism.

Palms: Blessed palms are a sac-ramental. They are blessed and distributed on the Sunday of the Passion in commemoration of the triumphant entrance of Christ into Jerusalem. Ashes of the burnt palms are used on Ash Wednesday.

Pantheism: Theory that all things are part of God, divine, in the sense that God realizes himself as the ultimate reality of matter or spirit through being and/or becoming all things that have been, are, and will be. The theory leads to hopeless confusion of the Creator and the created realm of being, identifies evil with good, and involves many inherent contradictions.

Papal Election: The pope is elected by members of the College of Cardinals in a secret conclave or meeting convened ordinarily in secluded quarters of the Vatican Palace between 15 and 20 days after the death of his predecessor. Cardinals under the age of 80, totaling no more than 120, are eligible to participate in a papal election. The ordinary manner of election is by scrutiny, with two votes each morning and afternoon in the Sistine Chapel until one of the candidates receives a two-thirds plus one vote majority. Ordinarily, the first indication that a new pope has been elected is a plume of white smoke rising from the Vatican on burning of the last ballots. The pope is elected for life. If one should resign, a new pope would be elected.

Paraclete: A title of the Holy Spirit meaning, in Greek, Advocate, Consoler.

Parental Duties: All duties related to the obligation of parents to provide for the welfare of their children. These obligations fall under the Fourth Commandment.

Parish: A community of the faithful served by a pastor charged with responsibility for providing them with full pastoral service. Most parishes are territorial, embracing all of the faithful in a certain area of a diocese: some are personal or national, for certain classes of people, without strict regard for their places of residence.

Parousia: The coming, or saving presence, of Christ which will mark the completion of salvation history and the coming to perfection of God's kingdom at the end of the world.

Paschal Candle: A large candle, symbolic of the risen Christ, blessed and lighted on the Easter Vigil and placed at the side of the altar until the end of the Easter season. Traditionally it is ornamented with five large grains of incense, representing the wounds of Christ, inserted in the form of a cross; the Greek letters Alpha and Omega, symbolizing Christ the beginning and end of all things, at the top and bottom of the shaft of the cross; and the figures of the current year of salvation in the quadrants formed by the cross. The candle is used to light the baptismal candles of newly baptized persons; it is also used as a symbol of resurrection in funeral liturgies.

Paschal Precept: Church law requiring reception of the Eucharist in the Easter season unless, for a just cause, once-a-year reception takes place at another time. (See *Easter Duty, Season.*)

Passion of Christ: Sufferings of Christ, recorded in the four Gospels.

Pastor: An ordained minister charged with responsibility for the doctrinal, sacramental and related service of people committed to his care; e.g., a bishop for the people in his diocese, a priest for the people of his parish.

Peace, Sign of: A gesture of greeting — e.g., a handshake — exchanged by the ministers and participants at Mass.

Pectoral Cross: A cross worn on a chain about the neck and over the breast by bishops and abbots as a mark of their office.

Penance or Penitence: (1) The spiritual change or conversion of mind and heart by which a person turns away from sin, and all that it implies, toward God, through a personal renewal under the influence of the Holy Spirit. In the apostolic constitution *Paenitemini,* Pope Paul VI called it "a religious, personal act which has as its aim love and surrender to God." Penance involves sorrow and contrition for sin, together with other internal and external acts of atonement. It serves the purposes of reestablishing in one's life the order of God's love and commandments, and of making satisfaction to God for sin. A divine precept states the necessity of penance for salvation: "Unless you do penance, you shall all likewise perish" (Lk. 13:3) . . . "Be converted and believe in the Gospel" (Mk. 1:15). In the penitential discipline of the Church, the various works of penance have been classified under the headings of prayer (interior), fasting and almsgiving (exterior). The Church has established minimum requirements for the common and social observance of the divine precept by Catholics — e.g., by requiring them to fast and/or abstain on certain days of the year. These observances, however, do not exhaust all the demands of the divine precept, whose fulfillment is a matter of personal responsibility; nor do they have any real value unless they proceed from the internal spirit and purpose of penance. Related to works of penance for sins actually committed are works of mortification. The purpose of the latter is to develop — through prayer, fasting, renunciations and similar actions — self-control and detachment from things which could otherwise become occasions of sin. (2) Penance is a virtue disposing a person to turn to God in sorrow for sin and to carry out works of amendment and atonement. (3) The sacrament of penance and sacramental penance.

Perjury: Taking a false oath, lying under oath, a violation of the honor due to God.

Persecution, Religious: A campaign waged against a church or other religious body by persons and governments intent on its destruction. The best known campaigns of this type against the Christian Church were the Roman persecutions which occurred intermittently from about 54 to the promulgation of the Edict of Milan in 313. The most extensive persecutions took place during the reigns of Nero, the first major Roman persecutor, Domitian, Trajan, Marcus Aurelius, and Diocletian. Besides the Roman persecutions, the Catholic Church has been subject to many others, including those of the 20th century in communist-controlled countries.

Personal Prelature: A special-purpose jurisdiction — for particular pastoral and missionary work, etc. — consisting of secular priests and deacons and open to lay persons willing to dedicate themselves to its apostolic works. The prelate in charge is an Ordinary, with the authority of office; he can establish a national or international seminary, incardinate its students and promote them to holy orders under the title of service to the prelature. The prelature is constituted and governed according to statutes laid down by the Holy See. Statutes define its relationship and mode of operation with the bishops of territories in which members live and work. Opus Dei is a personal prelature.

Peter's Pence: A collection made each year among Catholics for the maintenance of the pope and his works of charity. It was originally a tax of a penny on each house, and was collected on St. Peter's Day, whence the name. It originated in England in the eighth century.

Petition: One of the four purposes of prayer. In prayers of petition, persons ask of God the blessings they and others need.

Polytheism: Belief in and worship of many gods or divinities.

Poor Box: Alms-box; found in churches from the earliest days of Christianity.

Pope Joan: Alleged name of a woman falsely said to have been pope from 855-858, the years of the reign of Benedict III. The myth was not heard of before the 13th century.

Portiuncula: (1) Meaning little portion (of land), the Portiuncula was the chapel of Our Lady of the Angels near Assisi, Italy, which the Benedictines gave to St. Francis early in the 13th century. He repaired the chapel and made it the first church of the Franciscan Order. It is now enshrined in the Basilica of St. Mary of the Angels in Assisi. (2) The Portiuncula Indulgence, or Pardon of Assisi, was authorized by Honorius III in 1216. Originally, it could be gained for the souls in purgatory on August 2 only in the chapel of Our Lady of the Angels; later concessions extended the grant to other Franciscan and parish churches.

Possession, Diabolical: The extraordinary state of a person who is tormented from within by evil spirits who exercise strong influence over his powers of mind and body.

Postulant: One of several names used to designate a candidate for membership in a religious institute during the period before novitiate.

Poverty: (1) The quality or state of being poor, in actual destitution and need, or being poor in spirit. In the latter sense, poverty means the state of mind and disposition of persons who regard material things in proper perspective as gifts of God for the support of life and its reasonable enrichment, and for the service of others in need. It means freedom from unreasonable attachment to material things as ends in themselves, even though they may be possessed in small or large measure. (2) One of the evangelical counsels professed as a public vow by members of an institute of consecrated life. It involves the voluntary renunciation of rights of ownership and of independent use and disposal of material goods; or, the right of independent use and disposal, but not of the radical right of ownership. Religious institutes provide their members with necessary and useful goods and services from common resources. The manner in which goods are received and/or handled by Religious is determined by poverty of spirit and the rule and constitutions of their institute.

Pragmatism: Theory that the truth of ideas, concepts and values depends on their utility or capacity to serve a useful purpose rather than on their conformity with objective standards; also called utilitarianism.

Prayer: The raising of the mind and heart to God in adoration, thanksgiving, reparation and petition. Prayer, which is always mental because it involves thought and love of God, may be vocal, meditative, private and personal, social, and official. The official prayer of the Church as a worshiping community is called the liturgy.

Precepts: Commands or orders given to individuals or communities in particular cases; they establish law for concerned parties. Preceptive documents are issued by the pope, departments of the Roman Curia and other competent authority in the Church.

Presence of God: A devotional practice of increasing one's awareness of the presence and action of God in daily life.

Presumption: A violation of the theological virtue of hope, by which a person striving for salvation either relies too much on his own capabilities or expects God to do things which He cannot do, in keeping with His divine attributes, or does not will to do, according to His divine plan. Presumption is the opposite of despair.

Preternatural Gifts: Exceptional gifts, beyond the exigencies and powers of human nature, enjoyed by Adam in the state of original justice: immunity from suffering and death, superior knowledge, integrity or perfect control of the passions. These gifts were lost as the result of original sin; their loss, however, implied no impairment of the integrity of human nature.

Pride: Unreasonable self-esteem; one of the seven capital sins.

Priesthood of the Laity: Lay persons share in the priesthood of Christ in virtue of the sacraments of baptism and confirmation. They are not only joined with Christ for a life of union with Him but are also deputed by Him for participation in His mission, now carried on by the Church of worship. St. Peter called Christians "a royal priesthood" (1 Pt. 2:9) in this connection. St. Thomas Aquinas declared: "The sacramental characters (of baptism and confirmation) are nothing else than certain sharings of the priesthood of Christ, derived from Christ himself." The priesthood of the laity differs from the official ministerial priesthood of ordained priests and bishops — who have the power of holy orders for celebrating the Eucharist, administering the other sacraments, and providing pastoral care. The ministerial priesthood, by divine commission, serves the universal priesthood.

Primary Option: The life-choice of a person for or against God which shapes the basic orientation of moral conduct. A primary option for God does not preclude the possibility of mortal sin.

Prior: A superior or an assistant to an abbot in a monastery.

Privilege: A favor, an exemption from the obligation of a law. Privileges of various kinds, with respect to ecclesiastical laws, are granted by the pope, departments of the Roman Curia and other competent authority in the Church.

Probabilism: A moral system for use in cases of conscience which involve the obligation of doubtful laws. There is a general principle that a doubtful law does not bind. Probabilism, therefore, teaches that it is permissible to follow an opinion favoring liberty, provided the opinion is certainly and solidly probable. Probabilism may not be invoked when there is question of: a certain law or the certain obligation of a law; the certain right of another party; the validity of an action; something which is necessary for salvation.

Pro-Cathedral: A church used as a cathedral.

Promoter of the Faith: An official of the Congregation for the Causes of Saints, whose role in beatification and canonization procedures is to establish beyond reasonable doubt the validity of evidence regarding the holiness of prospective saints and miracles attributed to their intercession.

Prophecy: (1) The communication of divine revelation by inspired intermediaries, called prophets, between God and His people. Old Testament prophecy was unique in its origin and because of its ethical and religious content, which included disclosure of the saving will of Yahweh for the people, moral censures and warnings of divine punishment because of sin and violations of the Law and Covenant, in the form of promises, admonitions, reproaches and threats. Although Moses and other earlier figures are called prophets, the period of prophecy is generally dated from the early years of the monarchy to about 100 years after the Babylonian Exile. From that time on the written Law and its interpreters supplanted the prophets as guides of the people. Old Testament prophets are cited in the New Testament, with awareness that God spoke through them and that some of their oracles were fulfilled in Christ. John the Baptist is the outstanding prophetic figure in the New Testament. Christ never claimed the title of prophet for himself, although some people thought He was one. There were prophets in the early Church, and St. Paul mentioned the charism of prophecy in 1 Cor. 14:1-5. Prophecy disappeared after New Testament times. The Apocalypse or Book of Revelation is classified as the prophetic book of the New Testament. (2) In contemporary non-scriptural usage, the term is applied to the witness given by persons to the relevance of their beliefs in everyday life and action.

Province: (1) A territory comprising one archdiocese called the metropolitan see and one or more dioceses called suffragan sees. The head of the archdiocese, an archbishop, has metropolitan rights and responsibilities over the province. (2) A division of a religious order under the jurisdiction of a provincial superior.

Prudence: Practical wisdom and judgment regarding the choice and use of the best ways and means of doing good; one of the four cardinal virtues.

Punishment Due for Sin: The punishment which is a consequence of sin. It is of two kinds: (1) Eternal punishment is the punishment of hell, to which one becomes subject by the commission of mortal sin. Such punishment is remitted when mortal sin is forgiven. (2) Temporal punishment is a consequence of venial sin and/or forgiven mortal sin; it is not everlasting and may be remitted in this life by means of penance. Temporal punishment unremitted during this life is remitted by suffering in purgatory.

Purgatory: The state or condition in which those who have died in the state of grace, but with some attachment to sin, suffer for a time before they are admitted to the glory and happiness of heaven. In this state and period of passive suffering, they are purified of unrepented venial sins, satisfy the demands of divine justice for temporal punishment due for sins, and are thus converted to a state of worthiness of the beatific vision.

R

Racism: A theory which holds that any one or several of the different races of the human family are inherently superior or inferior to any one or several of the others. The teaching denies the essential unity of the human family, the equality and dignity of all men because of their common possession of the same human nature, and the participation of all men in the divine plan of redemption. It is radically opposed to the virtue of justice and the precept of love of neighbor. Differences of superiority and inferiority which do exist are the result of accidental factors operating in a wide variety of circumstances, and are in no way due to essential defects in any one or several of the branches of the one human family. The theory of racism, together with practices related to it, is incompatible with Christian doctrine.

Rash Judgment: Attributing faults to another without sufficient reason; a violation of the obligations of justice and charity.

Rationalism: A theory which makes the mind the measure and arbiter of all things, including religious truth. A product of the Enlightenment, it rejects the supernatural, divine revelation, and authoritative teaching by any church.

Recollection: Meditation, attitude of concentration or awareness of spiritual matters and things pertaining to salvation and the accomplishment of God's will.

Relativism: Theory which holds that all truth, including religious truth, is relative, i.e., not absolute, certain or unchanging; a product of agnosticism, indifferentism and an unwarranted extension of the notion of truth in positive science. Relativism is based on the tenet that certain knowledge of any and all truth is impossible. Therefore, no religion, philosophy or science can be said to possess the real truth; consequently, all religions, philosophies and sciences may be considered to have as much or as little of truth as any of the others.

Relics: The physical remains and effects of saints, which are considered worthy of veneration inasmuch as they are representative of persons in glory with God. First-class relics are parts of the bodies of saints, and instruments of their penance and death; second-class relics are objects which had some contact with their persons. Catholic doctrine condemns the view that relics are not worthy of veneration. In line with norms laid down by the Council of Trent and subsequent enactments, discipline concerning relics is subject to control by the Congregation for the Causes of Saints.

Religion: The adoration and service of God as expressed in divine worship and in daily life. Religion is concerned with all of the relations existing between God and man, and between man and man because of the central significance of God. Objectively considered, religion consists of a body of truth which is believed, a code of morality for the guidance of conduct, and a form of divine worship. Subjectively, it is a person's total response, theoretically and practically, to the demands of faith; it is living faith, personal engagement, self-commitment to God. Thus, by creed, code and cult, a person orders and directs his life in reference to God and, through what the love and service of God imply, to his fellow men and all things.

Reliquary: A vessel for the preservation and exposition of a relic; sometimes made like a small monstrance.

Reparation: The making of amends to God for sin committed; one of the four ends of prayer and the purpose of penance.

Reserved Case: A sin, or censure, absolution from which is reserved to religious superiors, bishops, the pope or confessors having special faculties. Reservations are made because of the serious nature and social effects of certain sins and censures.

Restitution: An act of reparation for an injury done to another. The injury may be caused by taking and/or retaining what belongs to another or by damaging either the property or reputation of another. The intention of making restitution, usually in kind, is required as a condition for the forgiveness of sins of injustice, even though actual restitution is not possible.

Retreat: A program of religious activities undertaken alone or with others for purposes of self-examination and progress in spiritual life. Elements include personal prayer, participation in the liturgy, conferences by leaders, spiritual reading, meditation, discussion, consideration of personal experience in the light of faith.

Ring: In the Church a ring is worn as part of the insignia of bishops, abbots, et al.; by sisters to denote their consecration to God and the Church. The wedding ring symbolizes the love and union of husband and wife.

Ritual: A book of prayers and ceremonies used in the administration of the sacraments and other ceremonial functions. In the Roman Rite, the standard book of this kind is the *Roman Ritual.*

S

Sabbath: The seventh day of the week, observed by Jews and Sabbatarians as the day for rest and religious observance.

Sacramentary: One of the first liturgical books, containing the celebrant's part of the Mass and rites for administration of the sacraments. The earliest book of this kind, the Leonine Sacramentary, dates from the middle or end of the sixth century. The *Sacramentary* in current use is the same as the *Roman Missal.*

Sacred Heart, Enthronement: An acknowledgment of the sovereignty of Jesus Christ over the Christian family, expressed by the installation of an image or picture of the Sacred Heart in a place of honor in the home, accompanied by an act of consecration.

Sacred Heart, Promises: Twelve promises to persons having devotion to the Sacred Heart of Jesus, which were communicated by Christ to St. Margaret Mary Alacoque in a private revelation in 1675. (1) I will give them all the grace necessary in their state in life. (2) I will establish peace in their homes. (3) I will comfort them in all their afflictions. (4) I will be their secure refuge during life and, above all, in death. (5) I will bestow abundant blessing upon all their undertakings. (6) Sinners shall find in My Heart the source and the infinite ocean of mercy. (7) By devotion to My Heart tepid souls shall grow fervent. (8) Fervent souls shall quickly mount to high perfection. (9) I will bless every place where a picture of My Heart shall be set up and honored. (10) I will give to priests the gift of touching the most hardened hearts. (11) Those who promote this devotion shall have their names written in My Heart, never to be blotted out. (12) I will grant the grace of final penitence to those who communicate (receive Holy Communion) on the first Friday of nine consecutive months.

Sacrilege: Violation of and irreverence toward a person, place or thing that is sacred because of public dedication to God; a sin against the virtue of religion. Personal sacrilege is violence of some kind against a cleric or Religious, or a violation of chastity with a cleric or Religious. Local sacrilege is the desecration of sacred places. Real sacrilege is irreverence with respect to sacred things, such as the sacraments and sacred vessels.

Sacristy: A utility room where vestments, church furnishings and sacred vessels are kept and where the clergy vest for sacred functions.

Salvation: The liberation of persons from sin and its effects, reconciliation with God in and through Christ, the attainment of union with God forever in the glory of heaven as the supreme purpose of life and as the God-given reward for fulfillment of His will on earth. Salvation-in-process begins and continues in this life through union with Christ in faith professed and in action; its final term is union with God and the whole community of the saved in the ultimate perfection of God's kingdom. The Church teaches that: God wills the salvation of all men; men are saved in and through Christ; membership in the Church established by Christ, known and understood as the community of salvation, is necessary for salvation; men with this knowledge and understanding who deliberately reject this Church, cannot be saved. The Catholic Church is the Church founded by Christ.

Salvation History: The facts and the record of God's relations with men, in the past, present and future, for the purpose of leading them to live in accordance with His will for the eventual attainment after death of salvation, or everlasting happiness with Him in heaven. The essentials of salvation history are: God's love for all men and will for their salvation; His intervention and action in the world to express this love and bring about their salvation; the revelation He made of himself and the covenant He established with the Israelites in the Old Testament; the perfecting of this revelation and the new covenant of grace through Christ in the New Testament; the continuing action-for-salvation carried on in and through the Mystical Body of Christ, the Church; the communication of saving grace to men through the merits of Christ and the operations of the Holy Spirit in the here-and-now circumstances of daily life and with the cooperation of men themselves.

Salvation outside the Church: The Second Vatican Council covered this subject summarily in the following manner: "Those also can attain to everlasting salvation who through no fault of their own do not know the Gospel of Christ or His Church, yet sincerely seek God and, moved by grace, strive by their deeds to do His will as it is known to them through the dictates of conscience. Nor does divine Providence deny the help necessary for salvation to those who, without blame on their part, have not yet arrived at an explicit knowledge of God, but who strive to live a good life, thanks to His grace. Whatever good or truth is found among them is looked upon by the Church as a preparation for the Gospel. She regards such qualities as given by Him who enlightens all men so that they may finally have life" (*Dogmatic Constitution on the Church,* No. 16).

Satanism: Worship of the devil, a blasphemous inversion of the order of worship which is due to God alone.

Scandal: Conduct which is the occasion of sin to another person.

Scapular: (1) A part of the habit of some religious orders like the Benedictines and Dominicans; a nearly shoulder-wide strip of cloth worn over the tunic and reaching almost to the feet in front and behind. Originally a kind of apron, it came to symbolize the cross and yoke of Christ. (2) Scapulars worn by lay persons as a sign of association with religious orders and for devotional purposes are an adaptation of monastic scapulars. Approved by the Church as sacramentals, they consist of two small squares of woolen cloth joined by strings and are worn about the neck. They are given for wearing in a ceremony of investiture or enrollment. There are nearly 20 scapulars for devotional use: the five principal ones are generally understood to include those of Our Lady of Mt. Carmel (the brown Carmelite Scapular), the Holy Trinity, Our Lady of the Seven Dolors, the Passion, the Immaculate Conception.

Scapular Medal: A medallion with a representation of the Sacred Heart on one side and of the Blessed Virgin Mary on the other. Authorized by St. Pius X in 1910, it may be worn or carried in place of a scapular by persons already invested with a scapular.

Scapular Promise: According to a legend of the Carmelite Order, the Blessed Virgin Mary appeared to St. Simon Stock in 1251 at Cambridge and declared that wearers of the brown Carmelite Scapular would be saved from hell and taken to heaven by her on the first Saturday after death. The validity of the legend has never been the subject of official decision by the Church. Essentially, it expresses belief in the intercession of Mary and the efficacy of sacramentals in the context of truly Christian life.

Schism: Derived from a Greek word meaning separation, the term designates formal and obstinate refusal by a baptized person, called a *schismatic,* to be in communion with the pope and the Church. The canonical penalty is excommunication. One of the most disastrous schisms in history resulted in the definitive separation of the Church in the East from union with Rome about 1054.

Scholasticism: The term usually applied to the Catholic theology and philosophy which developed in the Middle Ages.

Scruple: A morbid, unreasonable fear and anxiety that one's actions are sinful when they are not, or more seriously sinful than they actually are. Compulsive scrupulosity is quite different from the transient scrupulosity of persons of tender or highly sensitive conscience, or of persons with faulty moral judgment.

Seal of Confession: The obligation of secrecy which must be observed regarding knowledge of things learned in connection with the confession of sin in the sacrament of penance. The seal covers matters whose revelation would make the sacrament burdensome. Confessors are prohibited, under penalty of excommunication, from making any direct revelation of confessional matter; this prohibition holds, outside of confession, even with respect to the person who made the confession unless the person releases the priest from the obligation. Persons other than confessors are obliged to maintain secrecy, but not under penalty of excommunication. General, non-specific discussion of confessional matter does not violate the seal.

Secularism: A school of thought, a spirit and manner of action which ignores and/or repudiates the validity or influence of supernatural religion with respect to individual and social life. In describing secularism in their annual statement in 1947, the bishops of the United States said in part: "... There are many men — and their number is daily increasing — who in practice live their lives without recognizing that this is God's world. For the most part they do not deny God. On formal occasions they may even mention His name. Not all of them would subscribe to the statement that all moral values derive from merely human conventions. But they fail to bring an awareness of their responsibility to God into their thought and action as individuals and members of society. This, in essence, is what we mean by secularism."

Seminary: A house of study and formation for men, called seminarians, preparing for the priesthood. Traditional seminaries date from the Council of Trent in the middle of the 16th century; before that time, candidates for the priesthood were variously trained in monastic schools, universities under church auspices, and in less formal ways. At the present time, seminaries are undergoing change for the adaptation of academic and spiritual programs to contemporary needs.

Sermon on the Mount: A compilation of sayings of our Lord in the form of an extended discourse in Matthew's Gospel (5:1 to 7:27) and, in a shorter discourse, in Luke (6:17-49). The passage in Matthew, called the "Constitution of the New Law," summarizes the living spirit of believers in Christ and members of the kingdom of God. Beginning with the Beatitudes and including the Lord's Prayer, it covers the perfect justice of the New Law, the fulfillment of the Old Law in the New Law of Christ, and the integrity of internal attitude and external conduct with respect to love of God and neighbor, justice, chastity, truth, trust and confidence in God.

Seven Last Words of Christ: Words of Christ on the Cross. (1) "Father, forgive them; for they do not know what they are doing." (2) To the penitent thief: "I assure you: today you will be with Me in Paradise." (3) To Mary and His Apostle John: "Woman, there is your son . . . there is your mother." (4) "My God, My God, why have you forsaken Me?" (5) "I am thirsty." (6) "Now it is finished." (7) "Father, into Your hands I commend My spirit."

Shrine, Crowned: A shrine approved by the Holy See as a place of pilgrimage. The approval permits public devotion at the shrine and implies that at least one miracle has resulted from devotion at the shrine. Among the best known crowned shrines are those of the Virgin Mary at Lourdes and Fatima. Shrines with statues crowned by Pope John Paul in 1985 in South America were those of Our Lady of Coromoto, patroness of Venezuela, in Caracas, and Our Lady of Carmen of Paucartambo in Cuzco, Peru.

Shroud of Turin: A strip of brownish linen cloth, 14 feet, three inches in length and three feet, seven inches in width, bearing the front and back imprint of a human body. A tradition dating from the seventh century, which has not been verified beyond doubt, claims that the shroud is the fine linen in which the body of Christ was wrapped for burial.

Sick Calls: When a person is confined at home by illness or other cause and is unable to go to church for reception of the sacraments, a parish priest should be informed and arrangements made for him to visit the person at home. Such visitations are common in pastoral practice, both for special needs and for providing persons with regular opportunities for receiving the sacraments. If a priest cannot make the visitation, arrangements can be made for a Eucharistic minister to bring Holy Communion to the homebound or bedridden person.

Sign of the Cross: A sign, ceremonial gesture or movement in the form of a cross by which a person confesses faith in the Holy Trinity and Christ, and intercedes for the blessing of himself, other persons, and things. In Roman-Rite practice, a person making the sign touches the fingers of the right hand to his forehead, below the breast, left shoulder and right shoulder while saying: "In the name of the Father, and of the Son, and of the Holy Spirit." The sign is also made with the thumb on the forehead, the lips, and the breast. For the blessing of persons and objects, a large sign of the cross is made by movement of the right hand. In Eastern-Rite practice, the sign is made with the thumb and first two fingers of the right hand joined together and touching the forehead, below the breast, the right shoulder and the left shoulder; the formula generally used is the doxology, "O Holy God, O Holy Strong One, O Immortal One." The Eastern manner of making the sign was general until the first half of the 13th century; by the 17th century, Western practice involved the whole right hand and the reversal of direction from shoulder to shoulder.

Signs of the Times: Contemporary events, trends and features in culture and society, the needs and aspirations of people, all the factors that form the context in and through which the Church has to carry on its saving mission. The Second Vatican Council spoke on numerous occasions about these signs and the relationship between them and a kind of manifestation of God's will, positive or negative, and about subjecting them to judgment and action corresponding to the demands of divine revelation through Scripture, Christ, and the experience, tradition and teaching authority of the Church.

Simony: The deliberate intention and act of selling and/or buying spiritual goods or material things so connected with the spiritual that they cannot be separated therefrom; a violation of the virtue of religion, and a sacrilege, because it wrongfully puts a material price on spiritual things, which cannot be either sold or bought. In church law, actual sale or purchase is subject to censure in some cases. The term is derived from the name of Simon Magus, who attempted to buy from Sts. Peter and John the power to confirm people in the Holy Spirit (Acts 8:4-24).

Sin: (1) Actual sin is rejection of God manifested by free and deliberate violation of His law by thought, word or action. (a) Mortal sin — involving serious matter, sufficient reflection and full consent — results in total alienation from God, making a person dead to sanctifying grace, incapable of performing meritorious supernatural acts and subject to everlasting punishment. (b) Venial sin — involving less serious matter, reflection and consent — does not have such serious consequences. (2) Original sin is the sin of Adam, with consequences for all men.

Sins against the Holy Spirit: Despair of salvation, presumption of God's mercy, impugning the known truths of faith, envy at another's spiritual good, obstinacy in sin, final impenitence. Those guilty of such sins stubbornly resist the influence of grace and, as long as they do so, cannot be forgiven.

Sins, Occasions of: Circumstances (persons, places, things, etc.) which easily lead to sin. There is an obligation to avoid voluntary proximate occasions of sin, and to take precautions against the dangers of unavoidable occasions.

Sins That Cry to Heaven for Vengeance: Willful murder, sins against nature, oppression of the poor, widows and orphans, defrauding laborers of their wages.

Sister: Any woman Religious, in popular speech; strictly, the title applies only to women Religious belonging to institutes whose members never professed solemn vows. Most of the institutes whose members are properly called Sisters were established during and since the 19th century. Women Religious with solemn vows, or belonging to institutes whose members formerly professed solemn vows, are properly called nuns.

Sisterhood: A generic term referring to the whole institution of the life of women Religious in the Church, or to a particular institute of women Religious.

Situation Ethics: A subjective, individualistic ethical theory which denies the binding force of ethical principles as universal laws and preceptive norms of moral conduct, and proposes that morality is determined only by situational conditions and considerations and the intention of the person.

Slander: Attributing to a person faults which he does not have; a violation of the obligations of justice and charity, for which restitution is due.

Sloth: One of the seven capital sins; spiritual laziness, involving distaste and disgust for spiritual things; spiritual boredom, which saps the vigor of spiritual life. Physical laziness is a counterpart of spiritual sloth.

Sorcery: A kind of black magic in which evil is invoked by means of diabolical intervention; a violation of the virtue of religion.

Soteriology: The division of theology which treats of the mission and work of Christ as Redeemer.

Species, Sacred: The appearances of bread and wine (color, taste, smell, etc.) which remain after the substance has been changed at the Consecration of the Mass into the Body and Blood of Christ.

Spiritism or **Spiritualism:** Attempts to communicate with spirits and departed souls by means of seances, table-tapping, ouija boards, and other methods; a violation of the virtue of religion. Spiritualistic practices are noted for fakery.

Spiritual Works of Mercy: Works of spiritual assistance, motivated by love of God and neighbor, to persons in need: counseling the doubtful, instructing the ignorant, admonishing sinners, comforting the afflicted, forgiving offenses, bearing wrongs patiently, praying for the living and the dead.

Stational Churches, or Days: Churches, especially in Rome, where the clergy and lay people were accustomed to gather with their bishop on certain days for the celebration of the liturgy. The 25 early titular or parish churches of Rome, plus other churches, each had their turn as the site of divine worship in practices which may have started in the third century. The observances were rather well-developed toward the latter part of the fourth century, and by the fifth they included a Mass concelebrated by the pope and attendant priests. On some occasions, the stational liturgy was preceded by a procession from another church called a *collecta*. There were 42 Roman stational churches in the eighth century, and 89 stational services were scheduled annually in connection with the liturgical seasons. Stational observances fell into disuse toward the end of the Middle Ages. Some revival was begun by John XXIII in 1959.

Stigmata: Marks of the wounds suffered by Christ in His crucifixion, in hands and feet by nails, and side by the piercing of a lance. Some persons, called stigmatists, have been reported as recipients or sufferers of marks like these. The Church, however, has never issued any infallible declaration about their possession by anyone, even in the case of St. Francis of Assisi, whose stigmata seem to be the best substantiated and may be commemorated in the Roman-Rite liturgy.

Stipend, Mass: An offering given to a priest for applying the fruits of the Mass according to the intention of the donor. The offering is a contribution to the support of the priest. The disposition of the fruits of the sacrifice, in line with doctrine concerning the Mass in particular and prayer in general, is subject to the will of God. In the early Christian centuries, when Mass was not offered for the intentions of particular persons, the participants made offerings of bread and wine for the sacrifice and their own Holy Communion, and of other things useful for the support of the clergy and the poor. Some offerings may have been made as early as the fourth century for the celebration of Mass for particular intentions, and there are indications of the existence of this practice from the sixth century when private Masses began to be offered. The earliest certain proof of stipend practice, however, dates from the eighth century. By the 11th century, along with private Mass, it was established custom.

Stole Fee: An offering given on certain occasions; e.g., at a baptism, wedding, funeral, for the support of the clergy who administer the sacraments and perform other sacred rites.

Supererogation: Good and virtuous actions which go beyond the obligations of duty and the requirements enjoined by God's law as necessary for salvation. Examples of these works are the profession and observance of the evangelical counsels of poverty, chastity, and obedience, and efforts to practice charity to the highest degree.

Supernatural: Above the natural; that which exceeds and is not due or owed to the essence, exigencies, requirements, powers and merits of created nature. While man has no claim on supernatural things and does not need them in order to exist and act on a natural level, he does need them in order to exist and act in the higher order or economy of grace established by God for his salvation. God has freely given to man certain things which are beyond the powers and rights of his human nature. Examples of the supernatural are: grace, a kind of participation by man in the divine life, by which man becomes capable of performing acts meritorious for salvation; divine revelation by which God manifests himself to man and makes known truth that is inaccessible to human reason alone; faith, by which man believes divine truth because of the authority of God who reveals it through sacred Scripture and tradition and the teaching of His Church.

Superstition: A violation of the virtue of religion, by which God is worshiped in an unworthy manner or creatures are given honor which belongs to God alone. False, vain, or futile worship involves elements which are incompatible with the honor and respect due to God, such as error, deception, and bizarre practices. Examples are: false and exaggerated devotions, chain prayers and allegedly unfailing prayers, the mixing of unbecoming practices in worship. The second kind of superstition attributes to persons and things powers and honor which belong to God alone. Examples are: idolatry, divination, magic, spiritism, necromancy.

Swearing: Taking an oath; calling upon God to witness the truth of a statement; a legitimate thing to do for serious reasons and under proper circumstances, as in a court of law. To swear without sufficient reason is to dishonor God's name; to swear falsely in a court of law is perjury.

Syllabus, The: (1) When not qualified, the term refers to the list of 80 errors accompanying Pope Pius IX's encyclical *Quanta Cura,* issued in 1864. (2) The *Syllabus* of St. Pius X in the decree *Lamentabili,* issued by the Holy Office July 4, 1907, condemning 65 heretical propositions of Modernism. This schedule of errors was followed shortly by that pope's encyclical *Pascendi,* the principal ecclesiastical document against Modernism, issued September 8, 1907.

T

Te Deum: The opening Latin words, Thee, God, of a hymn of praise and thanksgiving prescribed for use in the Office of Readings of the Liturgy of the Hours on many Sundays, solemnities and feasts.

Temperance: Moderation, one of the four cardinal virtues.

Temptation: Any enticement to sin, from any source: the strivings of one's own faculties, the action of the devil, other persons, circumstances of life, etc. Temptation itself is not sin. Temptation can be avoided and overcome with the use of prudence and the help of grace.

Thanksgiving: An expression of gratitude to God for His goodness and the blessings He grants; one of the four ends of prayer.

Theism: A philosophy which admits the existence of God and the possibility of divine revelation; it is generally monotheistic and acknowledges God as transcendent and also active in the world. Because it is a philosophy rather than a system of theology derived from revelation, it does not include specifically Christian doctrines, like those concerning the Trinity, the incarnation and redemption.

Theological Virtues: The virtues which have God for their direct object: faith, or belief in God's infallible teaching; hope, or confidence in divine assistance; charity, or love of God. They are given to a person with grace in the first instance, through baptism and incorporation in Christ.

Theology: Knowledge of God and religion, deriving from and based on the data of divine revelation, organized and systematized according to some kind of scientific method. It involves systematic study and presentation of the truths of divine revelation in sacred Scripture, tradition, and the teaching of the Church. The Second Vatican Council made the following declaration about theology and its relation to divine revelation: "Sacred theology rests on the written word of God, together with sacred tradition, as its primary and perpetual foundation. By scrutinizing in the light of faith all truth stored up in the mystery of Christ, theology is most powerfully strengthened and constantly rejuvenated by that word. For the sacred Scriptures contain the word of God and, since they are inspired, really are the word of God; and so the study of the sacred page is, as it were, the soul of sacred theology" *(Constitution on Revelation,* No. 24). Theology has been divided under various subject headings. Some of the major fields have been: dogma (systematic theology), moral, pastoral, ascetics (the practice of virtue and means of attaining holiness and perfection), mysticism (higher states of religious experience). Other subject headings include ecumenism (Christian unity, interfaith relations), ecclesiology (the nature and constitution of the Church), Mariology (doctrine concerning the Blessed Virgin Mary), the sacraments, etc.

Tithing: Contribution of a portion of one's income, originally one-tenth, for purposes of religion and charity. The practice is mentioned 46 times in the Bible. In early Christian times, tithing was adopted in continuance of Old Testament practices of the Jewish people, and the earliest positive Church legislation on the subject was enacted in 567. Catholics are bound in conscience to contribute to the support of their church, but the manner in which they do so is not fixed by law. Tithing, which amounts to a pledged contribution of a portion of one's income, has aroused new attention in recent years in the United States.

Transubstantiation: "The way Christ is made present in this sacrament (Holy Eucharist) is none other than by the change of the whole substance of the bread into His Body, and of the whole substance of the wine into His Blood (in the Consecration at Mass) . . . this unique and wonderful change the Catholic Church rightly calls transubstantiation" (encyclical *Mysterium Fidei* of Paul VI, September 3, 1965). The first official use of the term was made by the Fourth Council of the Lateran in 1215. Authoritative teaching on the subject was issued by the Council of Trent.

Treasury of the Church: The superabundant merits of Christ and the saints from which the Church draws to confer spiritual benefits, such as indulgences.

Triduum: A three-day series of public or private devotions.

U-Z

Usury: Excessive interest charged for the loan and use of money; a violation of justice.

Viaticum: Holy Communion given to those in danger of death. The word, derived from Latin, means provision for a journey through death to life hereafter.

Virginity: Observance of perpetual sexual abstinence. The state of virginity, which is embraced for the love of God by Religious with a public vow or by others with a private vow, was singled out for high praise by Christ (Mt. 19:10-12) and has always been so regarded by the Church. In the encyclical *Sacra Virginitas,* Pius XII stated: "Holy virginity and

that perfect chastity which is consecrated to the service of God is without doubt among the most perfect treasures which the founder of the Church has left in heritage to the society which He established."

Virtue: A habit or established capability for performing good actions. Virtues are natural (acquired and increased by repeating good acts) and/or supernatural (given with grace by God).

Vocation: A call to a way of life. Generally, the term applies to the common call of all men, from God, to holiness and salvation. Specifically, it refers to particular states of life, each called a vocation, in which response is made to this universal call; viz., marriage, the religious life and/or priesthood, the single state freely chosen or accepted for the accomplishment of God's will. The term also applies to the various occupations in which persons make a living. The Church supports the freedom of each individual in choosing a particular vocation, and reserves the right to pass on the acceptability of candidates for the priesthood and religious life. Signs or indicators of particular vocations are many, including a person's talents and interests, circumstances and obligations, invitations of grace and willingness to respond thereto.

Vow: A promise made to God with sufficient knowledge and freedom, which has as its object a moral good that is possible and better than its voluntary omission. A person who professes a vow binds himself or herself by the virtue of religion to fulfill the promise. The best known examples of vows are those of poverty, chastity and obedience professed by Religious (see Evangelical Counsels, individual entries). Public vows are made before a competent person, acting as an agent of the Church, who accepts the profession in the name of the Church, thereby giving public recognition to the person's dedication and consecration to God and divine worship. Vows of this kind are either solemn, rendering all contrary acts invalid as well as unlawful; or simple, rendering contrary acts unlawful. Solemn and perpetual vows are for life; simple vows are for a definite period of time or for life. Vows professed without public recognition by the Church are called private vows. The Church, which has authority to accept and give public recognition to vows, also has authority to dispense persons from their obligations for serious reasons.

Week of Prayer for Christian Unity: Eight days of prayer, from January 18 to 25, for the union of all Christian bodies in the Church established by Christ. On the initiative of Father Paul James Francis, S.A., of Graymoor, N.Y., it originated in 1908 as the Chair of Unity Octave. In recent years, its observance on an interfaith basis has increased greatly.

Witness, Christian: Practical testimony or evidence given by Christians of their faith in all circumstances of life — by prayer and general conduct, through good example and good works, etc.; being and acting in accordance with Christian belief; actual practice of the Christian faith.

Zucchetto: A skullcap worn by bishops and other prelates.

General Index

A